DATE DUE

AU 2 '99			
AG 9 '01			
AG 2 '05			
AG 6 '08			

DEMCO 38-296

Worldwide Trends in Youth Sport

Paul De Knop, PhD
Vrije Universiteit Brussel (VUB)

Lars-Magnus Engström, PhD
Stockholm Institute of Education

Berit Skirstad, PhD
Norwegian University of Sport and Physical Education

Maureen R. Weiss, PhD
University of Oregon

Editors

Human Kinetics

loging-in-Publication Data

Knop . . . [et al.].

Includes bibliographical references and index.
ISBN 0-87322-729-8 (case)
  1. Sports for children—Cross-cultural studies. 2. Sports for
children—Social aspects—Cross-cultural studies. I. De Knop, Paul.
GV709.2.W67   1996   95-33994
796'.01922--dc20   CIP

ISBN: 0-87322-729-8

Acquisitions Editors: Rik Washburn and Rick Frey, PhD; **Developmental Editors:** Mary
Fowler and Julie Rhoda; **Assistant Editors:** Jacqueline Blakley, Sandra Merz Bott, Ann
Greenseth, and Susan Moore; **Editorial Assistants:** Jennifer J. Hemphill and Andrew T.
Starr; **Copyeditor:** Lee Erwin; **Proofreader:** Sue Fetters; **Indexer:** Barbara E. Cohen;
Typesetter and Layout Artist: Yvonne Winsor; **Text Designer:** Robert Reuther; **Cover
Designer:** Judy Henderson; **Illustrator:** Studio 2-D; **Photo Editor:** Boyd LaFoon;
Printer: Edwards Brothers

Printed in the United States of America   10 9 8 7 6 5 4 3 2 1

Human Kinetics
Web site: http://www.humankinetics.com

United States: Human Kinetics, P.O. Box 5076, Champaign, IL 61825-5076
1-800-747-4457
e-mail: humank@hkusa.com

Canada: Human Kinetics, Box 24040, Windsor, ON N8Y 4Y9
1-800-465-7301 (in Canada only)
e-mail: humank@hkcanada.com

Europe: Human Kinetics, P.O. Box IW14, Leeds LS16 6TR United Kingdom
(44) 1132 781708
e-mail: humank@hkeurope.com

Australia: Human Kinetics, 57A Price Avenue
Lower Mitcham, South Australia 5062
(08) 277 1555
e-mail: humank@hkaustralia.com

New Zealand: Human Kinetics, P.O. Box 105-231, Auckland 1
(09) 523 3462
e-mail: humank@hknewz.com

Contents

Foreword

This book is the outcome of the collaborative efforts of the Committee on Sport and Leisure of the International Council of Sport Science and Physical Education (ICSSPE). It deals with the organization, the developments, and the promotional campaigns concerning youth sport in 20 countries, and represents the first time that the structure, recent initiatives, trends, and dynamics of development of youth sport have been described from a multinational perspective. It compares the situations in countries from North and South America, Asia, Europe, and Oceania, countries with different histories, socioeconomic contexts, political structures, and stages of development.

The Sport and Leisure Committee has taken a leading role in expanding knowledge about youth participation in sport and about youth sport promotional campaigns. It held an international seminar, "Children, Youth and Sport—A Multinational Comparison" in Stockholm in 1993 to keep pace with the growth of youth sport worldwide. The idea of convening such a seminar was accepted and supported by the Swedish Sports Confederation.

From many perspectives, this seminar was a success. It brought together invited experts on youth sport to share their research, experience, and knowledge. It resulted in thought-provoking interactions between presenters and attendees. Finally, it resulted in the publication of this book, which should be of value to a broad array of sport students, scholars, practitioners and policy-makers interested in worldwide trends in youth sport.

Juan Antonio Samaranch
Marqués de Samaranch
President
International Olympic Committee

Preface

This book is organized into six parts. In Part I we provide an overview of the purpose, the benefits, and the problems of cross-national and comparative research, as well as of the role of sport in a changing society. The discussion focuses upon growing sport awareness (sportification) in many societies and the variety of alternative sport forms (e.g., leisure sports, adventure sports, health sports) that are being developed. How these developments are related to participation, organization, and socioeconomic trends is further described as well as social changes among youths themselves.

In Parts II through V we look specifically to youth sport in 20 countries on five continents—North and South America, Asia, Europe, and Oceania. We introduce each country by examining the organizational network of youth sport in that country (club sport, school sport, local authorities, private nonprofit organizations). We then explore youth sport participation, dropout issues, problems in youth sport, and youth sport promotional campaigns. Each chapter concludes with a look into the future of youth sport in the country reported.

In Part VI, we bring it all together to address the following questions.

- Are there any worldwide trends and developments in youth sport?
- What are the trends in youth sport participation?
- What are the main problems facing youth sport?
- What are the main trends in the youth sport policy, organization, and campaigns?
- Which policy steps should be taken concerning youth sport?
- What is the future of youth sport?

It is our hope that *Worldwide Trends in Youth Sport* will provide the reader with encyclopedic knowledge on the topic from different parts of the world. Besides that, we hope to have introduced some of the problems and the benefits of this collected cross-national knowledge. We have tried to maintain a consistent professional and academic standard as far as possible in treating the topics. Accordingly, we hope that some of the methodological considerations in evidence here will be helpful for students in the field as well as for more advanced researchers, and that the facts collected will be the starting point for further research and will stimulate others to address current issues and problems in sport systematically. People in sport will thus be able to get good ideas about workable and cost-effective ways to achieve the aims of youth sport.

For the exchange of students in sport, as for example ERASMUS (European Community Action Scheme for the Mobility of University Students), the book contains useful information about the situation of sport for children and youth around the world. Another aim of this book is to provide information that can be useful for coaches and sport politicians. The field of youth sport has created new career opportunities in several countries. It is our hope that through this book we have achieved a cross-fertilization of ideas and ways for those in this developing professional field to solve common problems in youth sport.

Paul De Knop, Lars-Magnus Engström,
Berit Skirstad, Maureen R. Weiss

Acknowledgments

We wish to thank the following sponsors: the International Olympic Committee (IOC), the International Council of Sport Science and Physical Education (ICSSPE), the Free University of Brussels (VUB), the Norwegian University of Sport and Physical Education, and the Swedish Sports Confederation. We also thank Marc Theeboom, PhD, for his assistance in editing the book and Carine Van den Houcke for her administrative work.

Part I

Introduction:
An International Comparative
Study on Youth Sport

Chapter 1

Purposes, Methodology, and Problems of a Cross-National or International Comparative Project on Youth Sport

Teus J. Kamphorst
Kenneth Roberts
Paul De Knop
Berit Skirstad
Lars-Magnus Engström

The international project "Children, Youth, and Sport," from which this book results, was conceived as a collaborative venture among some members of the ICSSPE Committee on Sport and Leisure. Subsequently, at a meeting of this committee held in Malaga in July 1992, other youth sport researchers were invited to contribute to the project. Some 20 representatives from around the world expressed their interest, and at a further meeting in Stockholm in May 1993, a plan was agreed upon for a book on multinational trends in youth sport. The main objective of the project is (a) to contribute to the general knowledge about how youth sport in contemporary societies is organized, (b) to explain how and why youth sport patterns change and develop, (c) to provide information concerning interesting campaigns, and (d) to look into the future of youth sport.

At the outset it was decided that the project would be loosely structured to enable different countries to participate according to their resources and interests. A secondary but important aim was to foster international collaborative work on youth sport, while seeking to gain a better understanding of the peculiar features

This methodological chapter draws heavily on the content of the introduction in T.J. Kamphorst and K. Roberts. (1989). *Trends in sports: A multinational perspective.* Culemborg, The Netherlands: Giordano Bruno. Adapted with permission.

of each society through cross-national comparison. As originally conceived, the project was not intended to be strictly comparative, but the guidelines drawn up at the Malaga meeting for the collection and analysis of data were designed to make the materials correspond as closely as possible to the criteria which normally form the basis of cross-national comparative research projects.

A study can be said to be cross-national and comparative if it compares one or more units in two or more societies, cultures, or countries in respect to the same concepts, and if it concerns the systematic analysis of phenomena, usually with the intention of explaining them and generalizing from them. The expectation is that the researcher gathers data about the object of study in different contexts and thereby gains a greater awareness and a deeper understanding of social reality. The larger system is taken to influence the characteristics of the units examined, and at the same time it becomes possible to generalize about the relations between variables from the analysis of the same concepts or phenomena in different national contexts.

Benefits

A number of important benefits can be gained from undertaking cross-national as well as international studies. These can be summarized as extending knowledge about other societies, about social behavior and social issues in general, and about the research going on elsewhere. In more specific terms:

• Participation in international research is a way of making the research done by individuals and groups in one country known elsewhere, and it can also extend knowledge about institutions, systems, and practices from one national context to another.

• International research offers a means of learning about research methodology from the experience of researchers in other organizations and national frameworks, providing opportunities to assess the applicability of such a methodology and a forum where different conceptual approaches can be compared and evaluated.

• International research can lead to new insights into and a deeper understanding of issues which are of central concern in different countries and point to possible directions that could be followed, about which the researcher may not previously have been aware.

• International projects bring together researchers to discuss issues, concepts, and theories and to look for common ground. They can also lead to the identification of gaps in knowledge which prevent effective cross-national comparisons, thereby suggesting useful avenues for future research.

• By formulating and testing the generalizability of statements about common patterns in different cultures and by universalizing sociological theory and reassessing its propositions, cross-national comparative research can provide systematic knowledge about universal concepts in human societies.

• Cross-national projects give researchers a means of confronting findings in an attempt to identify and illuminate similarities and differences, not only in the observed characteristics of particular institutions, systems, or practices, but also in their possible explanation in terms of national likeness and unlikeness.

Methodology

In many respects the methodology adopted in cross-national comparative research is no different from that used for comparisons within nations or for other areas of sociological research. It can be descriptive, evaluative, analytical, or all three. The descriptive or survey approach, which will usually result in a review of the state of the art, is generally the first stage in any large-scale international comparative project and it is also the method adopted in this book.

The comparative approach gives rise to a number of problems, some of which may not exist in a single-nation study, and many of which are particularly acute in cross-national work. If they go unresolved, these problems can affect the quality of the results of the whole project. The three main problem areas which will be considered here are the definition of the research parameters, access to comparable data sets, and the management of the research.

Research Parameters

First, there must be agreement on the *research parameters*, that is, what is being compared. In a longitudinal study of sport behavior, if the researchers are to discern trends, they need to know the time period involved, the social categories to be studied, whether they are looking at the provision and availability of facilities and/or the actual use being made of those facilities, the time span (e.g., last 12 months or 4 weeks) of the activities about which subjects are being asked, the frequency and/or regularity of the activities, and their duration. They need to decide whether sport is to be defined objectively or subjectively and whether respondents should be asked to list spontaneously the activities they have undertaken or to select from a prescribed list. A decision must also be made about which forms of time use qualify as sport. For example, is playing soccer in the street considered a sport? Although "korfball" might be classified by the researcher as a sport activity in Holland, it is doubtful whether it would be included in any list of leisure activities in Japan or Australia. Even if agreement can be reached about which terms to use for sport activities and what is meant by them, the national data for the past 10 years will most probably not have adopted a uniform definition. If activity checklists have been used, the items may have been changed. In addition, it may not in any case be possible to measure the same thing in different contexts, given the differences in institutional frameworks.

For the present study the period between 1983 and 1993 was suggested. By "children" or "youths" we mean youngsters between 6 and 18. "Sport" means all sport activities outside the physical education curriculum, including extracurricular school sport. The definition of sport activity is left to each of the contributing authors.

Access to Data

If agreement can be reached on the research parameters and the method of data collection, the second major and generally insoluble problem (if secondary sources are to be used) is the *availability of comparable data*, and this involves a number of related issues. The source of the data, the purpose for which they are gathered, and the method of collection may vary considerably from one country to another.

If national data exist, do the statistics refer to the same population in terms of age, gender, family, geographical, and socio-occupational status? Most of these types of profile information are routinely collected in national surveys, but surveys of sport and leisure tend to be selective about, for example, the age category to include. In addition, it is very difficult to reach agreement over the definition of socioeconomic categories cross-nationally. Yet, if social "class" and, indeed, gender and geographical location are not taken into account, the researcher may be neglecting explanatory factors which indicate greater intranational than international differences.

Managing the Research

The ways in which the data are collected and collated will produce different results. Can researchers gain access to the raw data for checking and reanalysis or must they base their results on data which have already been processed for a specific purpose? Reanalysis is a very time-consuming exercise.

Hantrais and Kamphorst (1987) describe some additional practical problems of international comparative research such as *funding and management*, which also may affect the outcome, and some of the more specific problems of the multinational enquiry. Most of the problems they discuss are equally relevant in this study of youth sports. Rereading the observations makes it clear that Hantrais and Kamphorst refer to, and reflect upon, that type of international comparative research that allows for direct comparison of basic, mainly quantitative data, as, for example, percentages of the respective countries' populations involved in soccer during a specified period. Hantrais and Kamphorst's "idealtype," their frame of reference, seems to be a comparative project in which all the participating researchers use exactly the same concepts, the same operationalizations, the same measurement instruments, and the same methods of analysis. Indeed, only when these conditions are fulfilled is it possible and fully justified to compare basic data, such as the exact time spent on rugby union by participants in a specified category, as, for example, youngsters under 19, among the populations in the participating countries. However, there is usually a sharp difference between idealtype and reality. The reality is that in this multinational book on youth sport, 20 countries, from various regions of the world, are involved, countries with differing histories and a variety of socioeconomic and political situations and backgrounds. Furthermore, the people in the countries involved have different ideas about, and attribute different meanings to, sport, and display a wide variety of sporting activity patterns. To make the situation even more complex, research traditions differ from country to country, as do the stages of development of the social sciences on whose outcomes this book is based. What to do in what appears, at first glance, to be a nearly chaotic situation? There are three options.

Forget about cross-national or international comparative research.   Following Hantrais and Kamphorst's argument, indeed, one conclusion could be that international comparative research is simply too difficult to attempt. This does not mean that a book like this should not be published at all. However, in this option, perhaps its value lies primarily in its encyclopedic, rather than its comparative, character.

Insist on the prerequisites of the idealtype for international comparative research.   There is a point at which the organizers of an international project are faced with the decision whether to continue their efforts to achieve comparability by asking participants to search for yet more data and/or rewrite their contributions, or to accept that there will always be national if not individual personality differences in approach and coverage (Hantrais & Kamphorst, 1987).

Accept, or even welcome, the fact that variety, distinction, diversification, and difference are integral—and often the most interesting—aspects of reality, and to continue with the project.   However, from this moment on, it would be wise not to call such a project "an international comparative project," because seemingly this combination of terms can easily lead to misunderstandings and false expectations or interpretations. For this reason, we chose as our title *Worldwide Trends in Youth Sport*.

Besides choosing a title with care, there is within this final option more that can be done to avoid misinterpretation. Returning again to Hantrais and Kamphorst's observations, it is clear that the difficulties of international comparative research mainly concern the comparison of basic quantitative data, such as the exact time spent per week on "aerobics" by the female inhabitants of Canada and Finland. Some of these difficulties can be overcome by concentrating the analysis on trends and developments, and not on the basic, mainly quantitative data as such. The following example may illustrate this difference in approach. Suppose that in Canada participation in aerobics is measured in terms of frequency per month, and in Finland by time spent per week. It is clear that a direct comparison of these basic statistical data is impossible. On the basis of these statistics no conclusion could be drawn about differences in participation in aerobics in Canada and in Finland. But what about when we compare data on female aerobics participants in both countries, with, say, the data on male aerobics participants? Very probably the data will allow us to conclude, that—though measured by different parameters—in both countries a common trend is that women are more actively involved in aerobics than men. The same holds for comparison over a certain timespan. On the basis of comparing data about female aerobics participants in Canada in 1991 and 1981, and data for female aerobics participants in Finland in, say, 1986 and 1976, we would very likely be able to conclude that—though measured by differing parameters and therefore not directly comparable—there had been a general rising trend in female participation in aerobics during the last ten years in both countries. Furthermore, suppose we had time series data on aerobics involvement in other countries; we might be able to conclude that there had been a general increase in aerobics involvement all over the world.

References

Hantrais, L., & Kamphorst, T.J. (1987). *Trends in the arts: a multinational perspective*. Culemborg, The Netherlands: Giordano Bruno.

Kamphorst, T.J., & Roberts, K. (1989). *Trends in sports: A multinational perspective*. Culemborg, The Netherlands: Giordano Bruno.

Chapter 2 Sport in a Changing Society

Paul De Knop
Berit Skirstad
Lars-Magnus Engström
Marc Theeboom
Helena Wittock

Sport has become an important social phenomenon in our societies. This is not only illustrated by an increase in sport participation by the population of Western Europe during the last decades, but also by an overall growth in sport awareness, which Crum (1991) labels the *sportification* of society. This sportification is evidenced by the expanding variety of sports and ways to practice sports in many countries, the generalization of the word "sportiveness," the growing use of sports as a marketing instrument, the increasing interest of tourists in sport activities, and so forth.

However, at the same time sport itself has been influenced by changes occurring within society. This has led to the development of a variety of "sport models." Besides the evolution toward a further development of top-level sports, there is also a growing alternative sport experience with immediate enjoyment, relaxation, and recreation as its main characteristics, resulting in different forms of sport such as leisure sports, adventure sports, and health sports. Dietrich and Heinemann (1989) refer to these alternative sport forms as *Nicht-sportliche Sport* (nonsporting sport), while Crum (1991) describes this evolution as the *desportification of sports*, pointing at the loss of the traditional concepts of sport within these alternative sport forms. As a result of this evolution, the actual content and meaning of sport in general becomes less clear. This is in sharp contrast with the clearly defined phenomenon of traditional sport of the past. These two evolutions concerning the identity and role of sports within society have been brought about by a number of factors, as described by various authors (Crum, 1991; De Knop et al., 1994; Heinemann, 1986; Kamphorst & Roberts, 1989).

We will give an overview here of the most important changes described in the literature that have an influence on sport, including youth sport. Then in the next chapters contributors from 20 different countries will present information about the evolution of youth sport, and in the final chapter the worldwide trends will be described.

Demographic Trends

An important development which influences sport is a distinct change in the composition of the population. Before we go into this change in more detail, let us first look at the total population. In 1990 the total population of the European community, for instance, was almost 327 million people (Eurostat, 1992), a number that is expected to reach a peak of about 334 million at the turn of the century. During the first two decades of the 21st century, however, a decrease in the total population is expected. In 2020 there will be about 2.5 million fewer people in the European community than in 1990. As mentioned before, there is also a distinct change taking place in the composition of the population. Data from Eurostat (1992) indicate that in the coming 30 years fewer children will be born within the European community, meaning that there will be 16.8 million fewer youngsters (aged 0-19) in 2020 than in 1990. Because there is only a relatively small decrease in the total population, a tendency toward an aging of the population can be expected.

Besides these demographic trends, it is also important here to mention the increasing influence of immigration on the composition of the total population. In addition to the traditional immigration from people of Mediterranean origin into most Western European countries, new immigration waves are occurring as a result of the drastic political changes in Eastern Europe.

Participation Trends

Within this category of market trends, those changes are described that occur among the preferences of sport participants. Some of these preferences become clear when one looks at data on sport participation by various groups of the population. Research has indicated that the popularity of sports is increasing. However, the activities and the organizational forms chosen have changed. Although during the last three decades organized sport participation in general has increased distinctly in many countries (Ban, 1990; Clearing House, 1988a, 1988b; De Knop, Laporte, Van Meerbeek, & Vanreusel, 1991), the increase in participation by youngsters in organized sports was proportionately lower than the increase in participation by older people (van Maanen, 1985). Several studies also indicated that after the age of 14 there is a clear dropoff of membership in sport clubs (Campbell, 1988; Seppanen, 1982; Stensaasen, 1982).

Because youth has always been the most important target group for sport clubs, and because the population of youngsters is declining, a decrease in the number of sport club members can be expected during the coming years (Clearing House, 1989a). Moreover, as a result of the demographic trend toward the aging of the population, an increasing demand for recreation-oriented and less physically demanding activities can be expected.

Another cultural trend is the increasing level of individualization within today's society (Beckers, 1989; Kamphorst & Roberts, 1989). People's behavior and preferences are less determined by traditional links with family, neighborhood, political organizations, and so on, and more influenced by individual choices. As a result, leisure activities have become more informal (that is, less organized). Such a trend of individualization will be especially problematic for team sports (Sports Council, 1982). However, concerning youth sports, a trend toward less informal sport activities can be noticed. Another development which can be closely linked to individualization is the growing popularity of practicing sport within the private sphere (at home) (Dietrich & Heinemann, 1989). This trend is often referred to as *cocooning.*

Organizational Trends

Another set of developments can be categorized on the institutional level. One of these developments has a distinct political-economical character and can be described as the privatization within sport. Since the beginning of the 1980s, there has been a shift in the role of the government in sport policy from the provision of collective facilities toward a growing emphasis on private initiatives and enterprises. This trend is an evolution which endangers the continuance of public sport provision.

Changes are also occurring in the situation of sport as a leisure activity. As a result of the expansion of the so-called leisure industry, a growing competition among the differentiated offers of leisure activities will put sport in an altered concurrent position. Today, consumers can select from an increasing offer of programs, events, and facilities within the cultural, sport, recreational, and tourist domains. However, besides the competition with other leisure activities, the offer of sport activities itself undergoes different changes. On the one hand, we can see alternative forms within the same sport discipline (e.g., indoor soccer as an alternative to outdoor soccer, climbing walls next to outdoor rock climbing, etc.). This phenomenon results in an increasing competition between a growing number of sports. On the other hand, we see alternative organizations in which sport can be practiced. Next to the traditional sport clubs, we see other sport service institutes. A good example of the latter is the professional sport school, where people pay for participation in sports whenever they want, without being affiliated. These sport schools often establish joint ventures with partners from the industry. In this way, sport is being commercialized.

This process of economization has turned sport into big business, in which the economic value often supersedes the traditional values of sport. Sewart (1987) refers to the commodification of sport, which means that sport has turned into a commodity. At one extreme, namely top-level sports, this has led to the destruction of the idealized model of sport, with its traditional ritualistic meanings. According to Sewart, the commodification of sport is evidenced in three arenas: changes in rules, format, and scheduling; the abandonment of the ethic of skill democracy; and the inclination to spectacle and theatricality. He provides ample evidence of this commodification process of top-level sports (such as changing the rules of sports to create less boring events). The main purpose of this process is to attract more viewers and therefore make sport economically more profitable. Sewart describes the change of sport into mass entertainment as follows: "Instead of athletic contests which happen to be broadcast on television, the process of commodification has given us television events which happen to involve athletes" (sic) (p. 178).

We can also refer to a growing internationalization of top-level sport. This process, which gives sport a more international character, plays an influential role within the economization of contemporary top-level sport (e.g., by encouraging a greater differentiation among the three main types of sport: amateur sport for all, amateur competitive sport, and high-performance professional, or top-level, sport) (Kamphorst & Roberts, 1989).

However, as already indicated, commodification of sport occurs not only with regard to top-level sports. The average sport participant has become increasingly demanding with regard to sport participation. This also involves demands regarding the provision of sport infrastructure and supporting facilities (e.g., cafeterias, lodging, and sideline activities). For example, most public swimming pools need to adjust to the standards of private sport facilities. Research has indicated that pools with recreational facilities attract more visitors and are more profitable, compared to traditional swimming infrastructure (Smeets, 1990). It can also be expected that more sport disciplines will evolve into indoor activities, which means that the existing sport infrastructure will need to be modified. As a result, local authorities will be confronted with the choice of renovating their infrastructure or closing down.

Although Beckers (1989) indicates that a professionalization of sport organizations might counter the consequences of the growing economization of today's sport, the continuance of the voluntary character of the traditional sport club can be endangered by such professionalization. Fewer volunteers will be found to do an increasing number of tasks, and the disappearance of traditional motivations (such as affiliation to a club) will only make this problem more serious.

Socioeconomic Trends

Finally, some socioeconomic trends will also have an impact on developments in sport. One of these trends is the phenomenon of democratization in sport participation. Although studies indicate that the sport participation of the population has increased during the last decades (Clearing House, 1988c; Taks, Renson, & Vanreusel, 1991), it would be a mistake to conclude that sports today are fully democratized. There are still many differences among the various groups in society, differences that often favor the higher socioeconomic classes (Clearing House, 1989b; Taks, Renson, & Vanreusel, 1991).

Another trend is an expected increase in the amount of leisure time for most workers, which might lead to more possibilities for active sport involvement. However, the institution of flexible working hours (part-time, weekend, and night work) will require a more flexible type of organization of sports, especially competitive sports, which have always been characterized by a strict time schedule, and will be increasingly confronted with individual-oriented leisure sports or an offer of day-time sports.

In order to investigate the consequences these external developments are having for youth sports, an international comparative study was set up to analyze possible changes that might have occurred within youth sports over more than a decade.

An evaluation of these changes will provide more insight into the current situation of youth sports and might lead to an answer to the questions, Is youth sport changing, and is youth sport influenced by the social change of contemporary society?

Social Changes in Youth

Because traditional values, norms, and relations seem to be disappearing, the traditional image of youth is also changing. Some key elements may help us to describe this development:

- Together with a longer educational period a delay in entry into employment can be noticed.

- While youth in the past was above all a period to prepare for adulthood, a so-called transit period, it has become more and more a phase on its own, an independent period with a right of existence and goals of its own.

- The clear separations among childhood, puberty, adolescence, and adulthood have become diffuse (for example, think about consumer behavior and sexual intercourse, which in the past were reserved to adults).

- Education has been liberated; parents do not prescribe the rules anymore: children enter into negotiation with their parents.

- Adults are not always seen as more competent (due, among other things, to the development of computer technology and media, in which younger people are often more expert than their elders); this means that the importance of adults as agents of socialization decreases in favor of the youths' own age group.

- Adults are taking their bearings more and more according to the youth culture.

There is also a mutual influence between generations not only when dealing with computers, interactive video, and other electronic equipment, but also through consumer behavior in general. In the field of leisure—especially in fashion, music, and sport—the enhanced status of health and fitness, and the omnipresence of youth in commercials have had the effect of changing the power balance between the generations. Adolescents have become trendsetters for adults in many fields of everyday life. Adults who do body building or jogging, who try to keep up a youthful and sporty appearance at work and in their spare time, are sufficient evidence of such trends.

All this means that the traditional image of youth is disappearing and that several divergent youth subcultures can be noticed because of a process of internal differentiation. Furthermore, the Western influence on society is also changing it from a "survival" society into an "enjoyment" society, with its new purpose being "to live and to enjoy living." This means that as a youngster you need to have strong legs to be able to carry the increasing freedom and the growing number of alternatives.

Conclusion

The 1960s and 1970s, when sport-for-all movements and policies were launched, can be characterized as the years of growth for sport, so that we can speak of the sportification of society. However, when we concentrate on sport itself, a desportification of sport can be found, judging from features of the activities chosen to new organizational forms, to individualism and cocooning, to the economization, the spectatorization, and the commercialization of sport. Another general trend (government decentralization) is guiding sport, except for top-level sport, toward privatization. Those changes in society and in sport, together with demographic trends, are influencing sport in general and thus youth sport more specifically. To check this hypothesis, we have requested researchers from around the world to describe the evolution of youth sport in their countries during the last decade.

References

Ban, D. (1990). *Participation of youth in sports organizations.* Paper presented at the Fourth Congress of Yugoslav Pedagogics of Physical Culture, Bled, Yugoslavia.

Beckers, T. (1989). Heeft de sport nog toekomst [Does sport still have a future]? *Vrijetijd en Samenleving, 7,* 83-94.

Campbell, S.C. (1988). Youth sport in the United Kingdom. In M.R. Weiss & D. Gould (Eds.), *Sport for children and youths* (pp. 17-20). Champaign, IL: Human Kinetics.

Clearing House. (1988a). Sportparticipatie in de Bondsrepubliek Duitsland [Sport participation in the Federal Republic of Germany]. *Sports Information Bulletin,* **13,** 697-703.

Clearing House. (1988b). Sportparticipatie in Noorwegen [Sport participation in Norway]. *Sports Information Bulletin,* **13,** 719-721.

Clearing House. (1988c). Sportparticipatie in Spanje [Sport participation in Spain]. *Sports Information Bulletin,* **13,** 723-725.

Clearing House. (1989a). Noorwegen: Een nieuwe impuls voor de sportclubs [Norway: A new impulse for sport clubs]. *Sports Information Bulletin,* **18,** 982.

Clearing House. (1989b). Zweden: Statistieken met betrekking tot sporten en spelen [Sweden: Statistics with regard to sport and games]. *Sports Information Bulletin,* **18,** 1299.

Crum, B.J. (1991). *Over versporting van de samenleving* [About the sportification of society]. Rijswijk, The Netherlands: WVC.

De Knop, P., Laporte, W., Van Meerbeek, R., & Vanreusel, B. (1991). *Fysieke fitheid en sportbeoefening van de Vlaamse jeugd* [Physical fitness and sport participation among Flemish youth]. Brussels, Belgium: IOS.

De Knop, P., Wylleman, P., Theeboom, M., De Martelaer, K., Van Puymbroeck, L., & Wittock, H. (1994). *Youth-friendly sport clubs: Developing an effective youth sport policy.* Brussels, Belgium: VUBpress.

Dietrich, K., & Heinemann, K. (Eds.) (1989). *Der nicht-sportliche sport* [The nonsporting sport]. Schorndorf, Germany: Hofmann.

Eurostat. (1992). *Demographic statistics 1991.* Luxembourg: Author.

Hantrais, L., & Kamphorst, T.J. (1987). *Trends in the arts: A multinational perspective.* Amersfoort, The Netherlands: Giordano Bruno.

Heinemann, K. (1986). The future of sports: Challenge for the Science of Sport. *International Review for the Sociology of Sport, 21,* 271-285.

Kamphorst, T.J., & Roberts, K. (1989). *Trends in sports: A multinational perspective.* Culemborg, The Netherlands: Giordano Bruno.

Seppanen, P. (1982). Sport clubs and parents as socializing agents in sport. *International Review of Sport Sociology, 17,* 79-90.

Sewart, J.J. (1987). The commodification of sport. *International Review for the Sociology of Sport, 22,* 171-191.

Smeets, P.J.X. (1990). Overdekte zwembaden 1988: Inrichting, bezoek en exploitatie [Indoor swimming pools 1988: Arrangement, visits and exploitation]. *Sociaal-culturele berichten, 16,* 1-10.

Sports Council. (1982). *Sport in the community: The next ten years.* London: Author.

Stensaasen, S. (1982). A coordinated comparative study of sports involvement among Scandinavian youngsters. *Scandinavian Journal of Sports Sciences,, 1,* 17-25.

Taks, M., Renson, R., & Vanreusel, B. (1991). *Hoe sportief is de Vlaming? Een terugblik op 20 jaar sportbeoefening 1969-1989* [How sport active are the Flemish? Looking back at 20 years of sport participation 1969-1989]. Leuven, Belgium: SOCK.

van Maanen, P. (1985). Dat is toch geen sport [Surely this is no sport]. *Spel en Sport, 1,* 33-35.

Part II

Youth Sport in North
and South America

Chapter 3 Brazil

Lamartine P. DaCosta

This Latin American nation has the eighth-largest gross national product in the world, but is otherwise considered a "third-world" country because of its extreme socioeconomic inequalities.

The Organizational Network

Youths up to 18 years of age in Brazil currently practice sports mainly in clubs and as an extracurricular activity in the school system, in addition to informal or recreational sport events at the grassroots level.

Sport Clubs

Whether community-based or elite initiatives, sport clubs are an outstanding tradition in Brazil. The first sport club was founded in Southern Brazil in 1852 at the initiative of European immigrants. Since then, this type of social enterprise has spread all over Brazil and now, according to the 1969 National Survey of the Sports Sector, totals nearly 40,000 sport clubs existing throughout the country's 27 states, which are subdivided into 4,500 municipalities or counties (DaCosta, 1971).

At the time of the survey, there were nearly 10,000 clubs classified in the elite category, based on their normative links with local sport leagues, state federations of sport disciplines, and various levels of government agencies and institutions. In this particular group of associations, there were 870,698 athletes, approximately 30% of whom were under 18 years of age. Later, in 1984, the Brazilian federal government held another survey, according to which there were 9,872 elite clubs, with 934,452 athletes, of whom there were 346,791 children and adolescents (up to 18 years of age) (Ministério da Educação, 1986). This increase of 7% in 15 years suggests a growing trend toward participation by younger athletes.

School Sport Programs

Although there is a lack of nationwide data due to an unprecedented economic recession beginning in the mid-1980s, current assessments continue to point to the expansion of youth groups in sports. That is the case of sport practice by adolescents as an extracurricular activity, detected primarily by the latest federal government survey on this subject with children and adolescents in school. According to these official data, in 1984 there were 4,693,885 children and adolescents participating in school-related competitions in Brazil. For 1985, the total was 6,078,889. As the total number of participants in physical education programs changes slightly from one year to the next, the evidence emerging from these figures points to a fast-growing movement of students toward practice in sports. This explanation is equally consistent with the fact that the number of student competitions increased from 143,304 in 1984 to 183,575 in 1985 (Ministério da Educação, 1986).

Because the number of youths 10 to 19 years old totalled 28,860,000 in 1985, 20% participation is now acknowledged significant for involvement in sports in relation to the 1980 national census. In short, 20% is a high rate of participation in extracurricular sports, because nearly 30% of Brazilian adolescents live in rural areas, where they start working at an earlier age and enjoy fewer educational opportunities. Likewise, roughly 20% of the 10-to-14-year-olds and 55% of the 15-to-19-year-olds drop out of school in both urban and rural settings, mainly in order to work, which further underscores the significance of having 20% of school-related participants in sports (this figure is even higher if one uses the 18-year cutoff point from previous surveys).

The growing trend of sport practice outside schools by adolescents was also quite evident to sport leaders in the late 1980s and early 1990s. The reason for the growth was the continuous nationwide expansion of the National School Games program ("Jogos Escolares Brasileiros"—"JEBs" in Portuguese). A pyramid-shaped system, the JEBs have included extracurricular sport competitions since 1969. At the base of the pyramid, annual competitions take place in the respective state capitals, bringing together athletes from primary and secondary educational levels, representing schools or municipalities or even both, depending on the possibilities in each state. At the top, 4,000 athletes chosen from all the states of Brazil are entitled to meet every year in the national capital (Brasília) to compete in 13 different sports.

By 1989, the JEBs were considered the main point of reference for school sports, although they are a parallel system in relation to the primary school system, as emphasized during the first Brazilian Conference on School Sports (Freire da Silva, 1989). In fact, the same technical meeting stressed that the successful mobilization of JEBs was due to flexible organization at lower levels of the pyramid. For instance, in the state of Parana, which is wealthy by Brazilian standards, JEBs occurred in 1989 as a 13-region competition, with 252 municipalities, 863 schools, and 20,673 athletes participating (Eiras, 1989). On the other hand, in Pernambuco, a state located in the poorest region of Brazil, eligibility for the JEBs in the 1970s was obtained through organized sport clubs managed by students and supported by state grants (Galvão, 1989).

Furthermore, the excessive concentration on competition and selection under JEB guidelines in the 1980s sparked a number of conflicts similar to the amateur/professional controversy in elite sports. Because some students were performing as professional athletes, in 1985 the federal government intervened as the major sponsor of the JEBs, prohibiting young professional athletes with links to sport federations from participating in the games.

In 1989, too, the same government authority decided to change the rationale for competition, favoring educational principles as well as participation, integration, and cooperation through the sharing of collective procedures in the games' development (Tubino, 1988). On the other hand, all track and field coaches participating in the final round of the JEBs made a public announcement against changes in competition rituals and rules which focused more on teams than on individuals (Pereira, 1989).

Overall, whether reflecting the JEBs' campaign or other factors, the present major trend is toward the replacement of physical education with sport training and competitions for the under-18 population group enrolled in schools. This new trend is currently acknowledged by Brazilian researchers and scholars as a significant synthesis: "sports in the school instead of school sports" (Soares, Taffarel, Varjal, Castellani, Escobar, & Bracht, 1992).

Confirmation of this phenomenon was brought to light by a professional follow-up survey carried out by Rezende and Costa Ferreira in 1984 with a sample of 503 graduates from four physical education colleges (university level) in the state of Rio de Janeiro. This study made clear the steady migration of professionals from the educational sector to other occupations, particularly to sports and leisure activities.

Another of Rezende and Costa Ferreira's conclusions was that physical education graduates develop an avoidance relationship with their own profession. As they become sport coaches they maintain deference to their original values and corpus of knowledge, which may differ from training and competition essentials. Regardless of difficulties in making generalizations based on these conclusions in a continental country like Brazil, more recent evidence was provided by overview studies like those developed by Faria Júnior (1989). A remarkable example is the breakdown of 316 masters' theses from 1973 to 1988 in the field of physical education, showing a concentration of majors in teaching but only as a front area of professional knowledge.

In addition, Farinatti (1991) further interpreted these theses and demonstrated that only 4.5% of them could be related in any way to actual physical education needs in school activities. This researcher's ultimate conclusion pointed more to physical education professionals' loss of enthusiasm than to a cognitive dissonance or even an identity crisis.

Sport Participation

Thus, these overview studies confront values with facts, although this is seldom stated by Brazilian authors themselves. As a consequence, "physical education" continues to be the fundamental value of sports practiced on an extracurricular basis in schools. Moreover, it was specifically school sports that were favored over club and federation sports in the recently approved 1988 Federal Constitution of Brazil (Tubino, 1989).

Also, extracurricular sports are the central focus of the latest trend in physical education in Brazilian schools. The presupposition now rests on the needs and aspirations of pupils and even of their families as well as on an empirical basis for building knowledge and providing legitimacy for interventions by teachers and coaches.

An example of this new trend is found in the research by Lovisolo, Soares, and Santos (1993), who designed a sample that surveyed 703 pupils ages 10 to 14 from several schools located in the Greater Rio de Janeiro Metropolitan Area, as well as 432 heads of families (either fathers or mothers). This group was selected in order to give statistical validity in terms of family economic status, that is, to obtain results that were representative of the major urban populations in Brazil (approximately 85% of the total Brazilian population live in urban areas).

Aside from not considering Brazil's regional cultural diversity, the survey results confirmed the full adherence of children and adolescents to sport participation: 87.86% of them practiced some form of sport outside of school, in addition to 86.1% of the same age group who joined extracurricular sport activities inside school. Table 3.1 breaks down these findings in profiles of sport activities, including both options.

Notwithstanding the breadth of participation revealed by these data, the profile for sports inside school is primarily related to the availability of facilities and programs, whereas options outside of school reveal cultural traditions in sports, in addition to a search for social participation through such activities. Answers

Table 3.1   Percentages of Sport Options by Pupils Aged 10-14 Years (1992-1993)

Inside school		Outside school	
Running and jogging	23.95	Soccer	19.33
Gymnastics	22.70	Gymanstics	16.82
Basketball	13.58	Volleyball	12.36
Soccer	13.52	Dancing	9.00
Volleyball	10.65	Swimming	6.56
Handball	6.94	Basketball	5.47
Dancing	3.17	Track and field	4.54
Track and field	1.76	Handball	4.20
Traditional games	1.12	Judo/Karate	4.20
Others	1.48	Others	7.37
		No one	10.00
No answer	1.18	No answer	7.25
$N = 703$			

Note. From *Educação Física em Escolas do Rio de Janeiro* [Physical Education in Rio de Janerio Schools] by H. Lovisolo, A.J.G. Soares, & M.D. Santos, 1993, Rio de Janeiro, Brazil: Universidade Gama Filho/Conselho Nacional de Pesquisas. Copyright 1993 by Universidade Gama Filha/Conselho Nacional de Pesquisas. Adapted by permission.

by fathers and mothers indicated these distinctions between the latter group (soccer, volleyball, basketball, etc.) and the former, which accounts for 44.5% of options, (gymnastics, dancing, swimming, judo, etc.) Still according to Lovisolo and colleagues, families are voluntarily paying for such outside involvement in sports, which often stretches their financial possibilities and may express an emerging value for the working class. Children's and youths' sport perceptions are in agreement with this supposition, because they trust in "sport practice" and "learning to compete" as useful skills for them (24.9% of respondents), following close behind "body development" and "health protection," with 34.99% of free responses.

Equally significant were the responses about the difference between physical education and sports: among pupils, 47.5% saw no distinction between the two, while 34.7% were not able to answer and 12.8% declared the existence of differences but without citing any of them. In turn, 54% of their parents were not able to cite distinctions, but the 40% who could set down supposed requirements (not descriptions) of physical education, such as "to provide health" (35%), "a prerequisite" (20%), or "discipline" (10%). The researchers thus concluded that physical education in Brazil has lost its specificity, sharing the same identity with sports.

New cultural value patterns should also shed light on children's and youths' motives in ranking physical education (that is "sports") as the subject they like most in school. Table 3.2 clearly shows this finding, with significant comparisons.

While the pupils' choices make a clear distinction between preference and importance, it is equally clear why they rank sports or physical education in third place (9.59%), following "teachers" (28.07%) and "friends" (9.68%), in choosing what attracts them to daily life in school. Contemporary interpretation

Table 3.2   Ranking of Pupils' Preference in School Subjects in Rio de Janeiro (1992-1993)

Choices	Like most	Like least	Most important
Sports	382 (1st)	54 (10th)	129 (7th)
Mathematics	318 (2nd)	260 (2nd)	439 (1st)
Portuguese	315 (3rd)	196 (7th)	432 (2nd)
Sciences	244 (4th)	203 (5th)	292 (3rd)
English	204 (5th)	203 (5th)	153 (7th)
Others	489	1,032	546

Note. From *Educação Física em Escolas do Rio de Janeiro* [Physical Education in Rio de Janeiro Schools] by H. Lovisolo, A.J.G. Soares, & M.D. Santos, 1993, Rio de Janeiro, Brazil: Universidade Gama Filha/Conselho Nacional de Pesquisas. Copyright 1993 by Universidade Gama Filha/Conselho Nacional de Pesquisas. Adapted by permission.

by researchers refers to intersubjectivity prevailing over all other factors, but as an overreaction to Brazilian public schools' current decadent environment.

This assumption proved to be empirically consistent, as students pointed to "dirtiness" (24.99%), "disorder" (19.48%), "lack of maintenance" (16.72%), and other shortcomings in school organization, management, and discipline, when asked what their dislikes were in the context of school. In short, sports must be giving them self-esteem and self-achievement, seldom obtained by means of other opportunities found in school.

Perceptions by fathers and mothers provided a complementary view of the pupils' defensive reaction to deficiencies in the schools. Table 3.3 shows the items chosen by heads of families when they were asked about what they expected from school sports practiced by their sons and daughters. Here, respondents referred to the development of attitudes that would supposedly suit their children's sport life needs.

This utilitarian interpretation from pupils and their parents corresponds to an outstanding demand for an increase in sport activities: some 93.7% of fathers and mothers were in favor of expanding opportunities for sports, with 15.2% requesting extracurricular solutions. Yet on this point, the research showed no relationship between high involvement in sports by pupils (86.1%) and the compulsory status of physical education in Brazilian school systems. In fact, whether it was compulsory (54.1%) or not (43.5%), pupils would continue to participate in school sports.

In view of these findings and in an attempt to further elaborate on the conclusions by Lovisolo et al. (1993), the following remarks compare the Brazilian

Table 3.3   Parents' Expectations Concerning School Sports in Rio de Janeiro (1992-1993)

Accomplishment	Percentage
To learn sport practice	27.5
To learn to compete	26.2
As a source of relaxation	13.8
To build personality	11.4
To control fears	10.8
To learn sportsmanship	8.9
No answer	1.4
$N = 432$	100.0

Note. From *Educação Físca em Escolas do Rio de Janeiro* [Physical Education in Rio de Janeiro Schools] by H. Lovisolo, A.J.G. Soares, & M.D. Santos, 1993, Rio de Janeiro, Brazil: Universidade Gama Filho/Conselho Nacional de Pesquisas. Copyright 1993 by Universidade Gama Filha/Conselho Nacional de Pesquisas. Adapted by permission.

situation with results from similar European research carried out by the Council of Europe (1982); McIntosh & Charlton (1985); the Belgium Sociological Research Unit (1991); and the Italian National Olympic Committee (1991):

- Brazilian children and adolescents share with their European counterparts the conspicuous tendency to make sports a key social norm in their day-to-day lives, while not abandoning sport practices inside schools as observed in many countries.
- This full adherence to extracurricular sports is done with the support and stimulus of parents and physical education teachers, mostly as a reaction to emerging cultural values and much less as a response to requirements and objectives of the schools. This social mobilization is due more to the failure of the Brazilian school system than to its possibilities.
- Contrary to the situation in affluent societies, in Brazil, lower income urban families do not necessarily reduce their level of participation in sports inside or outside schools. Also, the competition drive appears to be more evident among poor urban families.
- The main sports practiced in Brazil have a similar profile to those of both Italy and the French-speaking community in Belgium in the 10-to-14-year age bracket, suggesting that cultural rather than psychological factors primarily affect the choices made by young people in terms of sports.
- Virtually nothing is known about the typology of sport participation (regularity, intensity, gender difference, abandonment, etc.) in Brazil, an area which should cover the nationwide dimensions of child and adolescent populations, mainly because Brazilian scholars have placed empirical research after discussion of values and changes in both physical education and sports.

Promotional Campaigns

In spite of an economic crisis leading to an entire decade of decline and decadence in most sectors of Brazilian society, sports continue to uphold their potential. There are now nearly 150,000 teachers and coaches working with school sports and sport clubs, while as of 1992 there were a total of 122 Schools of Physical Education offering university-level courses to meet the needs of the country's 150 million inhabitants.

Of course, the indisputable social inequalities in Brazil make these figures at least questionable under the current situation. At any rate, positive developments are found frequently around the country, providing evidence of a latent capacity for mobilization. In club and federation sports, the 1980s boom of ''minischools'' is a vivid example of this statement.

As an instrument for training, competition, and talent scouting, the so-called sport minischools (''escolinhas de esporte'' in Portuguese) have operated symbolically and symptomatically inside recreational clubs rather than schools. Although this trend is widespread in many sport disciplines, once again there is not much data available. However, swimming stands to illustrate this new solution for the practice of sports by children and adolescents, because according to unconfirmed estimates, some 800,000 young athletes are currently participating. This figure is roughly the same for participants of all ages in the 14 major sport disciplines, who totalled 98% of elite club athletes in 1970 (DaCosta, 1971).

One relevant explanation for continued expansion of sports in the depressed Brazilian economy is the regular flow of financial support at the municipal level. According to the government nationwide school census in 1988, sports (5.9%) were second only to elementary schools (75.4%) in municipal educational expenditures nationwide. Educational organization/management ranked third with 5.5%, culture fourth with 4.9%, and all other items totalled 8.3% (Ministério da Educação, 1991).

Considering this effort at the grass roots level, the results that were expected explicitly for the JEBs when created in 1969 were not surprising: at that time, Brazil was a fast-growing economic power and the JEB system was expected to identify young talents in view of the representative nature of Brazilian sports (Ministério da Educação, 1989).

Contrary to that expectation, by 1981 it was clear that the JEBs had strayed from their original purpose: 54% of the athletes participating in JEB finals were not selected through school sport competitions, but rather included on the respective state all-star teams because of their performances in club and federation events. Thus, the intervention undertaken by the federal government also raised the need for new proposals for the JEBs. That was the scope of the "First National Conference on School Sports," held in Brasília in July 1989, which issued the "Brazilian Charter for School Sports" initiating a process of innovations that is still underway.

In short, this declaration aimed at providing backing for general recommendations for the organization and development of school sports, striving to hold back excess stress on performance that could possibly impede fair play and sporting attitudes. This objective should be considered achieved when "each athlete can make his or her individual contribution to benefit collective activities and accomplishments."

Because it was argued that the JEBs promoted school sports in a superficial, loose way, the charter established a legitimacy process in order to evaluate its own proposals. This conditional state is still valid now, as assumed by many Brazilian institutions and researchers. The study by Corbucci (1991) is an example of this step-by-step approach, because this researcher tested the charter's principles.

Prior to this task, Corbucci studied activities in a school setting according to a repression-emancipation continuum in which social actors' statements can be appropriately tabulated and submitted to categorical analysis. In the case of the JEBs, Corbucci studied the discourse of referees, team leaders, coaches, and young athletes as gathered through interviews. After having processed these statements in light of the charter's principles, Corbucci drew the following conclusions:

- Norms for competition are subject to change by participants for most sport disciplines.
- The significance of winning in sports is primarily related to fair play.
- Sport practice varies and is constantly reelaborated.
- Young athletes are capable of recreating sportsmanlike gestures themselves.
- Reward for competition occurs if all parties concerned achieve mutual development.
- Participants in any capacity take an intrinsically multidimensional approach to sport.

Along the same line of reasoning, Montenegro Passos and Menezes Costa (1989) surveyed the 1984-1988 reports on JEBs, adopting the Parlebas model of observation, which implies a cross-analysis involving athletes and the environment and athletes with athletes.

These researchers aimed to examine the solidarity or antagonism prevailing among JEB participants. Their final conclusions emphasized the impossibility of competitions in these games providing any motricity interaction, suggesting that they encourage individualism.

In another attempt to assess JEBs in relation to the School Sports Charter, Montenegro Passos and Menezes Costa in 1990 interviewed athletes, coaches, referees, and group leaders participating in the games to observe their managerial skills. This study's concluding remarks stressed the proven ability of pupils to perform self-management.

On the institutional side, it is important to mention the Program of Integral Support for Children and Adolescents, a $2-billion (Brazilian dollars) program included in the Brazilian federal budget. This program is an intervention to correct the decline of the Brazilian school system.

Beginning in 1992, this program has been building schools with a new concept according to which children and adolescents transfer their daily lives to school. In this case, the organization and management of school settings are supposed to be efficient. Pupils' cultural backgrounds are also a key reference for intra- and extracurricular activities and a basis for future actions.

In early 1993, the program added to its original concept that of full involvement in sports, which is now in the stage of planning a center for experimentation, demonstration, and dissemination to develop appropriate solutions for its target groups and for Brazilian education in general.

Conclusion

Overall, youth sports in Brazil have shown similar trends to European countries, but Brazilian specificities remain obscure due to lack of research. Despite this scarcity of data, sport proved to be among the key values of adolescents both outside school or inside it as an extracurricular activity. Very often, sport plays the role of a hidden curriculum for physical education in the school system, because it lies at the core of current culture.

As a future perspective, the sociocultural status of youth sports in Brazil is becoming a crucial source of proposals for renewing the educational system.

References

Belgium Sociological Research Unit. (1991). *The sporting practices of young people in the French community of Belgium*. Brussels, Belgium: Author.

Corbucci, P.R. (1991). *Um esporte na escola em busca da emancipação do homem* [School sport in search of man's emancipation]. Dissertação de Mestrado, Faculdade de Educação, Universidade de Brasília.

Council of Europe. (1982). *Sport in European society: A transnational survey into participation and motivation*. Strasburg, France: Author.

DaCosta, L.P. (1971). *Diagnostico de educação física e desportos no Brazil* [National survey of physical education and sport in Brazil]. Rio de Janeiro, Brazil: Ministério da Educação e Cultura.

Eiras, R.A.O. (1989). *Jogos escolares do Paraná: Rumo a democratização*. [School sport in Parana: Toward democratization]. Brasília, Brazil: Secretaria de Educação Física e Desporto, Primeira Conferência Brazileira de Esporte na Escola.

Faria Júnior, A.G. (1989). *Produção científica brasileira em educação física, 1973/1988* [Scientific works on physical education in Brazil, 1973/1988]. Rio de Janeiro, Brazil: Primeiro Congresso Internacional de Educação Física de Países de Lingua Portuguesa.

Farinatti, P.T. (1991). Pesquisa em educação física no Brazil: Por um compromisso com a evolução [Research on physical education in Brazil: In search of evolution]. In A.G. Faria Júnior & P.T. Farinatti (Eds.), *Pesquisa e produção do conhecimento em educação física* (pp. 34-68). Rio de Janeiro, Brazil: Ao Livro Técnico Editora.

Freire da Silva, J.B. (1989). *A competição e o esporte na escola: Valores e contradições* [Competition and sport in school]. Brasília, Brazil: Secretaria de Educação Física e Desportos, Primeira Conferência Brazileira de Esporte na Escola.

Galvão, N.A.V. (1989). *Desporto escolar* [Sport in school]. Brasília, Brazil: Secretaria de Educação Física e Desportos, Primeira Conferência Brazileira do Esporte na Escola.

Italian National Olympic Committee. (1991). *Survey on young people and sport: The factors influencing participation by young people*. Rome, Italy: Author.

Lovisolo, H., Soares, A.J.G., & Santos, M.D. (1993). *Educação física em escolas do Rio de Janeiro* [Physical education in Rio de Janeiro schools]. Rio de Janeiro, Brazil: Universidade Gama Filho/Conselho Nacional de Pesquisas.

McIntosh, P., & Charlton, V. (1985). *The impact of the Sport for All policy, 1966-1984*. London, England: Sports Council.

Ministério da Educação. (1986). *Sinopse da educação física e desportos, dados 1984-1986* [Summary of data: Physical education and sports 1984-1986]. Brasília, Brazil: Serviço de Estatística da Educação e Cultura.

Ministério da Educação. (1989). *Esporte na escola: Os XVIII JEBs como marco reflexivo* [School sport: Reflections on the XVIII JEBs]. Brasília, Brazil: Secretaria de Educação Física e Desportos.

Ministério da Educação. (1991). *Censo educacional de 1989: Prefeituras municipais* [Census of the educational sector 1989: Municipalities]. Brasília, Brazil: Serviço Estatística da Educação e Cultura.

Montenegro Passos, K.C., & Menezes Costa, V.L. (1989). *Uma lógica de solidariedade ou de antagonismo* [A logic of solidarity or antagonism]. Foz do Iguaçu, Brazil: IV Congresso Internacional da FIEP.

Montenegro Passos, K.C., & Menezes Costa, V.L. (1990). *Esporte na escola: educação para a democracia* [School sport: education for democracy]. Foz do Iguaçu, Brazil: V Congresso Internacional da FIEP.

Pereira, L.E. (1989). *O grêmio escolar: gestão democrática ou autogestão* [The school club: Democratic or self-managed]. Brasília, Brazil: Secretaria de Educação Física e Desporto, Primeira Conferência Brasileira do Esporte na Escola.

Rezende, H.G., & Costa Ferreira, V.L. (1984). *O espaço profissional ocupado pelo licenciado em educação física: Um estudo de mercado de trabalho* [The professional meaning of the physical education teacher: A labor market study]. Brasília, Brazil: Instituto Nacional de Estudos e Pesquisas Educacionais.

Soares, C.L., Taffarel, C.L.Z., Varjal, E., Castellani, L., Escobar, M.O., & Bracht, V. (1992). *Metodologia do ensino de educação física* [Methodology of physical education teaching]. São Paulo, Brazil: Cortez Editora.

Tubino, M.J.G. (1988). A interpretação do esporte na educação brasileira [The interpretation of sport in Brazilian education]. Tese de Doutorado, Faculdade de Educação, Universidade Federal do Rio de Janeiro.

Tubino, M.J.G. (1989). *A hora e a vez do esporte-educação* [The very turn of sport-education]. Brasília, Brazil: Secretaria de Educação Física e Desportos, Primeira Conferência Brasileira de Esporte na Escola.

Chapter 4 Canada

Leonard M. Wankel
W. Kerry Mummery

Canada's recreational system is a multisectoral system comprising public, quasi-public, private, commercial, and voluntary sectors (Wankel & Sefton, 1992). Each of these different components is involved in some way in the delivery of youth sport programs.

The Organizational Network

The public sector, through municipal governments, provides the major sporting facilities, including playing fields, ice arenas, swimming pools, and so forth. Provincial grants support the construction of these facilities and assist with some programming costs. Many of the gymnasia or auditoria used for indoor youth sport activities are provided by the tax-supported educational systems. Quasi-public agencies such as the YMCA/YWCA and Boys and Girls Clubs also sponsor a variety of youth programs and have a number of their own facilities. Voluntary agencies contribute to youth sport programming in a number of ways. Service clubs (e.g., Kinsmen, Lions, Optimists) have contributed substantial sums of money to developing parks and sporting facilities and are heavily involved in sponsoring the operation of youth sport activities as well. Volunteers serving on the various sport governing organizations (e.g., Football Association, Figure Skating Association, Tennis Association) at the national, provincial, and local levels play a central role in the conduct of sport at all levels in Canada. A variety of private sport clubs (e.g., squash and racquet clubs, tennis clubs, winter clubs, golf clubs) offer instructional and competitive sport opportunities for their members. Finally, a wide variety of businesses provide facilities, equipment, and/or programs for sport enthusiasts of all ages.

Although the rich variety of sporting opportunities provided by these various agencies does not constitute a sport system as such, youth sport programs within Canada may be generally viewed as falling within two major categories—community-based sport and sport offered within the education system. Community sport programs are generally offered by the local municipal authority in collaboration with other local agencies. In some communities the local youth sport programs are organized and administered directly by the local recreation department, whereas, in others, the department plays a more indirect role in facilitating the provision of recreation services by other agencies. The variety and extent of the offerings vary with the size and population of the area. Paralleling the community sport system, the major school systems, both public and sectarian (e.g., the Catholic School Board and the Anglican School Board) provide organized programs in a variety of sports. The relationship between the two general "systems" varies considerably. In a number of areas, especially smaller centers, the two systems may be closely coordinated with a view to providing the best overall sport opportunities for the area. In other cases, the two systems operate quite independently and may in fact compete in attempting to attract the best athletes.

Community-Based Youth Sport

The community-based youth sport system (frequently called "minor sport" in Canada) operates at two general levels. First, an inclusive community league or *house* system operates that caters to the participation of all those who are interested in participating in the particular sport. As many competitive units are organized as are necessary to accommodate the registered participants. These units are stratified according to age level, gender, and, when participant numbers are adequate, skill level.

Within most communities provision is made for a higher level of competition for the most skilled participants within the various age divisions. These *representative*, *all-star*, or *travel* teams provide a more intense level of sport involvement. They have a more extensive game schedule and more frequent, more highly organized practice sessions, and they travel greater distances to participate in competitions. Participation at this level, as compared to the community level, is much more time-intensive and expensive for the participants. Although in theory participation on these teams is open to any athlete, the number of participants is restricted and positions on the competitive units are determined through skill tryouts. Aspirants for these teams who are not selected by the coaches drop back to participate on a *house-league* team. This general bilevel model does not apply to all sports. For example, within such individual sports as swimming, track and field, and tennis, all participants may belong to the same club; however, highly skilled individuals are commonly selected for participation in meets to which the number of entrants is restricted.

Sports commonly offered on an organized-league basis by municipal recreation agencies in larger centers within Canada include baseball/softball, football, rugby, and soccer in the summer; and hockey, ringette, volleyball, and basketball in the winter. Individual sports such as swimming, skating, golf, tennis, racquetball, squash, and Alpine and Nordic skiing tend to be offered only on an instructional basis or on a drop-in recreational basis by municipal agencies. Competition in these sports occurs primarily through a club system. The clubs may be either voluntary nonprofit clubs (e.g., the South-West United Soccer Association, the Keyano Swim Club) or private agencies (e.g., the Squash and Racquet Club and the Golf and Country Club).

It is important to note that community-operated sport programs are collaborative ventures of various agencies within the community. Although the municipal government generally provides, or assists in the provision of, the sport facilities (e.g., playing fields, arenas, tennis courts), frequently the teams are sponsored by other agencies. These might be voluntary organizations (e.g., community leagues or associations), service clubs (e.g., Kinsmen, Lions, Optimists), or commercial firms. The local sport organization responsible for the sport will set guidelines for the sponsorship of teams and the selection and conduct of coaches, and will establish rules governing competition. Within these general guidelines the particular agency will select its coaches, who are responsible for the day-to-day operation of the team.

School Sport Programs

School sport programs typically can be divided into the instructional physical education class component; an intramural component geared to general participation with little emphasis on intense competition, schedules, or practices; and an interschool component for competition between schools in various sports. Intramural programs differ in orientation, ranging from established competitive units with set schedules to drop-in, spontaneously organized sport activities. These programs are organized and conducted autonomously within individual schools, so eligibility, rule modification, schedules, and so forth are determined by the particular school authorities. Leadership of the instructional and intramural programs is generally the responsibility of trained physical education teachers. Although the interscholastic program is also generally the responsibility of the physical education staff, in many schools other teachers or community volunteers who have backgrounds and expertise in the sport are frequently recruited as coaches.

Interschool competition falls under the jurisdiction of a school district governing body (e.g., the Edmonton High School Athletic Association) which, in turn, is a member of a corresponding provincial high school athletic association. In the case of basketball, for example, a provincial high school basketball association administers a system of annual playoffs to determine a champion in each unit (males and females each at several different levels, e.g., A, B, C, D, representing schools with different enrollments).

Although the situation varies somewhat from province to province, typically provincial championships at the senior high level (i.e., grades 10 to 12) are held for girls' and boys' teams in such sports as basketball, volleyball, soccer, badminton, track and field, and cross-country. Championships in wrestling and football as well are often held for boys.

At the junior high level (i.e., grades 7 to 9) competition is usually restricted to the local level. That is, a city or district junior high school champion in a given sport may be determined, and winners typically do not go on to compete at a higher level.

Sport at the elementary school level is generally not highly organized or structured. Occasionally, however, schools may join together for activity days in which students participate in a variety of activities and emphasis is placed on participation rather than competitive outcomes. Sport and physical education leadership at the elementary level is generally the responsibility of the classroom teacher, who frequently will have no specialized training or particular expertise in the subject.

Sport Governance

All competitive youth sport programs in Canada, whether they be offered through community agencies or the schools, fall under the overall supervision of the pertinent sport governing body. These voluntary agencies are hierarchically structured, paralleling the governmental structure of the country. That is, there are national, provincial (and territorial), and regional or local governing organizations for each sport. These organizations are responsible for establishing the rules and competitive guidelines, and for overseeing the operation of the particular sport at the appropriate level. The Canadian sport system is portrayed in Figure 4.1. (A more detailed description of the recreation and sport system in Canada is provided in Alberta Recreation and Parks, 1990.)

Sport Participation

There are few comprehensive statistics pertaining to youth sport participation in Canada. A 1988 national survey, the Campbell Survey of the Well-Being of Canadians, indicated that 42% of males and 37% of females 10 to 14 years old reported participating in competitive sport at least weekly (Stephens & Craig, 1990). The comparable figures for ages 15 to 19 were 44% for males and 28% and females who participated at least once during the year in various sports is presented in Table 4.1.

Information on the sport participation of 11-, 13-, and 15-year-old Canadian youths was collected as part of a World Health Organization-sponsored cross-national study of the health of children (King & Coles, 1992). The study indicated a progressive decline in sport involvement across the three ages studied as well as substantial gender differences. The percentages of boys and girls who were members of a community sport club were: age 11, 62% and 49%; age 13, 58% and 38%; age 15, 52% and 30%. The comparable figures for males and females who were members of a school sport team were: age 11, 45% and 45%; age 13, 51% and 37%; age 15, 42% and 35%. Comparative information for children from Finland, Wales, and Poland indicated that a greater percentage of Canadian youth, both males and females, were active in these forms of organized sports than were their counterparts from the other three countries.

A report on the program registrations in various sports in the city of Edmonton provides information concerning more regular sport involvement of boys and girls. The study of 73 minor-sport organizations indicated that 34% of eligible boys and 17% of girls, 18 years of age or younger, were involved in organized sport (Sanderson, 1993). The percentages of males and females comprised in the total registrations varied substantially across sports: aquatic programs, 43.7% male, 56.3% female; arena sports, 78.5% male, 21.5% female; field sports, 67.6% male, 32.4% female; indoor sports, 58% male, 42% female; outdoor sports, 43.4% male, 56.6% female. With respect to registrations in specific sports, males were

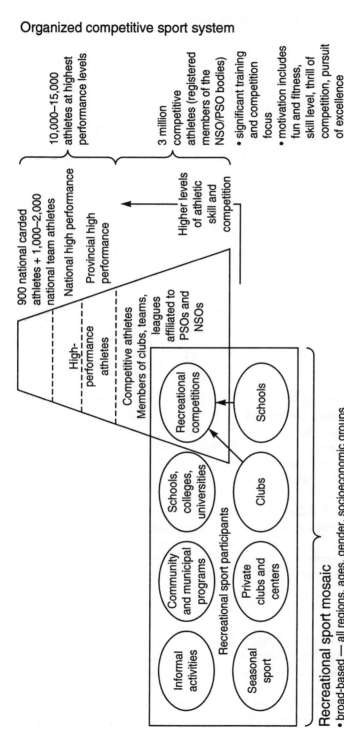

Figure 4.1 Sport in Canada. *Note.* From *Sport: The Way Ahead* (p. 30), by Minister's Task Force on Federal Sport Policy, 1992, Ottawa, Ontario: Ministry of Supply and Services Canada. Reprinted by permission.

Table 4.1 Percentage of Canadian Youth Participating in Individual Activities by Age and Sex (CSWB 1988)

	Age			
	10-14		15-20	
Sport	Male	Female	Male	Female
Skating	61	65	35	34
Cross-country skiing	26	33	21	26
Alpine skiing	40	43	48	35
Hockey	44	7	40	3
Swimming	78	87	58	69
Golf	15	5	28	10
Tennis	25	16	33	27
Baseball	59	41	44	30
Volleyball	6	16	8	16
Bowling	26	33	25	27

Note. From *The Well-Being of Canadians: Highlights of the 1988 Campbell's Survey*, by T. Stephens and C. Craig, 1990, Ottawa, Ontario: Canadian Fitness and Lifestyle Research Institute. (Calculations made on data tape made available from Canadian Fitness and Lifestyle Research Institute, Ottawa, Ontario.)

overrepresented in: boxing (100%), baseball (100%), Canadian football (100%), hockey (99.8%), lacrosse (96.9%), weight lifting (85.7%), soccer (69%), basketball (69%), and tennis (63%). Females were overrepresented in: synchronized swimming (100%), ringette (100%), rhythmic gymnastics (96.4%) and figure skating (69%). The proportions of males and females were relatively equal in such sports as: bowling, males 50%, females 50%; track, males 50%, females 50%; volleyball, males 50%, females 50%; gymnastics, males 44%, females 56%; curling, males 60%, females 40%; and softball, males 47.6%, females 52.4%.

Although more Canadian boys than girls participate in organized sport programs, there is a trend toward greater female involvement. The Alberta Soccer Association, for example, reported that the percentage of its membership that was female increased from 14.8% in 1985, to 27.9% in 1988, to 29.4% in 1992 (McConnel, 1993).

Trends

The absence of good statistics makes it impossible to conclusively document trends in participation. Nevertheless, the evidence available together with more casual observation suggests the presence of a number of trends in Canadian youth sports.

First, there is a progressive decline in the number of participants as age levels increase. While youth sport research has indicated that time constraints caused by the desire to do other activities is a major reason for leaving sport, negative experiences with adult leadership are also an important factor (Gould, 1987; Weiss & Chaumeton, 1992). This latter area is cause for concern if there is desire to maximize participation.

Second, there has been a professionalization of sport delivery. Although there are occasional criticisms of the adult-dominated nature of modern organized youth sport programs, and laments over the decline of spontaneous sport participation by children (Devereux, 1976), the trend has continued toward more highly organized, adult-led youth sport programs (Hall, Slack, Smith & Whitson, 1991). The demands from both parents and sport organizations for more effective skill development and better performance levels have fueled this trend. Sport facilities are heavily booked with organized practices and games. Little free time is left during the competitive season for spontaneous sport play.

Another indication of the increased organization of youth sport is the shift of control from the local level to provincial and national sport organizations. Rather than local individuals getting together to organize sport opportunities for youth according to what they think is best for the situation (e.g., accordingly adapt rules, playing time, eligibility), current practice is to shape local opportunities to fit the dictates of provincial and national guidelines to enable higher levels of competition. This higher level organization of youth sport has undoubtedly improved sport performance and has made competently led quality sport experiences available on a much broader basis. It has also, however, decreased spontaneity, local relevance, and flexibility.

A further manifestation of this organizational trend is the increasing standardization of equipment and facilities. Minor sport participants from the initial level onwards tend to be suited in professional-like gear and to play on standard-sized fields. Again, there are positive and negative features to this. Whereas more youth now play in comfortable, safe facilities with adequate protective equipment, these advances have greatly increased the cost of participation, which has created hardships for disadvantaged groups.

A third trend is the decreased dominance of a limited number of traditional sports (e.g., hockey, baseball, soccer) and increasing participation in a larger number of sports. This increased variety in particular sport participation may reflect a number of factors. The increasing multicultural makeup of the country has meant that a number of young Canadians do not have cultural affinity with the more traditional Canadian sports. The increased availability of indoor sport facilities has also made alternate sport activities (e.g., racquet sports, volleyball, basketball) more readily available. And increased costs of participation in certain sports has led to increased popularity of other less expensive sports (e.g., soccer or basketball in place of ice hockey).

Fourth, there has been a trend toward more gender equity in sport participation. Although a higher percentage of boys than girls participates in organized sport, the discrepancy has narrowed over the years (as is shown in the example mentioned earlier of the Alberta Soccer Association). The variety of sports available to girls has increased, and it has become more accepted for girls to participate on boys' teams when separate girls' teams are not available.

Problems in Youth Sport

Before discussing some of the current problems in Canadian youth sport, it should be clearly emphasized that youth sport is generally looked upon as a very positive element of Canadian life. Nearly all Canadian children participate in one sport or another, at some point, and in general they greatly enjoy their youth sport experience (Fry, McClements, & Sefton, 1981; Wankel & Kreisel, 1985). Further, most parents believe strongly in the potential benefits of youth sports (e.g., fitness, friendship development, discipline, character development, skill acquisition, and enjoyment) for their children (Dryden & MacGregor, 1989). Nevertheless, as in all things, there is room for improvement. Problems in youth sport may be classified as problems of equity, problems concerning values and ethical conduct in sport, and problems of leadership.

Problems of equity.   As a democratic country, Canada subscribes to a philosophy of sport for all, whereby individuals are entitled to participate in the sports of their choice. In reality, however, barriers do exist so that many Canadians do not have equitable access to the sport system. There are barriers along gender, cultural, regional, and economic lines.

Although progress has been made in providing greater opportunities for female participation in sport, girls are still disadvantaged in terms of sport opportunities relative to boys. The 1992 report of the Minister's Task Force on Federal Sport Policy states:

> The participation of females in physical activity and sport declines at a very young age. Fewer school sports and activities are offered to girls; teams are mainly segregated; opportunities are limited. Boys' teams tend to command the use of facilities. Rules and conventional practices in sport favor physical strength and development of boys. Sport is based on decades of traditions and practices which favor male participation (Sport: The Way Ahead, 1992, p. 149).

While overtly discriminatory practices impeding female involvement in sport have lessened over the years, more subtle practices persist. Parents, teachers, and other significant adults commonly do not provide as much encouragement for girls as for boys to participate in sport. A relative dearth of highly visible, well-publicized sporting role models for females weakens the supportive environment for involvement as well. The media continue to give most of their coverage to male sport events.

Canada's indigenous population is also disadvantaged in a number of ways. It suffers a lower standard of living, a higher crime rate, a greater incidence of illness, and a shorter life expectancy relative to other Canadian groups. With respect to sport participation, children in indigenous communities have fewer sporting opportunities. A study conducted in conjunction with the national task force on sport (Sport: The Way Ahead, 1992) indicated that few indigenous communities have adequate facilities for a well-rounded youth sport program, that the range of available activities provided is greatly restricted (most commonly hockey, softball, soccer, and volleyball), and that the programs offered frequently are lacking in quality as a result of unqualified coaches. Few leaders from this community participate in the National Coaching Certification Program.

Economic factors also have an impact on youth sport opportunities. The increased cost of ice time and required protective equipment for hockey, for example, has resulted in many young Canadians' dropping out of this sport. A study of dropouts from the Edmonton Minor Hockey Association programs indicated cost to be a primary reason for many participants leaving hockey (Sanderson, 1993). The federal task force on sport in Canada identified these gender, ethnic, and economic inequities and has targeted them for change in its proposals for improving the Canadian sport system. The vision of sport in Canada espoused by the task force emphasizes inclusion and equity.

Problems of ethical conduct. The official objectives for youth sport programs are above reproach. Typically, they espouse democratic ideals of participation, character development, enjoyment, and the promotion of health and fitness. In actual practice, however, a number of sport programs appear to focus more on winning games and pursuing championships than on the espoused objectives. Too frequently adults, whether as parents or coaches, tend to get carried away with their own agendas rather than providing a positive opportunity for skill development, success, and enjoyment for all participants. Although such undesirable practices are undoubtedly the minority in a field where caring, voluntary leaders provide countless hours of valuable service, nevertheless such practices have a significant impact. Poor leadership and adult pressure have been identified as contributing factors to premature withdrawal from sport (Gould, 1987).

Beyond the individual level, the increased professionalization of youth sport described previously and the more centralized control from national sport governing bodies have tended to alter the objectives. The linking of skill development to the profile of a sport and its status within the Canadian amateur sport hierarchy has affected the sport value system. Attempts to combine elitism for the talented few with recreational sport geared to the optimal development of all under one system often create an uncomfortable alliance.

On another level, pressures to be the best, to be stronger, and to be more muscular have resulted in an increasingly serious problem of drug abuse. In high-level sport, the desire to win at the highest competitive level has been implicated as a factor in the use of performance-enhancing drugs by international athletes (Dubin, 1990). More relevant to the current topic and of even greater concern is the more recent information that steroid use is not restricted to high-level athletes. A national survey of the use of performance-enhancing substances by school students in Canada indicated that over 30,000 Canadian males between the ages of 16 and 18 had used steroids in the previous 12 months (Canadian Centre for Drug-Free Sport, 1993; Cheadle, 1993). The survey indicated that the problem was not restricted to athletes. More than 47% of the steroid users in the survey indicated that they used the drug because they wanted to change their physical appearance, while 53.9% reported using the drug to do better in sports. These statistics signal a very serious problem and suggest that immediate attention should be given to how to redress the excessive pressures to succeed in sport and in society more generally. It would seem that what is needed is a total reorientation of values from the product-oriented outcome to a reestablishment of honor and integrity more characteristic of the original Olympic ideal.

A particular concern within the area of values is aggression or violence in sport. This is of particular interest in ice hockey. There has been an ongoing debate within hockey generally, and within youth hockey in particular, as to the acceptability of different levels of aggression. Debate continues as to the desirability of removing body-checking from the game for certain age levels.

The Fair Play movement is one reflection of such a shift in emphasis. A Fair Play Program introduced by the Edmonton Minor Hockey Program in Edmonton, Alberta, in January, 1991, emphasized four objectives:

- To reduce injuries
- To change the attitudes and values in the game
- To improve the quality of play
- To improve the image of the game (Knack, 1990).

This program, which rewards teams for playing penalty-free hockey during a delimited 6-week portion of the regular season, has now operated for three seasons and continues to grow in popularity. In the province of Quebec, a fair play scoring system has been employed wherein teams receive one point for scoring more goals than the other team and one point for not taking more than a certain number of penalties. The Fair Play movement and a move to eliminate body contact in the early years of hockey have been fostered by evidence such as that provided by Brust, Leonard, Pheley, and Roberts (1992) that body contact accounted for most injuries in youth hockey.

At the national level, a Commission for Fair Play was established by Canada's Minister of State for Fitness and Amateur Sport in 1986. The 20-member commission promotes fair play through

- advertising and promotional campaigns,
- informational and educational materials,
- encouragement and recognition of citizens who exemplify fair play, and
- proposing fair play initiatives to the minister.

The commission works with provincial and territorial representatives to further its ends throughout the country. The commission received recognition for its educational resource "Fair Play for Kids" when it was awarded a 1991 Diploma of Honour for the Promotion of Fair Play by the International Committee for Fair Play.

Problems with leadership.   The issue of leadership is closely tied to that of values. The Coaching Association, through the National Coaching Certification Program (NCCP), attempts to foster an athlete-centered approach to coaching. The majority of the thousands of volunteer coaches generally reflect this orientation in their coaching and perform a very creditable service. There are always a few, however, who are more committed to winning than to fairness and child development, or who focus on the talented few while overlooking the less talented. At times a "win at all cost" philosophy surfaces in the form of inappropriate coaching practices and "ugly incidents."

Promotional Campaigns

Despite the prevalence of these problems, it would be a fallacy to suggest that progress has not been made. In many ways Canada has been a leader in developing initiatives to address the problems identified. Of particular note has been the role of national agencies such as Sport Canada, the Coaching Association of Canada, Fitness Canada, and the Canadian Association for Health, Physical Education and Recreation.

Coaching Education

Canada has been a leader in coaching development programs. The National Coaching Certification Program (NCCP) was initiated by the Coaching Association of Canada, a division of Sport Canada, in 1974. The program consists of three components (theoretical, technical, and practical) and is structured into five levels. Levels 1 to 3 emphasize development, while levels 4 and 5 are oriented toward high-level performance. The theory component presents general information pertinent to all coaches (e.g., the psychology of coaching, the physiology of training, and the philosophy of coaching), while the technical component is sport-specific information offered in conjunction with the different sport associations. The practical component entails working in an actual coaching situation with an experienced coach. The program is directed nationally by the Coaching Association of Canada, but is delivered through the cooperating provincial authorities, who organize and administer the courses.

Although the program was initiated as a voluntary program, gradually certification at specified levels is beginning to be required for coaching at certain levels. For example, Level 4 certification is required to coach Canadian Olympic athletes, while Level 3 is needed to coach at the Canada Games level. Beyond this, various sport organizations or sponsoring clubs request specified levels of certification for their coaches. Although no major overall evaluation of the program has taken place, it is generally accepted that the program has had a positive influence on improving the quality of coaching in Canada. The level of acceptance is reflected in participation figures for 1992. In that year 1,798 courses were offered to 28,273 coaches. This included 1,322 courses with 21,506 coaches at Level 1, 382 courses for 5,711 coaches at Level 2, and 94 courses for 1,056 coaches at Level 3.

The focus of the initial levels of the NCCP is to foster more competent coaches who can facilitate skill development in young athletes and provide positive sporting experiences to all participants. It is hoped that this athlete-centered orientation will contribute to greater involvement and enjoyment by Canadian youths.

Involvement of Females

Sport Canada and the Coaching Association have also been attempting to promote greater female involvement in sport. A Women's Program Division has been established within Sport Canada, and a national advocacy/networking organization—the Canadian Association for the Advancement of Women in Sport—developed. These organizations have been effective in developing materials, organizing conferences and workshops, and communicating information. They have achieved some success in raising awareness of inequities. However, much still remains to be done, as indicated by both participation statistics and information concerning leadership positions in the sport system (Whitson & Macintosh, 1989).

Sport Competitions

The initiation of a system of Canada Games by Sport Canada, in collaboration with the pertinent provincial and territorial sport and recreation departments, has provided a positive stimulus for competitive sport for young Canadians. The Canada Winter Games and Canada Summer Games, which are held every four years, have provided a competitive outlet for and recognition to highly skilled young athletes. This system, in turn, has been extended downward in the form of Provincial Games by many of the provinces. Together, this system of games has promoted competitive sport for skilled young athletes and has stimulated the construction of sport facilities for the competitions in many communities across the country.

Fitness and Health-Related Activities

Fitness Canada, a federal government agency responsible for promoting and developing fitness in Canada, has played a leading role in developing initiatives to promote widespread physical activity. This agency works in collaboration with provincial recreation departments and representatives from various academic and professional groups. Its central emphasis in recent years has been on promoting the concept of Active Living and how it might apply to different target groups.

Active Living is a holistic perspective on physical activity encompassing the processes, experiences, and benefits associated with being physically active (Fitness Canada, 1991). Emphasis is placed on inclusiveness and equity—how physical activity can become an integrated component of daily living for all regardless of age, income, gender, or health status. Active Living emphasizes how physical activity can be made a lifelong, empowering developmental process to enhance self-realization and an improved quality of life. Leisure-time sport and physical activity are an important component of this message provided that they are offered in such a way as to emphasize positive outcomes, personal involvement and choices, and availability to all.

In promoting the philosophy of Active Living, Fitness Canada along with its collaborating partners identified a number of target groups and specific blueprints or frameworks for action in fostering active living within these groups. Children and youth were one such priority group. A planning guide was developed to assist agencies to cooperate in pursuing the goal of making active living a reality for the 7.3 million children and youth of Canada (Fitness Canada, 1990). To facilitate these initiatives, an Active Living Alliance for Children and Youth was established in March, 1991, comprising more than 30 fitness, sport, health, recreation, youth, and government organizations and agencies committed to facilitating active living and health in children and youth. The Alliance replaced the Children and Youth Fitness Office within Fitness Canada. Unfortunately, because of recent governmental cutbacks, Fitness Canada has discontinued its financial support for a number of programs, including the Alliance, and as a result it ceased operations in 1993.

Another collaborative initiative spearheaded by Fitness Canada is the development of the Canadian Active Living Challenge (Canadian Active Living Challenge, 1993). The Challenge was developed to replace the previous Canada Fitness Awards Program and is designed to foster the knowledge, attitudes, and skills pertinent to the practice of active living in young Canadians. The program includes four levels, catering to the age groups 6 through 18, which may be introduced through educational, recreational, or other youth agencies. A number of resource materials including pamphlets, workbooks, and videos have been developed to assist agencies in implementing the program.

Physical Education and Sport Development Activities

The Canadian Association for Health, Physical Education, Recreation and Dance (CAHPERD), the association for professionals in the fields of physical education and physical activity in Canada, has also been active in promoting widespread physical activity. For several years the association has been active in developing materials for and promoting Quality Daily Physical Education (QDPE) in the school system (Passmore, 1993). In 1993, this program received international recognition when it was awarded a prestigious UNESCO Award for Distinguished Services in the field of physical education and sport. To improve its educational and lobbying efforts for spreading the QDPE movement, CAHPERD in February 1993 joined with 13 national and allied associations, including the Canadian Medical Association, to form the Canadian Coalition for QDPE. Member groups are encouraged to use their networks and political influence to assist in the lobbying initiative.

A number of the specific sport organizations (e.g., the Canadian Amateur Hockey Association, the Canadian Figure Skating Association, Swimming Canada) have developed innovative programs to broaden their appeal. Alternatives to competitive programs have been developed with distinctive objectives, and attempts are being made to guide participants into ''streams'' compatible with their interests and abilities. The Alberta Hockey Association, for example, offers six different ability streams in an effort to accommodate diverse individuals. The

Canadian Figure Skating Association has introduced a learn-to-skate program for children as young as 4 to 5. Emphasis is placed on developing skill to increase competence and fostering lifelong interest in the sport. The vast majority of its 180,000 members are recreational rather than competitive skaters.

Finally, there are some noteworthy initiatives outside of the mainstream sport system. In Alberta, for example, a group of private individuals initiated the FunTeam concept to promote family sport activities outside of the mainstream organized sport programs. Funds were raised or obtained through granting agencies to provide materials and leadership to assist interested families and community groups to organize sport events designed to include all interested participants in healthy, enjoyable activities. In Edmonton, Alberta, a nonprofit organization called Sport Central was established in 1991 to "encourage participation in sport by all people through the provision of service and assistance to individuals and groups in the community" (Sport Central, 1993, p. 1). The organization pursues its goals by raising funds and offering programs, helping with communication, and providing equipment free of charge to those in need. Operating similarly to a food bank, the organization has addressed the problem of inequity in sport by providing sport equipment directly to disadvantaged youth. It also provides information on programs and arranges scholarships for programs and sport camps.

Conclusion

Youth sport is an important aspect of modern Canadian life. Nearly all young boys and girls participate at some time in organized sport. Research indicates that youths greatly enjoy participating in sport. Although a number of problem areas exist, these have been identified and attempts have been made to rectify them. Many of these problematic issues go beyond sport, reflecting general value issues within modern society. As a result, they are not subject to easy solutions within the sport setting. A number of initiatives have been taken within Canada to promote quality sport experiences for all youth, initiatives that may provide instructive examples for other countries. There is a lack of good information, however, concerning participation rates and trends in youth sport in Canada. Beyond such descriptive information concerning participation, it would also be desirable to have evaluative information concerning the outcomes of such programs. That is, do youth sport programs in fact produce the positive outcomes commonly claimed for them? There is need to document the organizational and leadership practices that are necessary for these outcomes to be realized (Wankel & Berger, 1990).

References

Alberta Recreation and Parks. (1990, September/October). The recreation and sport system in Canada. *Recreation News.*

Brust, J.D., Leonard, B.J., Pheley, A., & Roberts, W.O. (1992). Children's ice hockey injuries. *American Journal of Diseases of Children,* **146**, 741-747.

Canadian Active Living Challenge. (1993). *Leader's resource tool kit. (Program 4: Ages 15 to 18)*. Ottawa, Canada: Active Living Alliance for Children and Youth (Fitness and Amateur Sport).

Cheadle, B. (1993, June 2). Teenage athletes turning to drugs in 'scary' numbers. *The Edmonton Journal*, D5.

Canadian Centre for Drug-Free Sport. (1993). *National school survey on drugs and sport: Final report*. Gloucester, ON: Author.

Devereux, E.C. (1976). Backyard versus Little League baseball: The impoverishment of children's games. In D. M. Landers (Ed.), *Social problems in athletics: Essays in the sociology of sport*. Urbana and Chicago: University of Illinois Press.

Dryden, K., & MacGregor, R. (1989). *Home game: Hockey and life in Canada*. Toronto: McClelland and Stewart.

Dubin, C.L. (1990). *Commission of inquiry into the use of drugs and banned practices intended to increase athletic performance*. Ottawa: Supply and Services Canada.

Fitness Canada. (1990). *Because they're young: Active living for Canadian children and youth (A blueprint for action)*. Ottawa: Fitness Canada.

Fitness Canada. (1991). *Fitness Canada: Program description*. Unpublished manuscript.

Fry, D.A.P., McClements, J.D, & Sefton, J.M. (1981). *A report on participation in the Saskatoon Hockey Association*. Regina: Saskatchewan Sport.

Gould, D. (1987). Understanding attrition in children's sport. In D. Gould & M. Weiss (Eds.), *Advances in pediatric sport sciences* (pp. 61-85). Champaign, IL: Human Kinetics.

Hall, A., Slack, T., Smith, G., & Whitson, D. (1991). *Sport in Canadian society*. Toronto, Canada: McClelland & Stewart.

King, A.J.C., & Coles, B. (1992). *The health of Canada's youth: Views and behaviours of 11-, 13- and 15-year-olds from 11 countries*. Ottawa, Ontario: Minister of Supply and Services, Canada.

Knack, M. (1990, December 11). Minor hockey fair-play plan will hit city. *Edmonton Journal*, p. D2.

McConnel, R. (1993, May 15). Girls and sports: Greater expectations. *Edmonton Journal*, p. C3.

Passmore, R. (1993). The UNESCO award: A tribute to QDPE volunteers. *CAHPERD Journal*, **59**, 3, 7.

Sanderson, K. (1993). *Minor sport cost analysis study: Summary report*. Unpublished report submitted to Edmonton Parks and Recreation, Edmonton, Alberta.

Sport Central. (1993). *Information sheet*. Unpublished document.

Sport: The Way Ahead. (1992). *The report of the Minister's Task Force on Federal Sport Policy*. Ottawa, Canada: Ministry of Supply and Services Canada.

Stephens, T., & Craig, C. (1990). *The well-being of Canadians: Highlights of the 1988 Campbell's Survey*. Ottawa, Ontario: Canadian Fitness and Lifestyle Research Institute.

Wankel, L., & Berger, B. (1990). The psychological and social benefits of sport and physical activity. *Journal of Leisure and Recreation,* **22**(2), 167-182.

Wankel, L., & Kreisel, P. (1985). Factors underlying enjoyment of youth sports: Sport and age group comparisons. *Journal of Sport Psychology,* **7**, 65-74.

Wankel, L., & Sefton, J. (1992). Physical activity: Leisure and recreation. In C. Bouchard, B. MacPherson, & A. Taylor (Eds.), *Physical activity sciences* (pp. 155-165). Champaign, IL: Human Kinetics.

Weiss, M.R., & Chaumeton, N. (1992). Motivational orientations in sport. In T. Horn (Ed.), *Advances in sport psychology* (pp. 61-99). Champaign, IL: Human Kinetics.

Whitson, D., & Macintosh, D. (1989). Gender and power: Explanations of gender inequalities in Canadian national sport organizations. *International Review for the Sociology of Sport,* **24**, 137-150.

Acknowledgments

The authors express their appreciation to Candy Stothart, Active Living Alliance for Children and Youth; Kim Sanderson, Edmonton Parks and Recreation; and officers at a number of the sport governing associations and other agencies who helped provide information for this chapter.

Chapter 5   The United States

Maureen R. Weiss
Carl T. Hayashi

Competitive youth sport in the United States is practically a subculture of its own, with an estimated 20 to 35 million 5- to 18-year-old participants in nonschool sports (Ewing & Seefeldt, 1996) and 10 million 14- to 18-year-old participants in school sports (Seefeldt, Ewing, & Walk, 1992). Although these numbers likely represent overestimates due to participation in more than one sport by many youth, they nevertheless underscore the obsession Americans have with the importance and value of sport for children and adolescents. Whether it be competition in a local, agency-sponsored program, a school-sponsored intramural program, or free play in a neighborhood backyard, youth sport in the United States is alive . . . but is it well?

The public schools relinquished control over competitive sport for youth in elementary and middle schools around the 1930s. Nonschool programs such as national youth agencies (e.g., YMCA), national youth sport organizations (e.g., Little League Baseball), national governing bodies (NGBs; e.g., USA Gymnastics), and local service clubs (e.g., Eugene Emerald KidSports) picked up the slack, and athletic opportunities for children and teenagers have never looked back (Wiggins, 1996). Opportunities for youth to participate in a variety of sports in their own communities at a variety of skill levels are plentiful. Along with this shift of control from trained public educators to largely volunteer private professionals has come a continual debate on the cost/benefit ratio of children's sport participation. While advocates are quick to point out the potential physical, social, and psychological growth and development fostered by participation in adult-organized, competitive youth sport, critics are just as quick to point out the transfer of professional sport problems (e.g., ethics, undue stress, injuries) to its younger emulators.

Competitive sport for children is here to stay—children and their parents are enthusiastic consumers. It is critical to note that competitive youth sport is not inherently good or bad; it has been likened to a double-edged sword that can swing in either a positive or negative way (Martens, 1976). As sport social psychologists, our commitment is to conduct research and impart information that will maximize the positive and minimize the negative in children's sport. Eliminating the negative is, we believe, an unreachable goal. However, we remain highly optimistic that the history of children's and adolescents' sport illuminates a largely positive developmental phenomenon, and anticipates only better things for the future. To ensure this bright future will require that we step back and become introspective about the organization, participation trends, scientific progress, problems, and effectiveness of promotional campaigns in this country.

The Organizational Network

Youth sports in the United States can be divided into two categories of organizational networking: community-based (nonschool) and school-based programs. In general, community-based programs claim twice as many youth participants as school-based programs (Ewing & Seefeldt, 1996), largely because of diminishing resources in public schools over the last decade. This translates to fewer sports per school, fewer teams per sport, and fewer qualified individuals to coach. In contrast, community-based programs depend on volunteers (mostly parents) to administer, coach, and officiate children as young as 4 to 5 years of age in a large array of sports.

Community-based programs can be further divided into four types of organizations: agency-sponsored programs, national youth service organizations, club sports, and recreation programs (Seefeldt et al., 1992). For example, an agency-sponsored unit may include a local self-supporting community program that provides athletic opportunities for youth. This type of program depends heavily upon donations by service clubs and fundraising events. An agency-sponsored program could also be an affiliate of a larger national sponsor of a specific sport (e.g., Little League Baseball, American Youth Soccer Organization) that governs regulations for these sports. As an outgrowth of the U.S. Olympic Committee, NGBs are available for every sport (e.g., USA Wrestling, USA Swimming), and many local agencies serve as regional representatives of these organizations. By far, agency-sponsored programs have the largest number of youth participants in the United States.

National youth organizations (e.g., YMCA, YWCA, Boys and Girls Clubs of America), club sports (e.g., Amateur Athletic Union), and municipal recreational programs round out the other three categories of nonschool sports. National youth organizations claim more of the historical roots of providing youth sporting opportunities in America, with the YMCA emerging in the 1850s for the purpose of contributing to the social and moral development of children through athletic participation. Club sports are definitely on the rise in America with the trend toward earlier sport specialization. Nonschool clubs often serve either as a farm system to high school or college sports or as a legal outlet for year-round participation in a specific sport. For example, national tournaments are commonplace for nonsport clubs that often consist of the same high school lineups found during the school season. Scouts for universities and elite organizations are frequent visitors to these nonschool tournaments, Finally, city recreation departments have consistently been the mainstay of community athletic participation, with opportunities provided for a range of noncompetitive activities (e.g., rock climbing, whitewater rafting) as well as traditional competitive sports.

School-sponsored programs include intramurals (within-school competitions) and interscholastic athletics (between-school competitions). Intramural programs are rapidly becoming "dinosaurs" at the middle and high school levels because legislation has drastically cut funding for them. In response to the evaporating outlets for youth who are not skilled enough to make varsity teams or who prefer less intense levels of play, more and more agency-sponsored programs, both local service organizations and affiliates of national youth organizations, have emerged to fill the void that school programs have left. Unfortunately, agencies have primarily picked up responsibility for serving middle school youth (11- to 13-year-olds), leaving 14- to 18-year-old adolescents with after-school time on their hands and often nowhere to go.

Interscholastic athletics, governed by the National Federation of State High School Associations (NFSHSA) in Kansas City, Missouri, represents over 16,000 middle, junior, and senior high schools and over 5.6 million athletes ("High School Athletics Participation," 1995). The majority of these teenagers participate in more than one sport, which nearly doubles the numbers of sport participants in relative terms. The most current statistics show that participation has increased for the fifth consecutive year, with 3,478,530 male and an all-time high 2,124,755 female participants in school athletics ("High School Athletics Participation," 1995). It is somewhat paradoxical that the number of teenage school team participants continues to grow, given that school budgets have recently forced reductions in the number of available sports, teams, coaches, and athletic competitions. Perhaps this disconcerting downward trend of resources at the secondary school level will begin to reveal itself in survey statistics in the near future.

Sport Participation

The estimated numbers of youth participating in non–school-sponsored sports (20 to 35 million) and school-sponsored sports (over 5.6 million) are simply staggering when one considers comparable numbers documented in other countries (see chapters 3-22) and the lack of a centralized governance system for regulating nonschool youth sports. An inherent problem associated with these facts is an inability to maintain an accurate tracking mechanism, especially for the nonschool sport programs. Nevertheless, a recent nationwide survey conducted by the Youth Sports Institute at Michigan State University of nearly 8,000 girls (51%) and boys (49%) ranging in age from 10 to 18 years provides the most comprehensive, up-to-date participation rates in community-based and school-based sports by age, gender, and race conducted thus far (Ewing & Seefeldt, 1996; Seefeldt et al., 1992). The youth who participated in this survey responded for their activity involvement during the 1987-1988 school year.

Community-Based Sports

Over half (55%) of the sample surveyed reported that they participated in a community-based sport program. The highest participation rates were recorded by the 10-year-olds, with a steady decline in reported involvement for all sports from 10 to 18 years (see Table 5.1). Some consistent patterns of sport popularity were also observed. For 10- to 13-year-old participants, baseball, basketball, swimming, and soccer were cited by at least 25% and up to 43% of the sample. For the 14- to 16-year age group, baseball, basketball, and swimming were again the top three selections, followed by softball. The percentages for this age group and for these sports ranged from 19% to 27%. For the two oldest groups (ages 17 and 18), basketball, swimming, and softball were the top three, followed by baseball and volleyball. However, the percentages ranged from a low of 11% to a high of 20% for this age group. One other point to note is the higher percentage of participants in soccer than in football at ages 10 to 14 years. The popularity of soccer over the last decade has been a rather consistent shift from football, at least since the dramatic increase in participation rates recorded in 1986 (Martens, 1986). The steady decline in percentage of participation rates in community-based sports is perhaps not surprising when one considers that most of these programs serve youth 13 years and younger, and leave responsibility for sports at the high school level (ages 14 to 18) to the interscholastic leagues.

Survey results for participation rates by gender showed several similarities and some interesting differences (see Table 5.2). Boys participated most frequently in "the big three" of baseball, basketball, and football, with over 25% of the sample citing these sports. Soccer and swimming were the next most popular sports, respectively, with over 17% of the boys participating. Four sports were close in popularity for the girls: swimming, softball, basketball, and volleyball, all with over 20% of the sample participating. Gymnastics, soccer, tennis, and bowling clustered together as the next most popular activities (16% to 18%). These results are not surprising in light of the popularity of team sports such as baseball, softball, and basketball in American culture, as well as the endorsement of football

Table 5.1 Participation (%) in Community-Based Sports by Age During the 1987-1988 School Year

Sport	Age								
	10	11	12	13	14	15	16	17	18
Baseball	43	31	37	28	20	19	17	14	12
Basketball	40	33	32	30	27	26	25	20	18
Football	26	23	21	18	16	17	14	11	11
Swimming	42	32	27	26	21	21	20	16	12
Softball	27	22	20	22	21	20	20	16	11
Soccer	39	36	30	25	18	16	11	9	11
Volleyball	21	21	19	17	18	17	14	16	9
Gymnastics	25	20	15	18	11	9	6	5	3
Bowling	24	24	15	19	14	15	15	13	11
Tennis	17	22	15	19	15	14	13	11	8

Note. From *Overview of Youth Sport Programs in the United States*, by V. Seefeldt, M.E. Ewing, and S. Walk, 1992, Washington, D.C.: Carnegie Council on Adolescent Development.

as a more appropriate sport for boys than girls, and volleyball and gymnastics as more appropriate for girls than boys.

Little documentation exists of participation rates for youth who vary in race, ethnicity, or cultural roots. The survey results by the Youth Sports Institute are groundbreaking in this regard. Collecting their data from 17 regional sites across the United States, they recorded percentage of participation rates by race/ethnicity in these categories: Caucasian, African American, Hispanic American, Asian American, and Native American. These participation rates can be seen in Table 5.3. The only sport that held similar popularity across race/ethnicity (i.e., in the top five) was basketball. Baseball was in the top five for all but the Asian American group, soccer was in the top five for all but the African Americans, and swimming in the top five for all but the Hispanic Americans. These trends may reflect the lack of role models for these young athletes in these sports. The success of pitcher Hideo Nomo from Japan with the professional Los Angeles Dodgers team in 1995 may reverse this trend in later years. Note also that the percentage of Hispanic Americans who responded for each sport is considerably lower than all other racial/ethnic groups. Participation by race/ethnicity rates may also be influenced by socioeconomic status and family structure (e.g., single mother).

School Sports

Seefeldt et al. (1992) reported that the percentage of participants who reported they played interscholastic sports was half that of community-based sports. This

Table 5.2 Participation (%) in Community-Based Sports by Gender During the 1987-1988 School Year

Sport	Girls	Boys
Baseball	12	31
Softball	27	—
Swimming	27	18
Basketball	22	31
Football	—	27
Soccer	17	23
Volleyball	21	—
Tennis	16	12
Bowling	16	15
Gymnastics/Wrestling	18	12
Track and field	—	11
Flag football	—	12
Skiing	11	—

Note. From *Overview of Youth Sport Programs in the United States*, by V. Seefeldt, M.E. Ewing, and S. Walk, 1992, Washington, D.C.: Carnegie Council on Adolescent Development.

Table 5.3 Participation (%) in Community-Based Sports by Race/Ethnicity During the 1987-1988 School Year

Sport	Caucasian	African American	Hispanic American	Asian American	Native American
Baseball	24 (4)	22 (3)	16 (1)	18	28 (2)
Basketball	29 (1)	38 (1)	14 (2)	20 (5)	28 (2)
Football	18	21 (4)	12 (3)	14	21
Swimming	27 (2)	21 (5)	10	26 (4)	28 (1)
Softball	21 (5)	22 (2)	10	15	23 (5)
Soccer	25 (3)	13	11 (4)	34 (1)	24 (4)
Volleyball	18	21	10 (5)	27 (3)	21
Gymnastics	13	14	7	12	17
Bowling	20	14	6	20 (5)	18
Tennis	17	13	7	33 (2)	13

Note. Number in parentheses indicates rank of sport for an ethnic group. Football, softball, and volleyball were single gender sports.
Note. From *Overview of Youth Sport Programs in the United States*, by V. Seefeldt, M.E. Ewing, and S. Walk, 1992, Washington, D.C.: Carnegie Council on Adolescent Development.

is not surprising in light of factors mentioned previously in this chapter. Nevertheless, trends could be seen in the numbers by sport based on age, gender, and race/ethnicity. The greatest participation rates were found in the 13- to 15-year-olds with a steady decrease in participation from 15 to 18 years (see Table 5.4). Basketball, track and field, and volleyball were the three most popular sports for 12- to 13-year-old respondents, whereas football replaced volleyball in the top three for the age groups of 14 to 16 years. For the two oldest groups (17 and 18 years), baseball overtook basketball in the top three to go along with track and field and football.

At the interscholastic level of sport, boys and girls were more similar in the sports they played than they were for community-based programs. For boys, football, basketball, track and field, baseball, and soccer were the top five sports selected, ranging from 10% for soccer to 23% for football (see Table 5.5). For girls, track and field, basketball, softball, volleyball, and soccer were their five most popular sports, ranging from 7% for soccer to 12% for track and field. Thus four of the five top sports were similar (with baseball paralleling softball), the only difference being the traditionally male sport of football and traditionally female sport of volleyball.

Futher information on school-based sports for girls and boys can be found in statistics released by the NFSHSA ("High School Athletics Participation," 1995). They recorded the number of high school athletic participants during the 1993-1994 school year to be nearly 3.5 million boys and 2.1 million girls for a total

Table 5.4 Participation (%) in School Sports by Age During the 1987-1988 School Year

Sport	Age						
	12	13	14	15	16	17	18
Baseball	6	14	13	14	12	11	13
Basketball	15	24	26	22	16	11	11
Football	6	14	15	21	17	17	14
Swimming	5	12	8	8	6	5	6
Softball	5	12	12	11	9	8	4
Soccer	9	14	13	12	7	7	10
Volleyball	11	15	14	10	7	6	8
Gymnastics	8	13	5	4	2	3	3
Tennis	5	12	8	8	9	6	6
Track and field	10	24	21	21	18	14	14

Note. From *Overview of Youth Sport Programs in the United States*, by V. Seefeldt, M.E. Ewing, and S. Walk, 1992, Washington, D.C.: Carnegie Council on Adolescent Development.

Table 5.5 Participation (%) in School Sports by Gender During the 1987-1988 School Year

Sport	Girls	Boys
Baseball	2	15
Softball	11	—
Swimming	6	—
Basketball	12	16
Football	—	23
Soccer	7	10
Volleyball	10	—
Tennis	6	6
Flag football	—	5
Gymnastics	—	7
Track and field	12	16
Cross Country	6	6
Skiing	5	5

Note. From *Overview of Youth Sport Programs in the United States*, by V. Seefeldt, M.E. Ewing, and S. Walk, 1992, Washington, D.C.: Carnegie Council on Adolescent Development.

of 5.6 million athletes, the third highest in the survey's 24 years. While the number of boys participating in interscholastic sports has remained relatively stable since 1971 (range of 3.3 to 4.2 million), the number of girls has increased seven-fold since 1971, when the participation rate was a mere 300,000. The dramatic increase in participation rates since 1971 can be directly attributed to the passage of Title IX of the Educational Amendment Act, which called for abolishment of sex discrimination in any educational program, including sports. Since 1978, the number of girl participants has remained relatively stable (range of 1.7 to 2.1 million).

According to the 1993-1994 statistics released by the NFSHSA, the top five sports for boys were football, basketball, baseball, track and field, and soccer. These high participation rates are not surprising because these sports usually field a large number of team members. The next five popular sports for boys were wrestling, cross country, tennis, golf, and swimming and diving. For girls, the five most popular sports were basketball, track and field, volleyball, fast-pitch softball, and soccer. These rates follow the same trends as for boys. The next five sports most frequently cited were tennis, cross country, swimming and diving, field hockey, and slow-pitch softball. In all, the top five sports for boys and girls at the interscholastic level are congruent for both the NFSHSA and Youth Sport Institute samples.

Seefeldt et al. (1992) were also able to break down their school sport statistics by race/ethnicity as they did with the community-based sports (see Table 5.6). Some very interesting findings emerged with regard to sport preference. There was not a unanimous choice of top three sports across race/ethnic groups. Caucasians were highest for track and field, basketball, and football; African Americans for basketball, football, and baseball; Hispanic Americans for baseball, football, and track and field; Asian Americans for soccer, volleyball, and tennis; and Native Americans for track and field, football, and basketball. A comparably higher percentage of African Americans identified basketball than did any other group, while a small percentage of Asian Americans cited football as one of their sports. In contrast, the percentage of Asian Americans who cited soccer and volleyball was higher than all other groups.

Youth Participation in Competitive Sports: A Scientific Perspective

The demographic approach to understanding frequency of participation in various sports, as taken in the preceding section, is important for documenting numbers, age-related trends, and gender and race/ethnic differences. However, beyond the quantitative aspects of understanding youth participation lie the qualitative aspects of not only describing, but explaining and predicting participation behavior. A massive amount of scientific research has been conducted over the last 20 years on children's experiences in competitive sport. Among the contributions to the scientific knowledge base are books, symposia, coaching workshops, and empirical research studies. These contributions have been central to an understanding of children in sport in the United States, and they have made an impact on how

Table 5.6 Participation in School Sports by Race/Ethnicity During the 1987-1988 School Year

Sport	Caucasian	African American	Hispanic American	Asian American	Native American
Baseball	9	13 (3)	9 (1)	6	7
Basketball	14 (2)	26 (1)	7 (4)	14 (5)	12 (2)
Football	12 (3)	19 (2)	9 (2)	5	12 (2)
Swimming	6	7	3	6	9 (5)
Softball	7	10 (4)	4	11	6
Soccer	9 (4)	7	5	23 (1)	7
Volleyball	8 (5)	9 (5)	6 (5)	18 (2)	8
Gymnastics	4	6	2	7	10 (4)
Tennis	6	8	5	18 (3)	4
Track and field	14 (1)	9	9 (3)	15 (4)	19 (1)

Note. Number in parentheses indicates rank of sport for an ethnic group. Football, softball, volleyball, and gymnastics were single gender sports.
Note. From *Overview of Youth Sport Programs in the United States*, by V. Seefeldt, M.E. Ewing, and S. Walk, 1992, Washington, D.C.: Carnegie Council on Adolescent Development.

youth agencies operate their programs and how parents and coaches interact with their child athletes.

Over the last 10 years, several books and symposia have targeted the topic of the child in sport. At the Olympic Scientific Congress in Eugene, Oregon in 1984, one of the speciality themes was "competitive sport for children and youth," which included several programs on timely topics such as competitive stress, game modifications, minimal age at which children should compete, and youth sports around the world. These papers were complied into a book titled *Competitive Sport for Children and Youths* (Weiss & Gould, 1986), published by Human Kinetics. Human Kinetics has also published *Advances in Pediatric Sport Sciences, Volume 1: Biological Issues* (Boileau, 1984); *Advances in Pediatric Sport Sciences, Volume 2: Behavioral Issues* (Gould & Weiss, 1987); *Children in Sport* (Smoll, Magill, & Ash, 1988); and *Intensive Participation in Children's Sports* (Cahill & Pearl, 1993) following a symposium by the same name in Peoria, Illinois in 1990.

The proliferation of interest in youth sport participation is perhaps best seen in the sheer amount of empirical research conducted on the topic. For example, Weiss and Bredemeier (1983) conducted a content analysis of youth sport scientific studies conducted between 1970 and 1981. They were able to cite 143 studies or narrative reviews that focused on the child in sport. An identical content analysis conducted from 1982-1993 (Weiss & Raedeke, 1994) resulted in 404 studies and reviews, a nearly threefold increase in productivity on this topic in the same time span. The most popular topics were motivation (e.g., reasons for participation and attrition; Weiss, 1993), social influences (e.g., coaching behaviors; Horn, 1987), self-perceptions (e.g., self-esteem, perceived competence; Weiss & Ebbeck, 1995), anxiety and stress (Gould, 1993), socialization (Brustad, 1992), moral development (Shields & Bredemeier, 1995), and psychological skills training (Weiss, 1991). These scientific advances are significant because they go beyond the mere description of participation rates to understanding how, why, and under what conditions children's and teenagers' participation and behaviors in sport occur. The scientific study of youth in sport has made a significant contribution to the development of theory, as well as to practical applications for parents, coaches, and youth agencies in working with young athletes.

Problems in Youth Sport

The majority of research studies and demographic statistics point to positive outcomes outweighing negative outcomes in youth sport, namely high participation rates, greater participation by females than ever before, experiences of enjoyment more than stress, and positive interactions with parents, teammates, and coaches. However, there appear to be some consistent findings about children's experiences in sport that will require future investigation and proactive planning. First, fewer and fewer trained coaches are being hired to coach interscholastic sports. This has been a result of cuts to physical education programs where a large majority of athletic coaches were trained. Hiring untrained coaches has been and can be problematic in a number of ways: (a) lack of basic principles of child development may result in the use of inappropriate strategies for teaching and motivating youngsters; (b) lack of knowledge of proper training and conditioning principles may result in increased injuries; and, (c) lack of knowledge about adolescent growth and development may lead to misleading and inaccurate decisions with regard to skill development, nutrition, and motivational level. Clearly, the formal education and certification of untrained (i.e., high school) and volunteer (i.e., nonschool) coaches are essential for the future progress of youth sport participants (Seefeldt, 1996).

Another concern related to current data is the steady decline of athletic involvement of youth from ages 10 to 18 years. More specifically, the middle and late adolescent years of 14 to 18 years are especially susceptible to reduced physical activity, whether it come in the form of organized sport or informal exercise (Rowland, 1990). There are a multitude of reasons for this, including: (a) less opportunities for organized sport, as community-based programs target youth under 14 years and over 22 years, and high school sports usually field one team per sport that is available to only the talented athletes; (b) adolescents are concerned about their transition to adulthood, which may result in choices related to academics and work, rather than sports and physical activity (Coakley & White, 1992); and (c) teenagers remain unconvinced that they are susceptible to negative health consequences if they do not stay physically active. Whatever the reason, a future plan of action is for researchers, educators, and policy makers to collaborate on sustaining and enhancing adolescents' physical activity levels (Sallis & Patrick, 1994).

Promotional Campaigns

Children's involvement in sport and physical activity is a hot topic among researchers, educators, parents, politicians, administrators, and corporations. In this section, current projects that are under way that are designed to have a direct impact on children's and adolescents' quality of sport experiences are shared.

Education of Youth Sport Coaches

An estimated 2.5 million volunteers (mostly parents) serve as coaches each year in community-based youth sport programs. These individuals generally have little preparation in the field of coaching, with their prime credentials having experienced playing the sport in high school or college. Although the time and effort investment by these individuals is commendable, there is concern among educators that lack of credentialing or licensure in the profession of coaching is likely to lead to legal liability issues, psychological child abuse, and failure to develop basic skills adequately. Likewise, interscholastic programs that once required coaches to be employed as teachers within the school system are also struggling with the issue of coaching certification. Presently, only 13 states require their high school coaches to meet minimum coaching competencies as spelled out by the NFSHSA.

To quell concern, a number of national coaching education programs have emerged with specific teaching modules and competencies targeted at untrained coaches of youth. These programs include the American Sport Education Program (ASEP), founded by Rainer Martens, whose national center is located in Champaign, Illinois; Program for Athletic Coaches' Education (PACE), founded by Vern Seefeldt, located at the Youth Sports Institute at Michigan State University; and the National Youth Sports Coaches' Association (NYSCA), founded by Fred Engh, located in West Palm Beach, Florida. These programs have provided coaching workshops to thousands of individuals involved in coaching community-based and school-sponsored sports, but evaluation research is essential to determine the effectiveness of these training programs on increasing sport science knowledge and applications.

Girls and Women in Sports

Despite higher participation opportunites for girls and women in sport, there is continued concern about gender equity in sport, educating adolescent girls about the role of physical activity and health, and encouraging females to consider leadership positions in sport-related professions. All of these areas have been tackled by a number of organizations that are committed to sustaining and enhancing the quality of females' sport experiences from childhood through older adulthood.

Two national organizations have been effective in educating the public, helping to form networks among women, promoting gender equity, and effecting change in girls' and women's sport. They are the National Association for Girls and Women in Sport (NAGWS), a unit under the American Alliance for Health, Physical Education, Recreation and Dance (AAHPERD), and the Women's Sports Foundation (WSF). The NAGWS, which has been in operation for over 100 years, consists of leaders and members who are dedicated to making a difference at the elementary, secondary, and college levels in sport for girls and women. A quarterly newsletter is distributed to members and yearly projects are identified, enthusiastically embraced, and followed to completion. For example, two of the most recent projects include the Women's Support and Leadership Networks, and Links to Leadership. The former project is designed to recruit, train, and evaluate females for leadership positions such as coaching, officiating, and administration. Links to Leadership is a 5-year program that was funded by the United States Olympic Committee to identify individuals with potential for top leadership positions and to train them to conduct state and national governing body leadership workshops. The national governing bodies for track and field, cycling, field hockey, racquetball, shooting, and soccer, and weight lifting are participating in this innovative project.

The WSF was founded in 1974 by several progressive women leaders, including tennis star Billie Jean King, shortly after the passage of Title IX and her defeat of Bobby Riggs in the "Battle of the Sexes" competition. It serves as a national resource network of programs and services for girls and women in sport. Resources such as scientific reports, videos, books, and fact sheets are available to individuals who are trying to promote girls' and women's sports in their communities or states. On February 1 of each year, a National Girls and Women in Sports Day is sponsored by the WSF, in which leaders in every community across the United States are encouraged to promote female involvement in sport by recognizing student athletes, exemplary coaches, and girls and women who are active in sports and exercise.

Two major institutes in the Twin Cities area (St. Paul and Minneapolis) of Minnesota offer unique perspectives, services, and resources on girls and women in sports. The Melpomene Institute was founded in 1982 to help girls and women of all ages link physical activity and health through research, publications, and education. A board of directors and an advisory board are comprised of professionals, athletes, and researchers in a variety of fields related to physical activity, health, and well-being. Research is conducted by these individuals and others who are recruited on such timely topics as menopause and physical activity, adolescent girls' self-esteem and physical activity, infertility in physically inactive women, and osteoporosis and exercise. A quarterly journal, *Melpomene: A Journal of Women's Health Research*, revolves around a current theme such as young girls in sport, coaching issues, heroes, and careers.

Another Institute, the Center for Research on Girls and Women in Sport, is just getting off the ground at the University of Minnesota as a result of a generous endowment from an alumnus. The center's mission is to understand how participation in sport contributes to healthy physical, social, and psychological development of girls and women. Its goals are to specifically encourage interdisciplinary and collaborative research, develop and promote research that counts, and disseminate research findings to practitioners who work with girls and women in physical activity settings. Clearly, there are many active organizations and individuals who are committed to enhancing girls' and women's quality of sport experiences, whether as athletes, coaches, officials, or administrators.

Corporate Involvement

Because youth sport is such a visible and timely topic, it is not surprising that corporate America is jumping on the bandwagon to lend a hand. One of the more recent promotional campaigns to hit the market is Nike's P.L.A.Y. (Participate in the Lives of America's Youth) program. Fancy brochures, high-dollar television advertisements, and apparel bearing the acronym of their newest program abound. P.L.A.Y., according to the brochure, is designed to provide resources and create partnerships to keep recreation alive for kids. The specific targets appear to be at-risk children who are unable to pay for sport programs or who do not have available facilities in which to participate in sports. Nike has donated thousands of dollars in partnering with Boys and Girls Clubs of America to provide community-based sports and fitness programs for children, to provide safe facilities and recreation centers in urban areas, and to recycle worn-out Nike shoes to create indoor and outdoor sports courts, playgrounds, and running tracks. Finally, they have recruited Michael Jordan and Jackie Joyner-Kersee as their spokespersons on the project to encourage children and teenagers to get involved more frequently and intensely in sports and physical activity. Only time will tell whether Nike's clever and creative program will have an impact on today's youth when it comes to being physically active.

Conclusion

Youth sport in America attracts the attention and involvement of millions of participants, parents, officials, coaches, and administrators. Just about any sport and a variety of intensity levels are available to children as young as 4 or 5 years old, and both community- and school-based programs abound. Many challenges face today's educators and professionals involved in youth sport: (a) declining participation levels from 14 to 18 years, especially that of girls; (b) the prominence of untrained coaches at both the community and school levels; (c) the pressure by adults to specialize earlier in a sport, resulting in year-round seasons and the probability of earlier attrition or burnout; and, (d) creating more opportunities in sport for at-risk youth, such as those who have socioeconomic or physical disadvantages, as well as those youth who are susceptible to substance abuse or juvenile delinquency.

The large body of scientific knowledge on children and youth in sport paints a generally rosy picture, in contrast to what detractors of youth sports might think. However, we cannot deny that, with approximately 40 million youth ages

6 to 18 years participating in community and school sports, even a small percentage such as 5% who have negative experiences in sport results in 200,000 lives being impacted. Therefore, we must continue to demand that our children and teenagers get only the most qualified coaching, supportive parenting, and input into the decision-making of their sport experiences. If these goals can be reached and sustained, then there is no doubt that the long tradition of the value of youth sport in American society will continue to thrive.

References

Boileau, R. (1984). *Advances in pediatric sport sciences, Vol. 1: Biological issues.* Champaign, IL: Human Kinetics.

Brustad, R.J. (1992). Integrating socialization influences into the study of children's motivation in sport. *Journal of Sport & Exercise Psychology,* **14**, 59-77.

Cahill, B.R., & Pearl, A.J. (1993). *Intensive participation in children's sports.* Champaign, IL: Human Kinetics.

Coakley, J.J., & White, A. (1992). Making decisions: Gender and sport participation among British adolescents. *Sociology of Sport Journal,* **9**, 20-35.

Ewing, M.E., & Seefeldt, V. (1996). Patterns of participation and attrition in American agency-sponsored youth sports. In F.L. Smoll & R.E. Smith (Eds.), *Children in sport: A biopsychosocial perspective* (pp. 31-45). Indianapolis: Brown & Benchmark.

Gould, D. (1993). Intensive sport participation and the prepubescent athlete: Competitive stress and burnout. In B.R. Cahill & A.J. Pearl (Eds.), *Intensive participation in children's sports* (pp. 19-38). Champaign, IL: Human Kinetics.

Gould, D., & Weiss, M.R. (1987). *Advances in pediatric sport sciences, Vol. 2: Behavioral issues.* Champaign, IL: Human Kinetics.

High school athletics participation highest in 15 years. (1995, Winter). *National Association for Sport and Physical Education (NASPE) News,* 7.

Horn, T.S. (1987). The influence of teacher-coach behavior on the psychological development of children. In D. Gould & M.R. Weiss (Eds.), *Advances in pediatric sport sciences, Vol. 2: Behavioral issues* (pp. 121-142). Champaign, IL: Human Kinetics.

Martens, R. (1976). *Joy and sadness in children's sports.* Champaign, IL: Human Kinetics.

Martens, R. (1986). Youth sport in the USA. In M.R. Weiss & D. Gould (Eds.), *Sport for children and youths* (pp. 27-33). Champaign, IL: Human Kinetics.

Rowland, T.W. (1990). *Exercise and children's health.* Champaign, IL: Human Kinetics.

Sallis, J.F., & Patrick, K. (1994). Physical activity guidelines for adolescents: A consensus statement. *Pediatric Exercise Science,* **6**, 302-314.

Seefeldt, V. (1996). The future of youth sports in America. In F.L. Smoll & R.E. Smith (Eds.), *Children in sport: A biopsychosocial perspective* (pp. 423-435). Indianapolis: Brown & Benchmark.

Seefeldt, V., Ewing, M.E., & Walk, S. (1992). *Overview of youth sport programs in the United States.* Washington, DC: Carnegie Council on Adolescent Development.

Shields, D.L.L., & Bredemeier, B.J.L. (1995). *Character development and physical activity.* Champaign, IL: Human Kinetics.

Smoll, F.L., Magill, R.A., & Ash, M.J. (1988). *Children in sport* (3rd ed.). Champaign, IL: Human Kinetics.

Weiss, M.R. (1991). Psychological skill development in children and adolescents. *The Sport Psychologist, 5,* 335-354.

Weiss, M.R. (1993). Psychological effects of intensive sport participation on children and youth: Self-esteem and motivation. In B.R. Cahill & A.J. Pearl (Eds.), *Intensive participation in children's sports* (pp. 36-69). Champaign, IL: Human Kinetics.

Weiss, M.R., & Bredemeier, B.J. (1983). Developmental sport psychology: A theoretical perspective for studying children in sport. *Journal of Sport Psychology, 5,* 216-230.

Weiss, M.R., & Ebbeck, V. (1995). Self-esteem and perceptions of competence in youth sport: Theory, research, and enhancement strategies. In O. Bar-Or (Ed.), *The encyclopaedia of sports medicine, Vol. VI: The child & adolescent athlete.* Oxford: Blackwell Scientific.

Weiss, M.R., & Gould, D. (1986). *Competitive sport for children and youths.* Champaign, IL: Human Kinetics.

Weiss, M.R., & Raedeke, T.D. (1994, June). *Developmental sport psychology revisted: Current status and research directions for the millennium.* Paper presented at the annual NASPSPA conference, Clearwater, FL.

Wiggins, D.K. (1996). A history of highly competitive sport for American children. In F.L. Smoll & R.E. Smith (Eds.), *Children in sport: A biopsychosocial perspective* (pp. 15-30). Indianapolis: Brown & Benchmark.

Part III

Youth Sport in Asia

Chapter 6 Israel

Uriel Simri
Gershon Tenenbaum
Michael Bar-Eli

Youth sport in Israel is organized by independent sport federations such as the Israel Basketball Association (IBA), the Israel Football Association (IFA), the Israel Tennis Association, and the National Sport Federation (NSF, which comprises all other sports). These federations organize competitive sport activities on a weekly basis throughout the year. These activities are aimed at athletes who are members of sport clubs. Complementary and independent sport activities are organized by the Sport and Physical Education Authority (SPEA) under the auspices of the Ministry of Education and Culture. These activities are aimed at school children and are organized throughout the school year.

The sport activities organized by these organizations are, however, quite different. In team sports, which are the most popular sports in the country, the federations organize the league games according to seasons, whereas the SPEA schedules tournaments and cup competitions throughout the entire year. The youth program of the SPEA is limited to the sports of soccer, basketball, volleyball, team handball, track and field (including cross-country running), gymnastics, and the recently added table tennis and orienteering, all of which hold annual championships.

The Organizational Network

The general scheme presented in Figure 6.1 shows the sport activities that are independently organized by each of the sport organizations. Only recently, the National Olympic Committee, the SPEA, and the National Sport Federation cooperated in establishing a Unit of Youth Sport (UYS) at the Wingate Institute for Physical Education and Sport, Israel's national sport center. The unit concentrates on elite and talented athletes from all over the country, and organizes tournaments and other activities to enhance the athletic achievements of these young athletes.

The selection of young athletes for the various programs and sports, and the hierarchy of their development, are outlined in the model presented in Figure 6.2.

Sport Participation

In a study of the motives of Israeli youth for participation in sport (Weingarten, Furst, Tenenbaum, & Schaefer, 1984), a "reason for sport participation" questionnaire, consisting of 41 items, was administered to 446 young Israeli sport

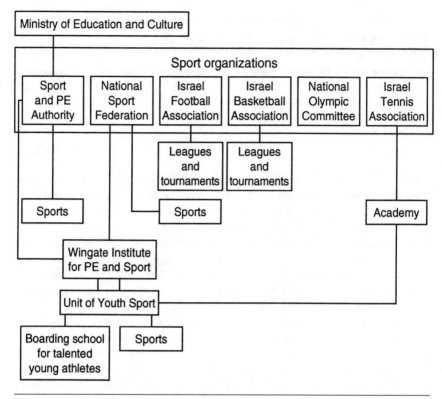

Figure 6.1   A scheme showing the institutional structure of youth sport in Israel.

participants (109 girls and 337 boys, aged 9 to 16 years). The sample consisted of children who had trained regularly for 1 to 6 years in either sport clubs or special municipal sport schools, in 10 different sports (table tennis, volleyball, gymnastics, basketball, swimming, team handball, tennis, fencing, soccer, and track and field).

A factor analysis applied to the children's responses revealed six main factors (motives):

- Familial/societal (reasons related to the influence of family and friends)
- Enjoyment of the sport lifestyle
- Future success orientation
- Achievement/competitiveness
- Affiliation/friendship
- Competence (skill and self improvement)

It was apparent that the familial/societal motive explained most of the total motivational variance (56.6%). However, its general mean rating of importance was the lowest. The second motive, enjoyment, received the highest ratings by the

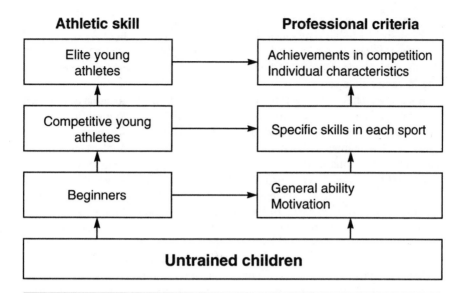

Figure 6.2 A general model of selective processes for young athletes and their developmental stages.

young participants, but accounted for less than 15% of the common motivational variance. The other four motives together accounted for less than 30% of the total variance. In other words, the motivation of young sport participants in Israel seems to have more of an internal, independent nature, rather than an external, dependent one. The young athletes were found to be motivated to take part in competitive sport primarily because it provides them with an opportunity to actualize their independence, to take responsibility, and to make their own decisions. In addition, Israeli children choose to be involved in sport for reasons having to do with values directly related to actual participation, namely, enjoyment of the sport lifestyle, future success, and achievement/competitiveness.

Recent Trends

The school population is made up of 1.5 million children and youths between the ages of 5 and 18. This number roughly equals the total number of children and youths in Israel up to the age of 18, since education is mandatory until 15 and officially free until the age of 18 (and most youths between 15 and 18 continue their studies). More than 80% of the children under 18 are engaged in physical activity within the formal school system. However, fewer than 10% participate in competitive sport.

The number of entries to the competitions organized by the SPEA for 1992 was 49,428, in comparison to 40,016 in 1989, 41,297 in 1990, and 42,589 in 1991. About one third of the participants are female—a much larger percentage than that prevailing in the events organized by the sport federations. It should be noted, however, that these numbers are not necessarily identical to the number of participants, because many students participate in more than one sport event. For the same reason, the dropout rate, according to a recent survey (Tenenbaum & Lustig, 1993) exceeded 80% of the total number of children and youths participating in competitive sport.

Soccer, which for years was not included in the physical education curriculum, has recently become very popular among the SPEA's activities. In contrast, participation in other sports, such as handball and gymnastics, is gradually decreasing. The number of soccer teams taking part in the school championships rose from 117 teams in 1989 to 171 in 1992. However, the number of handball teams has decreased from 118 in 1989 to 56 in 1992 (including only 12 female teams). Parallel figures for gymnastics also show a 50% decline, from 319 school teams in 1989 to 158 in 1992. Basketball continues to be by far the most popular sport among school teams, with the number of participating teams reaching 493 in 1992.

Most of the SPEA programs are aimed at high school students (grades 10-12), but a growing number of junior high school children (grades 7-9) are becoming involved in those programs from year to year. The only program provided by the SPEA to elementary children is gymnastics, and this is aimed primarily at female students.

Though indirectly relevant to the issues discussed here, 120 sport-oriented classes (with a total of 3,840 students) were established in the formal educational system. At the high school level, 27 schools offer a major in physical education and sport (and in many the emphasis is on elite sport). The educational system encourages students to specialize in such programs by adding more hours to the curriculum. In addition, the system provides students with special tutors, to facilitate higher academic achievement as well as excellence in athletic pursuits. The SPEA finances many sport activities of these students, and subsidizes their participation in European and world school championships. Most of the teachers in these programs are offered financial support to take part in special studies and workshops in Israel and abroad. An additional branch includes the recreational activities organized by the SPEA in cooperation with three nautical centers (Ginossar, at the sea of Galilee; Caesarea, on the Mediterranean Sea; and Eilat, on the Red Sea). Sport-class students and sport majors in high schools participate in these naval activities for one week each year. The students experience the various sea activities such as gliding, surfing, canoeing in all the centers during their school years.

The most popular programs initiated by the sport federations are those of the Israel Football Association (IFA) and the Israel Basketball Association (IBA). In 1992, the program of the IFA involved close to 20,000 players in 577 registered teams, whereas that of the IBA involved 850 teams with over 15,000 registered players. The football [soccer] federation runs organized leagues for the age groups 10 to 12, 12 to 14, 14 to 16, and 16 to 18, and has recently added seven leagues for the 8-to-10 age group, on a trial basis. The youth program of the IBA starts at the age of 10, with minibasketball leagues organized on a local or regional level.

As far as individual sports are concerned, the largest youth program organized by a sport federation is the age-group swimming program, which was adapted along the lines of the American program. These age-group competitions start at the age of 10, and in 1992 involved over 3,000 young Israeli swimmers. The National Sport Federation organizes programs in other sports as well, such as team handball, volleyball, track and field, fencing, judo, wrestling, and water polo, in which several thousand young athletes take part.

Another major federation is the Israel Tennis Association, which has initiated the construction of 10 modern centers located around the country. Approximately 3,000 young participants are now being trained in these centers. About one third of them are competitive players who actively participate in tournaments organized throughout the year. Twenty youngsters are enrolled at the Academy of Tennis located in Ramat-Hasharon, near Tel Aviv. They are top-level players, who are trained in a special daily program coordinated with the formal educational system. An additional 100 to 200 young tennis players are trained in their regions and are considered candidates for the academy. During the summer, a 2-week program is held by the academy for 7-to-11-year-old children, with the purpose of discovering new young tennis talents. The children who are evaluated as having a high potential are then trained on a daily basis.

International Activities

The sport federations and the SPEA have maintained a high level of activity in the international youth sport scene. The IFA, for example, was one of the initiators of the Asian Youth Championships, which was won by the Israeli team six times between 1964 and 1972. After the IFA was expelled from the Asian Football Confederation in 1974, it initiated an annual International New Year's Tournament, open to European teams of under 17 and under 19 years of age. This tournament has gained much popularity and has undoubtedly played a significant role in paving the way for Israeli youth teams to be accepted to United European Football Association (UEFA) competitions.

The SPEA has been active within the framework of the International School Sport Federation (ISSF) for over 20 years. In 1972, the SPEA organized the international volleyball championship of the ISSF, and since then has hosted a significant number of these championships, the most recent being table tennis (1991), windsurfing (1992), and soccer (1993). In the ISSF championships Israel's athletes have gained a number of titles, including three in volleyball (1971, 1973, 1974), two in table tennis (boys and girls in 1991), and one each in basketball (1983), soccer (1987) and team handball (1992). In 1992, Israel participated in the ISSF championships in team handball, volleyball, and cross-country running (with both boys' and girls' teams). In 1991, it was represented in the championships of soccer, basketball, track and field, and orienteering. It is worthwhile mentioning that Arab students were among those who have represented the State of Israel in the ISSF championships.

Promotional Campaigns

In 1991, a special program to promote talented youths in certain sports was initiated at the Wingate Institute for Physical Education and Sport. About 50 youths aged 11 to 16, gifted in gymnastics, swimming, tennis, and table tennis, were invited to attend a newly established boarding school at the institute, in order to provide them with the most advanced conditions available in the country. This program has already borne its first fruits, with one of the students of the boarding school (a female swimmer) being selected for the Israel Olympic team at the 1992 Barcelona Games.

In 1974, Israel's three major sport organizations (the Sport and Physical Education Authority, the Israel Olympic Committee, and the National Sport Federation) established the Unit of Youth Sport (UYS). The main target of the UYS is to develop a pool of talented young athletes in a variety of disciplines, and to support them with the most up-to-date scientific and professional means, within the framework of their clubs. One of the unit's most important goals has been to establish an organizational hierarchy based on objective tests, in order to enable selection and longitudinal development with maximal proficiency. The unit was given the mandate to organize workshops for physical education teachers, coaches, and instructors, and to provide them with the latest professional and scientific materials. These activities are financed by the major organizations mentioned above.

Since 1974, the UYS has developed and distributed short- and long-term training programs to various teams and individual athletes. In these programs special physical tests are given to athletes across the country. The results are then compared to national and international norms, and immediate feedback is given to the coaches. The UYS maintains close contact with the Ribstein Center for Research and Sport Medicine Sciences at the Wingate Institute. The center informs the unit about recent developments in the sport sciences, which are subsequently implemented in the field by the professional coordinators employed by the UYS.

To give an example, the UYS and the Behavioral Sciences Department at the Ribstein Center have developed a new computerized psychological instrument which measures mental and social variables in young athletes. The instrument has been administered thus far to more than 800 young athletes. The main psychological components found to be of predictive validity include behaviors following unsuccessful events and stressful or anxiety-evoking situations, attributions following unexpected negative and expected positive results, behaviors and cognitions during training and competition, social relations, and motives for competitive participation. This psychological tool, together with the physical examinations, provide valid and reliable criteria for the selection and treatment of talented athletes.

Once a year, large-scale tournaments and competitions are organized at the Wingate Institute so that observations and evaluations can be made. These competitive events are integrated into the yearly program provided to the coaches and clubs in advance.

According to UYS regulations, a club, school, or any other sport organization can benefit from its support only if several criteria are fulfilled. These criteria are

- presentation of a written yearly program,
- certification of coaches and professionals,
- attendance of professionals at workshops organized by the UYS,
- attendance of talented athletes at special programs organized by the UYS during the year,
- participation of athletes in tournaments and competitions organized by the UYS, and
- training of athletes in appropriate sport facilities.

The total budget for the sport schools is provided by the local municipalities, the families of the young athletes, and the UYS. Thus far, the program has promoted professional and scientific standards. However, its long-term influence on elite sport will have to be determined in the more distant future.

Sport clubs are provided with financial support for their athletes who participate in the sport events organized by the UYS. Financial support is also provided to coaches who participate in the workshops. In addition, the SPEA gives financial support to sport clubs for professional materials and the purchase of sport equipment.

During the 1992 season, the UYS distributed a document that presented the various sport disciplines and their organizational duties. The age ranges in each sport supervised by the UYS are presented in Table 6.1.

Table 6.1 Age Ranges of Sports Supervised by the Unit of Youth Sports (UYS)

Sport discipline	Age of final professional support (years)	Age range in which organizational and professional support is provided (years)
Volleyball	16	13-15
Handball	16	12-14
Water polo	16	14-16
Gymnastics—males	13	11-13
Gymnastics—females	11	8-11
Table tennis	13	11-13
Track and field	17	13-15
Fencing	15	11-15
Wrestling	16	11-14

Note. This table is based on data courteously supplied by Mr. Gili Lustig, director of the Unit of Youth Sport at the Wingate Institute for Physical Education and Sport.

Another institution involved in preparing and educating coaches for youth is the Nat Holman National School of Coaches and Instructors at the Wingate Institute. The school provides programs which train coaches and instructors in the various sport disciplines. Students are exposed to various scientific disciplines, such as exercise physiology; biomechanics and motor learning, development, and control; developmental and sport psychology; anatomy; training theory; pedagogy; and didactics. In addition, students are trained in sport centers and clubs in order to enhance their coaching skills. Recently, these programs have been substantially revised to emphasize coaching youths. The school also provides special yearly workshops for physical education teachers, who coach school teams within the formal education system. These activities are coordinated jointly by the school and the UYS.

In recent years attempts have been made to establish a National School Sport Federation, but so far the SPEA has not been able to realize this goal. In case such a federation is established, it may cause some conflicts among the existing sport associations, which may threaten athletes joining the new federation with sanctions. The SPEA, which has initiated the creation of the new federation with the claim that the current sport federations neglect the professional enhancement of sport-talented youth, has claimed that the School Sport Federation would only attempt to fill in the areas in which the associations are not sufficiently active. This would mean that the new federation would be quite limited, particularly in sports such as soccer, basketball, and swimming.

Conclusion

Israeli sport organizations offer young people ample opportunities to engage in both recreational and competitive sport. The number of opportunities for participating in sport and physical activities has risen substantially, particularly in the last 10 years. These programs have gained much popularity among youths, and this trend seems to be gaining momentum. Future effects of these programs on health and on recreational and leisure activities, as well as on elite sport, remain to be seen.

References

Tenenbaum, G., & Lustig, G. (1993). *A survey of drop-outs among Israeli youth in competitive sport*. Netanya, Israel: Wingate Institute.

Weingarten, G., Furst, D., Tenenbaum, G., & Schaefer, U. (1984). Motives of Israeli youth for participation in sport. In J.L. Callaghan (Ed.), *Proceedings of the International Symposium on "Children to Champions"* (pp. 145-153). University of Southern California and California State University at Northridge.

Chapter 7 Japan

Yasuo Yamaguchi

People in Japan are enthusiastic about sport with respect to both primary and secondary involvement. According to a national survey (Prime Minister's Office, 1994), 66.7% of Japanese citizens report participating in exercise or sport activities at least once per year. Recent figures indicate that, on an annual basis, 23 million people visit ball parks to see professional baseball games and 10 million sport newspapers are sold.

Before discussing youth sport in Japan, it is important to have some general information on Japanese children. Although the population of Japan has been increasing, totaling 124.2 million in 1992, the number of children and adolescents has been gradually decreasing. The average number of births per woman was 1.5 in 1993. The population of 5-to-19-year-olds is 25.5 million, or 20.5% of the total population.

The Organizational Network

Sport in Japan is organized at the local, prefectural, and national levels. In the amateur sport world, the Japan Amateur Sports Association (JASA) and the Japan Olympic Committee (JOC) govern 54 sport associations and 47 prefectural amateur sport organizations. At the national level, both JASA and JOC have close relationships with the Physical Education Bureau in the Ministry of Education, Science, Sports, and Culture, while local and prefectural boards of education have close links with local and prefectural sport associations. Thus, sport organizations in Japan have close relations with educational institutions.

Since the beginning of the Meiji Restoration in 1867, sport in Japan has been developing mainly within formal educational institutions and industries (Yamaguchi, 1984). A number of industries and corporations have sport clubs controlled by industrial sport associations. While there are both competitive and recreational sport clubs in industry and business, several sports, including rugby, soccer, volleyball, basketball, baseball, and ice hockey, have been attracting a number of spectators and fans.

With respect to youth sport, organizations are diverse, especially at the local level. Three major organizations can be identified: school sport clubs, Junior Sports Club Branches, and other sport-related bodies. Figure 7.1 presents an organization chart for youth sport in Japan, and in particular focuses on school sport clubs and junior sports clubs.

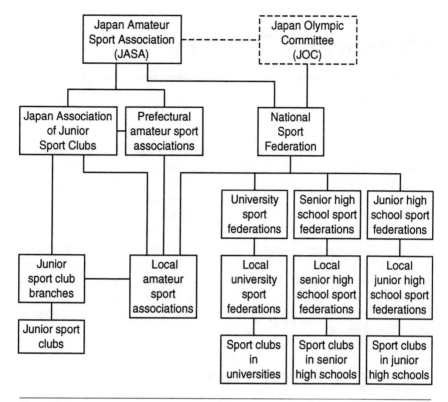

Figure 7.1   An organizational chart of youth sport clubs in Japan.

School Sport Programs

School sport clubs exist in elementary schools, junior and senior high schools, and universities. While there are several sport clubs in most elementary schools, most elementary school students belong instead to Junior Sports Club Branches. The picture changes in junior high school, however, and most junior high schools and high schools have more than 10 sport clubs. At the university level, there are both university teams and recreational sport clubs. All clubs at junior high schools, senior high schools, and universities can participate in local or prefectural leagues, whereas sport clubs in elementary schools are organized only at the local level to avoid a competitive orientation.

Club Sport Programs

Junior Sports Club Branches (JSCB) were organized by JASA in 1976, and immediately attracted 500,000 members. The JSCB are governed by local amateur sport associations and the Japan Association of Junior Sports Clubs. In 1993, there were 32,872 clubs with 1,017,030 members in Japan. The JSCB have their own facilities and club houses as do sport clubs in Germany. Approximately

70% of the clubs use school facilities, while 20% of the clubs practice at other public facilities. Most of the club members are elementary school children and are likely to leave the club when they enter junior high school. Junior high school and older students who want to play sports typically belong to school sport clubs.

Other sport-related bodies include private swimming schools, Little League Baseball Clubs, children's clubs, private kendo or karate schools, the YMCA, and so forth. A number of children go to private swimming schools, especially in urban areas. Most of the schools have elite swimmers' courses aimed at preparing youths for local and national championships. Olympic swimmers generally have belonged to such swimming schools.

The Japan Little League Baseball Association was established in 1964 and currently has approximately 1,500 teams. Children's clubs have also been organized within most towns. In addition to social activities, some clubs have baseball teams and leagues in larger cities. In addition, such traditional sports as kendo and karate have been taught at private schools in the community since Japan's medieval period, the Tokugawa era (1603-1867). It should be noted that some local police offices also hold kendo classes for children in the community. Thus, children and adolescents have a variety of sport opportunities within their communities and their schools.

Sport Participation

Recent trends in youth sport should be noted. First, there has been a decreasing number of youths joining baseball teams. Although the most popular sport in Japan had previously been baseball, recently children have become more interested in soccer. In 1993, a professional soccer league, called the "J league," started with 10 clubs and gained incredible attention and popularity among children and adolescents. It was estimated that the market of "J league goods" was 670 million in U.S. dollars, while the economic impact of the "J League" was 20 billion dollars during the past year.

Second, in contrast with the "soccer boom," baseball has been gradually losing popularity and players. Although the national championships of high school baseball are still very popular and supported by local fans and spectators, the number of baseball players at high school was 146,000 in 1993, which was less than the 161,000 soccer players. Thus, among children and adolescents, it seems that soccer has replaced baseball as the number one status sport in Japan.

Third, the number of children's clubs as well as the number of children in communities has been decreasing, especially in the downtown areas of towns and cities. This is mainly due to the fact that the number of children per household has been decreasing, as mentioned earlier. In recent years, Japan's total fertility rate, the average number of births per woman, has been gradually declining. The decreasing number of children's clubs is thus another factor contributing to the declining number of children participating in baseball in towns and cities.

Japanese educational institutions have paid considerable attention to the role of sport and physical education in their curricula. Physical education classes are required courses at all elementary schools, junior high schools, and senior high schools. Furthermore, full-time physical education teachers are employed at all junior and senior high schools.

In 1993, the Physical Education Bureau of the Ministry of Education, Science, Sports, and Culture presented the findings of a national survey of participation in sport by elementary school children. The survey showed that in addition to the physical activities associated with physical education classes, 55.4% of the children were active in other sports. The results indicated that they belong to school sport clubs (18.6%), Junior Sports Club Branches (18.6%), and other clubs (17.0%) (Physical Education Bureau, 1993).

Table 7.1 shows the popular sports at school sport clubs, Junior Sports Clubs Branch, and other clubs. At school clubs, popular sports are minibasketball, soccer, and baseball, in that order, while baseball, soccer, and volleyball are the top three most popular sports among Junior Sports Club members. Unique sports can be seen in other sport clubs as shown in Table 7.1. Swimming has been taught at private swimming schools according to teaching manuals and grade systems. The highest grade is an elite swimmers' course, which, as mentioned earlier, aims at local and national championships.

Kendo, which literally translated means "sword" (ken) "ways" (do), can be interpreted to mean "the way of the sword." This traditional martial art emphasizes "self-discipline," influenced by "Bushido," that is, the spirit of traditional sport. Bushido is an unwritten code of laws governing behavior and has its roots in thirteenth-century feudalism in Japan. Bushido incorporates elements from Confucianism, Buddhism, and Shintoism in stressing such values as loyalty, self-discipline, modesty, courage, simplicity, reverence for nature, and strict obedience to the law and moral code. All the names of these traditional sports have the suffix "do" (way). This reflects a unique Japanese value that people emphasize a process, as well as a product. Such traditional sports as kendo and karate have been taught at private schools in the community since feudal times.

Table 7.1   Popular Sports at School Sport Clubs, Junior Sport Clubs, and Other Clubs

Rank	School sport clubs		Junior sport clubs		Other clubs	
1	Minibasketball	(27.2%)	Baseball	(27.9%)	Swimming	(39.9%)
2	Soccer	(18.2%)	Soccer	(19.4%)	Kendo	(10.6%)
3	Baseball	(10.2%)	Volleyball	(12.3%)	Karate	(8.7%)
4	Track and field	(8.6%)	Softball	(10.4%)	Baseball	(7.2%)
5	Volleyball	(6.6%)	Minibasketball	(8.5%)	Minibasketball	(5.3%)
6	Swimming	(5.8%)	Kendo	(5.8%)	Volleyball	(4.0%)

Note. Percentages indicate participation rates of students who belong to the club. From *National Survey on Sport Activities of Elementary Schools* by Physical Education Bureau, 1993, Tokyo: Author.

Children are socialized into a variety of sport roles when they enter junior high schools and high schools. Most junior high schools and high schools have more than 10 kinds of sport clubs as extracurricular activities. National championships at the junior high school level were held in 17 sports, and in the high school level in 31 sports, in 1993.

Sport journalists have provided in-depth coverage of high school baseball since the first national championship in 1915. There are two national championships, one in spring and the other in summer. One of the reasons journalists have been paying such attention to high school baseball is that two major newspaper corporations have been the main sponsors of the two national championships. The greater the number of articles on high school baseball in newspapers, the greater their sales. The high school baseball association is a unique organization which is independent from the high school sport association. In the summer championship of 1992, 4,059 high school teams took part in local tournaments, compared to the 73 teams that participated in the first championships in 1915. The national championships are covered by national TV networks, while local tournaments are aired by local TV stations. It should be noted that a number of players at the national championships are scouted every year by professional baseball clubs. Thus, mass media have been making use of high school baseball for their sales promotions.

According to the national survey of junior and senior high school students conducted by the Ministry of Education, Science, Sports, and Culture (1993), 65.0% of junior high school students and 63.3% of high school students took part in sport and exercise activities more than once a week in addition to physical education classes. The results also indicate that 43.5% of junior high school students and 48.9% of high school students participated in sport and exercise activities more than three times a week in addition to physical education classes. It can be estimated that nearly half of them were active in school sport clubs in junior high and high schools.

Table 7.2 shows the participation rates of sport and exercise activities by students in the previous 12 months. Those sports in which more than 50% of the students participated are, in order, basketball, volleyball, swimming, and track and field. Surprisingly, 25.8% of the students had experience in skiing. Perhaps this is because the traditional graduation trips recently have been directed at ski areas. These data indicate that students of junior and senior high schools are socialized into a variety of sports within extracurricular activities as well as physical education classes.

Problems with Organization and Participation

Although children and adolescents have been quite active in sport and exercise activities in Japan, several problems in youth sport have recently emerged.

The number of sport injuries among children and adolescents has been increasing.   In a national survey of elementary school children conducted by the Ministry of Education, Science, Sports, and Culture (1993), 17.4% had taken a

Table 7.2 Participation Rates in Sport and Exercise Activities by Junior and Senior High School Students

Rank	Activities	Percentage
1	Basketball	63.7
2	Volleyball	63.5
3	Swimming	59.3
4	Track and field	56.3
5	Soccer	43.5
6	Badminton	32.5
7	Table tennis	28.6
8	Softball	26.8
9	Skiing	25.8
10	Skating	19.6
11	Baseball	19.0
12	Judo	17.4
13	Soft tennis	15.1
14	Gymnastics	14.4
15	Kendo	12.0
16	Tennis	9.8
17	Team handball	9.7
18	Sumo wrestling	6.1
19	Rugby football	5.4
20	Karate	2.4

Note. From *National Survey on Children's Sport* by Ministry of Education, Science and Culture, 1993, Tokyo: Author.

week off because of injury in games or training. Mutoh, Fukashiro, and Fukashiro (1985) reported that the number of injuries to the elbow, shoulder, lower back, knee, and ankle has been increasing because of overtraining. They referred to this phenomenon as the ''overuse'' syndrome.

The overuse syndrome has become more apparent since the start of national championships in junior high schools. It can be argued that the goal of participating in the national championships encouraged a strong winning orientation. Another reason for the overuse syndrome may be the advantage given elite athletes in entrance examinations to high schools and universities. A number of private universities and some national universities use the recommendation system of entrance examinations for elite athletes. If they have distinguished athletic records, they are likely to be accepted, in spite of low academic records. Therefore, athletic students try to perform their best athletically by means of hard training, in order to enroll in the best schools or universities.

In recent years, in fact, elite athletes among junior high school students have had some advantage in entrance examinations to high schools. It may be taken for granted that the winning orientation has become significant in consideration of the severe competition for entrance examinations into the best schools as a unique feature of the Japanese educational system.

The number of dropouts from organized sports has been increasing. Why do children withdraw from participation in organized youth sport? Ebihara (1988) administered a questionnaire to 908 junior and senior high school students in order to examine the characteristics of sport dropouts from school sport clubs. Approximately 30% of the sample were dropouts from school sport clubs because of conflict with other people, the clubs' strong winning orientation, or preparation for entrance examinations. Critics of youth sport have pointed to negative elements within sport environments, including the dominating influence of coaches and the winning orientation of sport programs, as being responsible for sport dropouts. In their review of North American sport literature, McPherson and Brown (1988) pointed out that withdrawal from organized sport was associated with such factors as an emphasis on competition, pressure to win, a lack of enjoyment, a lack of success, a dislike of team practices, a lack of skill development, or dissatisfaction with coaches. Similar tendencies influencing withdrawal from organized sport might be found in Japan.

It has been pointed out that adults organize and ultimately dominate the youth sport milieu. Based on a review of literature and fieldwork in youth sport, Yamamoto (1987) criticized the fact that adults control youth sport world and apply the commercialized values of their own sport and business worlds. As a result, children are socialized into an adult model of sport too early during childhood and face a variety of such problems as ''burnout'' and deviant behaviors. It can be said that children are ''burned out" in sport by adult coaches because of those coaches' desire to receive gratification and prestige by winning at all costs.

Parents in Japan have placed perhaps too great an emphasis on developing their children's mental and social discipline through sport. For example, one of the purposes of the Japan Junior Sports Club Association is to discipline children's bodies and spirits through sport. Many parents also expect their children to develop social manners and mental discipline. In a national survey of parents regarding youth sports (Ministry of Education, Science, Sports, and Culture, 1993), parents reported that they expected their children to develop both physically and mentally (69.2%), to enjoy sport (35.9%), to have confidence (32.4%), and to have self-discipline with a peer group. Thus, because of the strong concern with children's mental development by parents and coaches concerned with the physical demands of the sport, a number of such problems as overuse syndrome, burnout, and dropout have developed.

The number of overweight children has been increasing. This tendency is mainly caused by their lifestyle, which includes taking in too many calories a day as well as a lack of exercise. Children tend to be more enthusiastic about computer games than about playing outdoors.

In short, the number and severity of problems in youth sport have both increased and have become recognized. As suggested by McPherson and Brown (1988), there may be a need to initiate social changes in youth sport including alternative models, a new structure, or new rules to existing youth sport programs.

Promotional Campaigns

The Ministry of Education, Science, Sports, and Culture has been promoting two types of programs for regional governments since 1992. One program is "Sport for Children," which enhances sport opportunities for inactive children, including campaign activities. Another program is "Support Youth Sport Clubs," which promotes the establishment of sport clubs in the community. Both programs include leadership development seminars for adult leaders, with financial assistance.

There is no doubt that it is especially important for youth sport to reinforce leadership development. Social problems in youth sport often are caused by adults, including leaders, coaches, and parents. Recently, the Japan Junior Sports Club Association started a leadership development course for "Junior Sports Leaders" to be certified by the Ministry for Education, Science, Sports, and Culture. This certification course aims to develop the quality of leaders and coaches by offering seminars in a variety of sport sciences courses. The JJSCA strongly recommends that leaders and coaches of Junior Sports Club Branches take these seminars.

Conclusion

The key points regarding youth sport in Japan can be summarized as follows:

- Children and adolescents have a variety of opportunities for sport participation within the community and schools.
- The Japan Junior Sports Club Association is the major governing body in youth sport, while youth sport organizations are diverse, especially at local levels.
- In recent years, soccer has exceeded baseball's popularity among children and adolescents, influenced by the establishment of a professional soccer league called the "J League."
- Youth sport has been regarded as a major part of youth education by junior sport clubs as well as educational institutions.
- Several social problems including the increasing incidence of sport injuries, overuse syndrome, dropout, burnout, and overemphasis on winning and competition in youth sport have appeared, while leadership development programs for adult coaches and leaders have been initiated.

The discussion has been focused on two crucial points in youth sport. First, a differentiation of children has been accelerating: one is the child "jock" who often displays overuse syndrome and burnout, and the other is the overweight child, whose problem is due to a lack of exercise (Ikeda, Yamaguchi, & Ebihara, 1986). On the one hand, children and adolescents who belong to sport clubs are likely to get intensively involved in sport activities with a strong emphasis on winning. As a result, there have been increasing problems with overuse syndrome and sport injuries. On the other hand, the number of overweight children has been increasing because of the recent boom in computer games. Especially in Japan, a number of children get involved in computer games as a leisure activity. Thus, a differentiation of children has appeared, including severe social problems.

Second, youth sport should emphasize "enjoying sport" and "having fun" rather than the "educational context of youth sport" and "winning and competition." As discussed earlier, an educational context for youth sport has been emphasized by sport associations, educational institutions, and parents. This might lead to a misunderstanding of meanings and values of youth sport and distort the nature of youth sport among volunteer coaches, officials, and administrators. More attention should be given to the intrinsic motivation of children and adolescents in sport by coaches, officials, administrators, and parents.

References

Ebihara, O. (1988). Characteristics of sport dropouts from organized sport: A comparison among frequent participants, dropouts and non-participants. *Sociological Journal of Physical Education and Sport, 7*, 107-129.

Ikeda, M., Yamaguchi, Y., & Ebihara, O. (1986). Social changes in children's sport. *Japan Journal of Pediatrics,* **19(6)**, 912-928.

McPherson, B.D., & Brown, B.A. (1988). The structure, processes, and consequences of sport for children. In F.L. Smoll, R.A. Magill, & M.J. Ash (Eds.), *Children in sport* (pp. 265-286). Champaign, IL: Human Kinetics.

Ministry of Education, Science, Sports, & Culture. (1993). *National survey on children's sport.* Tokyo: Author.

Mutoh, Y., Fukashiro, S., & Fukashiro, T. (1985). *Children's growth and sport.* Tokyo: Tsukiji Shokan.

Physical Education Bureau. (1993). *National survey on sport activities of elementary schools.* Tokyo: Author.

Prime Minister's Office. (1994). *National poll on fitness and sport.* Tokyo: Author.

Yamaguchi, Y. (1984). A comparative study of adolescent socialization into sport: The case of Japan and Canada. *International Review for the Sociology of Sport,* **19**(1), 63-82.

Yamamoto, K. (1987). Children and sport: Today's situation and the direction of study of sport socialization in childhood. *Sociological Journal of Physical Education and Sport,* **6**, 27-49.

Chapter 8 China

Hai Ren

China is a unique, even mysterious land to many Westerners. Its uniqueness may be attributed to its diverse physical environment, with a varied landscape of approximately 9.6 million km². It has various types of islands, mountains, plateaus, basins, hills, and deserts, and equally varied climates. The social environment of China has contributed even more to its uniqueness:

- With its 1.2 billion citizens, it has the largest population in the world.
- It is one of the earliest Asian civilizations, with a recorded history of about 3,600 years.
- Its political system is based on socialism.
- It has the largest economy in the developing world.

But still more interesting is its current transformation from a planned economic pattern to a market-oriented one which is leading to rapid social changes.

These natural and social factors have had a series of deep and comprehensive impacts on youth sports in China, shaping their organizational systems and practice patterns, and guiding the directions of their development.

The government of China has played a leading role in youth sports, mainly through two agencies: the State Sport Commission and the Education Commission and their affiliated structures at various levels. They make all essential policies related to youth sport and take the initiative in organizing various national youth sport events.

Not surprisingly, then, the organization of youth sport in various parts of the country is closely related to the school system. Community-based sport clubs and sport centers are still in an embryonic stage, whereas schools already organize huge numbers of children and young people. In total, there are 169 million children and youngsters studying in 866,000 ordinary primary and secondary schools in China. Schools may also provide better facilities, experienced instructors, and reliable financial support and organizational systems. As a result, all forms of Chinese youth sports have direct or indirect relations to the educational system.

In addition to the governmental sport and education agencies, there are two student sport societies taking increasingly important roles in youth sport: the Sport Society of University Students and the Sport Society of Secondary School Students, established respectively in 1973 and 1975. In May 1991, the two societies held a joint workshop, passed new charters, and established their permanent organizational structures. The Sport Society of Secondary School Students also set up three specialized commissions in order to handle expanded youth sport activities: the Commission of Sport Competition and Refereeing, the Commission of Sport Training and Scientific Research, and the Commission for Instruction of Child and Youth Sport Activities.

The growth of youth sport is also indicated by the significant increase of physical education teachers in China, from 130,000 in 1983 to 310,000 in 1992 (Qu, Pan, & Mao, 1993). Currently, there are one university and 14 institutes of physical education, as well as 179 departments of physical education in normal universities in various parts of China. The graduates from these institutions are mainly physical education teachers and coaches engaged in youth sport (Zhang, 1990).

As in many nations, especially developing ones, sport in general and competitive sport in particular are highly regarded in China as a means for building the national image and assisting national integration. Since 1979, when China returned to the Olympic family and entered almost all international sport arenas, the pace of development of sport has been accelerated, and the youth sport organizational system has gradually taken its current shape.

The Organizational Network

During the early 1950s, the organizational system of Chinese youth sport was based on the former Soviet system. Many projects, such as the "Ready for Labor and Defense" national fitness program, the spare-time sport schools for youngsters, the physical educational institutes, and many others, were simply copied from the USSR. In later years, with the deterioration of the relationship between the two countries, this system changed. Since the mid-1980s, a youth sport system with Chinese characteristics has gradually been introduced. It is aimed at cultivating young high-level athletes through various means.

As Figure 8.1 shows, the current sport organizational structure in China consists of six main levels.

In this structure the first four levels from the bottom up are formed by various patterns of youth sports. They may be referred to as the spare-time sport system for youngsters. Most sport stars in this country start their sport careers from the low level of the system, where their sport talents are identified and they are consequently selected by one or another of the youth sport organizations. They receive systematic training for many years, until they finally become outstanding players. For example, of the 94 Chinese gold medalists at the 10th Asian Games held at Seoul in 1986, 93% came from the spare-time sport training system.

Grass Roots Level

To most Chinese children and adolescents, with or without sport talents, the first and most popular opportunities they have to participate in sport are the physical exercises, including all kinds of sport activities, in primary and secondary schools, which form the roots of the entire sport system of the country. In primary and secondary school, youth sports are provided mainly through the following three

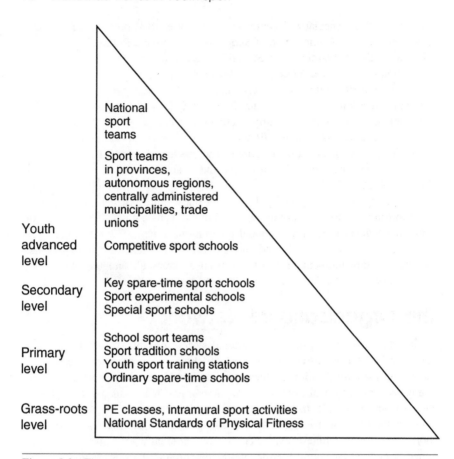

Figure 8.1   The sport organizational system in China.

basic forms: physical education classes, the National Standards of Physical Fitness Program, and intramural sport activities.

Physical education classes.   While in some Western countries physical education may be listed as an elective subject, in China physical education is compulsory for all primary schools up through the first two years of university. During this period, which usually lasts about 14 years, all students have to attend two classes of physical education each week. The total sum of physical education hours is 9 to 11% of the teaching hours of all subjects in primary and secondary schools. Beginning in 1994, three physical education classes a week for primary and secondary schools are required, according to the new program of nine-year compulsory education. During these nine years, there are 812 classes of physical education in total, which puts physical education in third place in teaching hours among subjects in primary schools and fourth in secondary schools.

Sports, especially ball games (soccer, volleyball, and basketball), track and field, and gymnastics are the essential components of the physical education curriculum in Chinese schools. It is thus through physical education classes that many children first come in contact with sports.

Since the early 1980s, physical exercises have been listed in some local areas as an item in the entrance examination to senior high school, with the purpose of encouraging school leaders to pay more attention to the health of youths. By 1993, this practice had spread to nine provinces and municipalities, and involved nearly 275 million junior high school graduates. It is expected that this practice will be introduced all over the country (Qu, 1994).

The National Standards of Physical Fitness Program. The National Standards of Physical Fitness Program is a nationwide youth program, not only for testing the fitness level of Chinese youngsters, but also for stimulating them to take part in fitness and sport activities. The test battery is designed for both evaluating and exercising. In 1981, the Ministry of Education (later renamed the State Education Commission) stipulated that college and university applicants who have passed the National Standards of Physical Fitness test will be given priority for admission when their other qualifications are the same as those of candidates who have failed the test.

The current standards program was issued on 1 September 1990 by the State Council, and carried out in 29 provinces and autonomous regions in the mainland. According to a 1993 survey of 620,000 schools, the program was conducted in 85% of the schools, involving more than 113 million students. Eighty-seven percent of the students were qualified. Fourteen percent of them reached the "excellent" standard and 46% the "fair" level. By 1993, the number of students who had met the fitness standards had reached 800 million (Progress, 1993).

A series of measurements has been developed in promoting the program and the performance of the program is listed as an evaluation item by schools and teachers in most provinces. The program has been carried out in combination with all kinds of school sport activities, such as intramural sporting events, physical education classes, and sport competitions. Games of the test battery items are organized through correspondence competition, duel competition, selecting competition, and so on, in order to reach as many students as possible. In 1993, the primary and secondary schools in the Tibet Autonomous Region also started the program. Some necessary changes were made to adapt to the local natural conditions (Progress, 1993).

Moreover, for the purpose of promoting Chinese traditional sports among the youth, some items of *wushu* (Chinese martial arts) have been added to the program. From 1993 to 1994, the new program was tested in 70 primary and secondary schools in Beijing and 622 schools in Hebei Province (Application Status, 1994).

Because physical education is obligatory and the National Standards of Physical Fitness Program has been widely carried out, a high sport participation rate of Chinese youth is predictable. Theoretically, all children and youngsters participate in sport activities as long as they are in school. As a result, some social surveys even take it for granted that all primary and secondary school students are regular sport participants. However, one cannot be so sure of this, if it is taken into account that 89% of the primary and secondary schools and 74% of all students in China are located in rural areas (Zou, 1988). In many schools, especially those in the poor rural areas, students have much less chance to be involved in sport due to the lack of necessary sport facilities and instructors.

Intramural sport activities.   Based on the regulations stipulated by the State Education Commission, the students in primary and secondary schools are expected to participate in extracurricular sport activities at least twice a week. In addition, students are also required to take part in exercises during breaks between classes. Usually these activities focus on the items in the National Standards of Physical Fitness and youth calisthenics to broadcast music.

In most schools, the annual games have become a routine, usually held in spring and autumn. They are mainly dominated by track and field events, lasting one or two days and often connected to holidays. During that time, all classes are canceled and all students have to attend the games either as athletes competing on the sport grounds or as spectators cheering for their classmates in competition.

To secure physical education and sport activities in schools, a document, the Standard Category of Sport Equipment for Primary and Secondary Schools, was worked out by the State Education Commission in 1989. However, to date, many schools have not yet reached the standards of sport equipment required in the document.

First Level

In general, all primary and secondary schools have their own teams consisting of students identified as being good at sports in physical education classes and intramural sport activities. These sport teams usually have training schedules (first level) to prepare for various interschool tournaments and district competitions.

Sport tradition schools.   During the 1950s and 1960s, some primary and secondary schools were good at certain sports such as table tennis, soccer, basketball, volleyball, track and field, swimming and so on, because they had specialized physical education teachers and the necessary facilities. Over the years, these sports, usually one or two, have gradually taken deep root in these schools and have turned into "traditions" of the schools.

In November 1983, the State Sport Commission and State Education Commission (the Ministry of Education at that time) decided to promote this type of school. One hundred of such schools and 500 of their outstanding physical education teachers were given awards. Since then, the State Sport Commission and the State Education Commission have given annual awards to the outstanding sport tradition schools and their sport instructors. The local governments have also set up related regulations to improve schools of this type. In Beijing, for example, a series of rules have been issued such as the Administration of Sport Tradition Schools, the Evaluation Standards for Sport Tradition Schools, the Regulation of Financial Aspect of Sport Tradition Schools, and the Standards for Outstanding Physical Education Teachers in Sport Tradition Schools (Li, 1992).

Based on their qualities, the sport tradition schools are divided into three levels, namely, provincial, municipal, and county. Each school has its certificate issued by sport and educational administrative agencies. To make a sport a school tradition, the school has to draw many students into participating in this sport. In these schools, the vast sport participation and elite sport training are usually interrelated, and promoting physical fitness and enhancing sport performance are easily combined. As a result, schools of this type have developed rapidly. To date, the number of the sport tradition schools has reached more than 26,000, resulting in a huge number of boys and girls receiving sport training there. These schools provide an important base for the high-performance sport of China and constantly supply "new blood" to the higher stages of the sport system. In 1990, for instance, of all Chinese gold medalists at the 11th Asian Games in Beijing, 311 had been trained in these schools. In 1992, 78,172 students from these schools went on to higher sport schools (Pan, 1994).

Sport tradition schools have regular competitions among themselves, usually organized by the State Sport Commission in order to improve the quality of their sport training. In 1993, for example, a national track and field tournament for the secondary sport tradition schools and a swimming competition for the primary sport tradition schools were organized.

Youth spare-time sport training stations.   The youth spare-time sport training stations are commonly established in those schools or universities with better sport facilities and coaches. They offer boys and girls from nearby schools with poorer sporting conditions opportunities to take part in sport in their spare time.

Ordinary spare-time sport schools.   Children who are good at a particular sport may also receive sport training after class and on holidays in spare-time sport schools where better sport facilities and professional coaches are available. Spare-time sport schools have systematic training plans that usually last for several years.

These schools were first set up in 1955 in the three central municipalities: Beijing, Shanghai, and Tianjin. Since then, they have spread all over the country. The sports offered in these schools are usually track and field, gymnastics, swimming, soccer, basketball, volleyball, table tennis, badminton, tennis, handball, diving, speed skating, figure skating, and wushu.

The regulations regarding spare-time sport schools are issued jointly by the State Sport Commission and the State Education Commission. According to the overall arrangement made by the State Sport Commission in 1980, the various provinces, municipalities, and autonomous regions reorganized their spare-time sport schools to emphasize their specialized sports.

There are 3,841 ordinary spare-time sport schools, and 340,000 students of primary and secondary schools are receiving training in these schools.

Second Level

The top young players of ordinary spare-time sport schools may be selected to continue their further training in so-called Key Sport Spare-Time Schools.

Key Sport Spare-Time Schools. These schools are mainly organized by the sport commissions at provincial, regional, or municipal level and supported by the governmental educational agencies at the same level. These schools usually have much better sporting conditions, such as experienced instructors, sufficient sport facilities and equipment, and good accommodation and boarding. The young trainees live, study, and train together in the schools, spending half the day in study and the other half in sport training.

This practice started in the late 1950s. The students of these schools are taking general subjects equivalent to junior and senior high school classes and have teachers of general subjects who take care of their academic learning. However, their study programs are quite flexible in order to adapt to the demands of training and frequent interruptions from sport competitions.

Sport experimental schools. To prepare high-quality sport reserve forces for high-performance sports, a new program has been put into practice since 1985 in some secondary schools that have high-quality physical education teachers and relatively better sport facilities. Because this practice is still in its experimental stage, these schools are "sport experimental schools for sport reserves." In 1989, the State Education Commission issued a formal document to develop this type of school, 216 secondary schools were named for the further experiment in a larger scale, and operational guidelines for these schools were proposed. The student athletes in these schools are provided with certain financial subsidies from the state, mainly for their nutrition and sporting equipment. Some students may postpone their graduation by one year in order to make up for the studying time lost to training and competition. Some experimental schools can even provide the student athletes with boarding and accommodation. In 1993, the number of secondary schools of this type increased to 289. In 1987, the State Education Commission started a similar experimental program in some universities with good sport facilities and sport instructors, in order to continue the training process begun in the secondary sport experimental schools and to train high-level athletes among university students (Xu, 1994). By the end of 1993, there were 59 universities named as sport experimental universities at the national level and nearly 100 at the provincial level. During the Seventh National Games, there were 150 student athletes from these universities competing, representing their provinces or trade unions (Pan, 1994).

Special sport schools. These schools are set up for those sports requiring specialized training from an early age, such as swimming, gymnastics, acrobatics, figure skating, diving, and so on. Each of these schools concentrates entirely on one sport. Special sport schools usually have much better training conditions, because most students in these schools are still young children who could easily be injured if the training were conducted improperly.

Advanced Level

At the top level of the system of youth sport in China are those so-called "competitive sport schools," which are secondary educational institutions oriented toward professional sports. They are either independent schools organized jointly by the sport and education administrative agencies at provincial and regional levels, or affiliates of higher institutes of physical education such as the Beijing University of Physical Education. They are the important schools for Chinese youth sport, gathering the young sport talents with the most brilliant prospects.

The students in these schools are provided with the best sport training facilities, and receive instruction from high-quality coaches. They study half a day and practice the other half.

After several years of training and studying, some outstanding youngsters in these schools are selected into high-level sport teams, which often leads to national or even international fame in the elite sports arena. The less talented may either continue their professional study in physical education institutes, if they have passed the university entrance examination, or take sport-related jobs as physical education teachers or coaches in primary or secondary schools.

Promotional Campaigns

Sport competitions are one of the most popular means used in China to promote youth sport. Besides the annual sport games in all schools described earlier, there are also the Youth Sport Games, mainly participated in by students. These games are held at various levels—city, county, district, province, and nation. All these games are connected with one another in a hierarchical order, forming a system of youth sport competition. At the top of the system there are the National Games of Secondary School Students, which are held every 3 years, in which the players are usually between 12 and 18 years old. The National Games of University Students are held every 4 years. A considerable number of students take part in the games. For example, 100,000 university students competed in a series of preliminary games leading to the National University Games in 1988.

In addition, there have been a series of sport competitions specially designed as promotional campaigns for youth sport, which are mainly organized by the Sport Society of University Students and the Sport Society of Secondary School Students, and which are often in cooperation with various organizations of particular sport events.

"Eaglets Taking Off" Sport Campaign

The "Eaglets Taking Off" sport campaign is specially aimed at the promotion of some popular sports like track and field, swimming, and table tennis among primary and secondary education students. The campaign was originally launched in 1987 to prepare athletes who were good in these sports for the 11th Asian Games held in Beijing in 1990. For that purpose, the State Sport Commission and the State Education Commission launched a nationwide campaign to encourage youth participation in these three sport events. Two hundred thousand yuan (US $60,000) were allocated annually from the central government to support the campaign. Since the campaign has mobilized a great number of youngsters to take part in sport, it was decided to prolong it until the year 2000 (Physical Education, 1991).

Associated with this campaign, a variety of sport tournaments, training clinics, and sport camps have been organized, such as the national "Eaglets Taking Off" Sport Camp which was held in August 1994 in Qinghai Province.

Summer Sport Camps

Various summer sport camps for children and youths are regularly held throughout the country during the summer vacations.

National "Cup of Rejuvenating China" volleyball summer camp for secondary school students.   This national sport camp has been organized for several years. For example, in Tianjin City in early August 1987 more than 150 games were organized among 46 volleyball teams made up of secondary school boys and girls from 14 provinces and 24 districts. In addition to volleyball games, there were other educational events held mainly for cultivating the patriotism of the youngsters. With the increasing influence of the campaign, more provinces have joined and the organizational board has set up three subcommittees to deal with organizational, coaching, and financial affairs (Lu & Bai, 1987).

Table tennis summer camp for primary school students.   Supported by the State Sport Commission, there are also some summer sport camps organized by the nongovernmental sector for primary school students, for example, the "Sunny Cup" and "Seeding Cup" table tennis summer camps.

Local Endeavors

There are several youth sport programs running locally for the purpose of cultivating high-performance players in the future, such as the "1014 Plan" in Tianjin City. This plan started in 1985 as a program for the strategic development of youth sport. The name "1014" refers to the age of the target group of the program: children and youngsters from 10 to 14 years old. The program is also called "The Hoping Star," with the purpose of increasing youth sport participation and preparing future outstanding players, especially in track and field, soccer, basketball, volleyball, and table tennis. The program, as an extracurricular activity, has been carried out in all primary and secondary schools of the city (Xu & Su, 1991). Following Tianjin's example, several similar youth sport programs in other local areas appeared, such as the "0714 Plan" in Hunan Province, focusing on youths aged from 7 to 14, and the "Stars of Tomorrow" program in Shenyang.

Conclusion

Youth sport in China is almost exclusively organized within a school context. School sport activities in physical education classes, as well as intra- and extramural programs, have formed its basis. Upon this basis, and with the direct support of the government, a multilevel structure of Chinese youth sport has been built up, with the sport tradition schools and all kinds of spare-time sport schools as its essential parts.

Because physical education is a compulsory subject and the National Fitness Standards Program is heavily emphasized from primary schools to universities, the rate of participation in sport by children and youths in China is very high. A number of trends for the future development of youth sport in China may be identified.

Organizational Decentralization

Youth sport in China is a diverse phenomenon, not only because of the significant differences among various regions, but also because of the large gaps between schools in urban and those in rural areas, between higher and lower educational institutions, between key and ordinary schools, and so on. For many years, this complex phenomenon was organized in a centralized and uniform way under the planned economy. However, it would be inefficient to go on dealing with this situation in the same way now. With the rapid social change occurring now, mainly characterized by the turn to a market-oriented economy, a new trend has appeared since the 1990s. Direct governmental involvement in youth sport has gradually shifted to a more indirect involvement, and some nongovernmental youth sport organizations, such as the sport societies of students, have taken more responsibilities for youth sport operation.

Financial Diversification

The financial shortage faced by youth sport has been a major problem bothering many youth sport administrators. It has often proved to be the main factor restraining the development of youth sport in China. Although there are 5.48 million students receiving sport training in one form or another through the spare-time sport system (Su & Lai, 1994), they are not more than 3.24% of the total student population of primary and secondary schools in China. As the governmental budget cannot possibly meet the great demands of Chinese youth sport, it has become necessary to develop other financial resources. With the increasing trend of organizational decentralization of Chinese youth sport, some new and nongovernmental resources may appear.

Olympic Sport Orientation

The performances of Chinese athletes at the Olympic Games have become a social focal point since the middle of the 1980s, and have tremendously influenced youth sport in China. It is certain that the main contents of youth sport in China will still concentrate on those sports in the Olympic program, especially track and field, basketball, volleyball, swimming, and table tennis. Meanwhile, as there is a trend in China to educate youths in traditional cultures, some Chinese traditional sports, especially wushu, may draw more attention for their unique cultural and educational values.

References

Application status of National Physical Fitness Standards 1992-1993. (1994). *School Physical Education in China*, **3**, 6.

Li, M. (1992). Report on workshop of Sport Tradition Schools in Beijing, Hebei and Liaoning. *School Physical Education in China*, **2**, 50.

Lu, S., & Bai, R. (1987). Report on the "Cup of Rejuvenating China" for secondary school students. *School Physical Education in China*, **6**, 74.

Pan, S. (1994). Report on national conference of school spare time sport training. *School Physical Education in China*, **1**, 11-12.

Physical education working plan of the State Sport Commission in 1991. (1991). *School Physical Education in China*, **1**, 8.

Progress of new National Physical Fitness Standards. (1993). *School Physical Education in China*, **3**, 5-7.

Qu, Z. (1994). Issues on physical education test in entrance examination of senior high school. *School Physical Education in China*, **4**, 4.

Qu, Z., Pan, Z., & Mao, Z. (1993). Reform and development of sport in schools in China. *School Physical Education in China*, **1**, 12-13.

Su, L., & Lai, T. (1994). Cultivation of elite sport reserve force through combination of sport and physical education. *School Physical Education in China*, **1**, 47.

Xu, Y. (1994). Report on workshop of general secretaries of sport societies in universities and secondary schools. *School Physical Education in China*, **1**, 9.

Xu, Y., & Su, L. (1991). "Hoping Star" and the phenomenon of hoping stars. *School Physical Education in China*, **4**, 9.

Zhang, C. (1990). Cradle of Stars in Asian Games and foundation of sport power. *School Physical Education in China*, **4**, 10-13.

Zou, S. (1988). Speech at national conference of school physical education and hygiene. *School Physical Education in China*, **5**, 7-10.

Part IV

Youth Sport in Europe

Chapter 9 Belgium

Paul De Knop
Bart Vanreusel
Marc Theeboom
Helena Wittock

Belgium has a surface of 30,518 km^2 and a population of about 10 million (i.e., 328 inhabitants per km^2), from which almost 1.6 million (15.8%) are youngsters between 6 and 18 (Nationaal Instituut voor de Statistiek, 1993). However, as in other Western countries, the composition of the population is changing rapidly and a clear decrease in the number of youngsters is expected during the upcoming decades (see Figure 9.1). Undoubtedly, this evolution will have a serious impact on the internal environment in the sport clubs that are still mainly oriented toward youngsters.

The 1980 constitutional revision divided Belgium into three communities (Flemish, French-speaking, and German-speaking) with separate responsibilities for several cultural matters, which include sports and outdoor recreational activities (Van Mulders, 1992). As a result, all three communities have their own separate sport administrations:

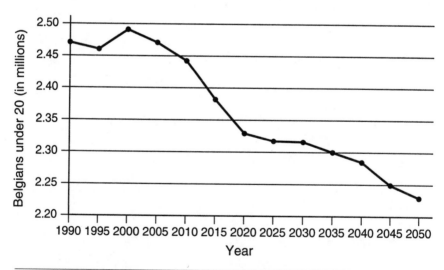

Figure 9.1   Demographic prognoses for the Belgian population under 20.
Note. From *Perspectives Démographiques 1992-2050* [Demographic Perspectives 1992-2050], by Nationaal Instituut voor de Statistiek, 1993, Brussels, Belgium: Author. Copyright 1993 by Nationaal Instituut voor de Statistiek. Reprinted by permission.

- The Flemish community has the Commissariaat-generaal voor de bevordering van de Lichamelijke Ontwikkeling, de Sport en de Openluchtrecreatie (BLOSO).
- The French-speaking community has the Direction d'Administration de l'Education Physique, des Sports et de la Vie en Plein Air (ADEPS).
- The German-speaking community has the Deutsche Gemeinschaftsanwalt für Sport.

Each sport administration is responsible for governmental affairs concerning sports within its area. The central government, however, retains a number of prerogatives also closely related to sports, like public safety at sport events. The role of public authorities, which is primarily complementary, is to intervene in favor of sport practice and to support private initiative, provided that certain general conditions (access, freedom, safety) are fulfilled. This public role does not preclude active involvement to foster sports (e.g., in sport infrastructure, or the Sport for All promotion). It is worth mentioning that Belgium was one of the first countries to accept a Sport for All policy, in which the promotion of youth sport has been one of the main strategies.

However, sports in Belgium, and especially youth sports, are mainly organized on a free and voluntary basis by the sport associations. Within sport clubs, youngsters can develop their motor and physical abilities as well as their social and personal skills. Sport clubs form parts of federations (national or community) which, in turn, are often members of the Belgian Olympic and Interfederal Committee (BOIC).

In this chapter, figures for all of Belgium will be used when available. However, because sport is a cultural matter, some of the research findings described in this chapter are uniquely valid for the situation within one community. We will therefore always clearly indicate to which population the described findings refer.

The Organizational Network

In Belgium the term "youth sport" has been applied to any athletic program that provides a systematic sequence of practices and contests for children and youths, on competitive or recreational levels, which are offered separately from the normal physical education curriculum at school. Opportunities for involvement in organized sports usually begin at ages 5 and 6 in most of the team sports (such as soccer, basketball, and handball) and in many of the individual sports (such as swimming and gymnastics).

In reality, these sport experiences differ greatly in competitive level, length of season, organizational context, cost to competitors, qualifications of coaches and officials, and skill levels of the athletes. They are conducted within schools, clubs, municipal sport services, private sport organizations, commercial sport centers, organizations set up by the governmental sport bodies, school sport federations, or sport federations (see Figure 9.2). Each of the programs is becoming more elaborate and enlisting younger participants every year. For almost every youth's or parent's ambition there is at this moment a well-organized outlet.

In this chapter only the programs which are most important to organized youth sport will be mentioned and illustrated with some examples of initiatives in the field. These are club sport programs, interscholastic activities, programs of private nonprofit organizations, and programs of the central and local governments.

Club Sport Programs

Club sports is a term commonly reserved for sport programs which conduct year-round practices and offer mainly competitive opportunities. Within these club sport programs we usually find a hierarchy of skill development that begins prior to age 6 and continues to age 18.

Although sport clubs also address themselves to adults and seniors, youngsters make up an important part of the total population of the clubs. This is also illustrated by the findings of a study on the structures and characteristics of sport clubs in Flanders (De Knop, Laporte, Van Meerbeek, & Vanreusel, 1991), which showed that 45% of the population of Flemish clubs consists of youngsters under the age of 19.

Most of the club sport programs are characterized by their fee-for-services structure. However, the membership fees demanded are too low to cover all the costs that clubs require for the organization of their sport programs. Bearing this in mind, it is not surprising that 40.9% of the clubs must deal with financial problems. Other problems clubs face are providing scheduling and facilities,

Figure 9.2   The organization of youth sport programs in Belgium.

recruiting and retaining youth members, finding board members, and recruiting qualified and motivated coaches (see Table 9.1).

Although some sport clubs have engaged salaried coaches and managers, usually all the technical and administrative work is done by volunteers. Unfortunately, 33% of Flemish clubs still do not require general pedagogical qualifications for their sport technical staffs, and an even smaller number require specific qualifications in teaching youngsters (De Knop et al., 1991).

School Sport Programs

Interscholastic athletic programs include the organized interschool sport participation of boys and girls at the lower, secondary, and university levels. Both in Flanders and in Wallonia, these activities at the lower and secondary levels are governed by the three school sport federations associated with their educational networks. The Flemish school sport federation is the umbrella organization of the three Flemish federations. The sport programs organized by the school sport federations are recreational as well as competitive.

Recreational Programs of the Local Authorities

Although recreational programs sponsor various levels of athletic competition, their main characteristics are enjoyment, physical development, and social interaction instead of a ''win-at-all-costs'' philosophy. The emphasis is on maximum participation rather than on high levels of competition. Competitions do exist in

Table 9.1 Problems Faced by Sport Clubs in Flanders

Kind of problems	n	%
Financial problems	201	40.9
Problems with infrastructure	125	25.4
Problems in recruiting and keeping youth members	117	23.8
Problems concerning board members	59	12.0
Problems finding capable and motivated coaches	48	9.8
Sport-specific problems (i.e., pollution of the rivers, etc.)	22	4.5
Problems concerning third persons	20	4.1
Need for recognition	16	3.3
Other problems	87	17.7
Number of clubs	492	100.0

Note. From *Fysieke Fitheid en Sportbeoefening van de Vlaamse Jeugd: Vol. 2. Analyse van de Georganiseerde Sport in Vlaanderen* [Physical Fitness and Sport Participation of Flemish Youth: Vol. 2. Analysis of Organized Sport in Flanders] (p. 66), by P. De Knop, W. Laporte, R. Van Meerbeek, and B. Vanreusel, 1991, Brussels, Belgium: IOS. Copyright 1991 by IOS. Adapted by permission.

recreational programs but they are usually confined to intracity competition or one-day programs.

An example of a recreational program organized by a number of Belgian municipal sport administrations is the sport academy. Its aim is to introduce school children in the lower grades to various sport disciplines by means of cooperation with the local sport clubs. Youngsters can either participate in the general sport program of the academy or follow the training courses of one or more sport clubs, without having to affiliate with a specific club. Both sport clubs and youngsters benefit from this initiative: for the clubs this academy helps to develop their youth structure, while the children can try out different sports or clubs before they really have to make a choice.

Another example of a successful recreational program is the sport camps organized during the holiday periods. Four types of sport camps can be identified: sport camps in one discipline (initiation or training), a combination of several sports, sport and education (languages, computers, outdoor education), and adventure sport camps. For instance, in 26 locations all over Flanders and Brussels, BLOSO organizes 972 sport camps in 102 different disciplines for youngsters from 8 up. During 1992, 14,054 children participated in the sport camps organized by the Flemish Community's sport administration. BLOSO also encourages private structures to organize sport camps of good quality by offering subsidies. In 1992, for instance, these private organizations received subsidies for 18,038 children.

Sport Programs of Other Private Nonprofit Organizations

Sports are also often incorporated into youth welfare programs in Belgium. Besides offering social and cultural activities, the sport programs they organize contain an ample package of recreational sport activities and are guided by people who are also responsible for the other activities.

Sport Participation

Several large representative surveys on sport participation by Belgian youth have been completed in the last 4 years. The results of this research offer important insights into changes in the levels of such participation (Bodson, 1991; Taks, Renson, & Vanreusel, 1991; Vanreusel & De Knop, 1992).

General Information on Youth Sport Participation

In Flanders, 41% of the boys and 54% of the girls between 12 and 18 are inactive or active only at a very moderate level. More encouragingly, 27% of the boys and 27% of the girls are active in sports for 3 to 6 hours a week. Moreover, 32% of the boys and 19% of the girls report being very active in sports, defined as participating for more than 6 hours a week. Comparative data between 1969 and 1989 show different tendencies in sport participation depending on age and gender. On the one hand, young adolescent boys (ages 12 to 15) now tend to be more active in sports than was the case 20 years ago. On the other hand, older boys (ages 16 to 18) are less active in sport compared to the same age group 20 years before. The number of low-active girls increased about 10% from 1979 to 1989, and the number of very active girls decreased about 10% over the same period (Taks et al., 1991). Research on youngsters in the French-speaking community of Belgium indicated that 66.6% of the youngsters between 6 and 18 are active in sports outside the school. Some 16.2% have never participated and 17.2% have dropped out (Bodson, 1991) (see Figure 9.3). Some 60% of the sport-active youth population participate in at least two sports.

The same study has also shown that boys and girls are not active in sports to the same degree. Of 100 youngsters who are active in sports, 47 are girls and 53 boys. Of those who have never participated in sports 65% are girls and only 35% are boys. Those who have dropped out of sport are 60% girls and 40% boys. It can be concluded, therefore, that girls are less active in sports than boys. Also the proportion of dropouts or nonparticipants is higher among girls than among boys.

Table 9.2 provides an overview of the most popular sport activities among Flemish youngsters from 12 to 18. Swimming is foremost of the favorite sports for both boys and girls. Next are soccer (for boys) and gymnastics (for girls). Some sport disciplines are strongly related to gender. For example, among the French-speaking community 94.5% of the participants in dance are girls and 95.4% of the soccer players are boys (see Table 9.3).

Other disciplines are strongly related to age: for example, among the French community gymnastics, dance, and swimming are typical activities for younger children (50% are younger than 12) (see Table 9.4). Tennis, jogging, and horseback riding are mainly practiced by adolescents (from 12 to 17).

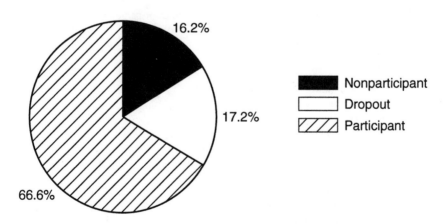

Figure 9.3 Distribution of 6-to-18-year-old youngsters' sport participation (*N* = 2,355). *Note.* The information regarding sport participation in the French-speaking community has been provided to us with permission from ADEPS and is extracted from the magazine *Sport*, n°136 and 140.

Table 9.2   Preferred Sports Among 12-to-18-Year-Old Flemish Youths

Boys (n = 872)		Girls (n = 897)	
Sport	Percentage of participants	Sport	Percentage of participants
Swimming	56	Swimming	59
Soccer	50	Gymnastics	48
Gymnastics	32	Volleyball	35
Volleyball	29	Track and field	23
Basketball	28	Basketball	22
Track and field	26	Badminton	21
Tennis	24	Tennis	20
Table tennis	24	Dance	16
Badminton	17	Handball	13
Cycling	13	Soccer	11

Note. From *Hoe Sportief Is de Vlaming? Een Terugblik op 20 Jaar Sportbeoefening 1969-1989* [How Sport-active Are the Flemish? Looking Back at 20 Years of Sport Participation 1969-1989] (pp. 25, 41), by M. Taks, R. Renson, and B. Vanreusel, 1991, Leuven, Belgium: SOCK. Copyright 1991 by SOCK. Adapted by permission.

Table 9.3   Differences of Practiced Sports According to Gender Among 6-to-8-Year-Old Youngsters in the French-Speaking Community

Sport	Percentage of participants (N = 2,355)	
	Boys	Girls
Swimming	42.9	57.1
Soccer	95.4	4.6
Tennis	49.8	50.2
Martial arts	75.8	24.2
Cycling	58.8	41.2
Gymnastics	25.0	75.0
Dance	5.5	94.5
Basketball	69.9	30.1
Jogging	42.7	56.4
Horseback riding	18.8	81.2

Note. From *Sport: Les Jeunes et le Sport en Communauté Française* [Sport: Youth and Sport in the French Community] (p. 4), by D. Bodson, 1991, Brussels, Belgium: ADEPS. Copyright 1991 by ADEPS. Adapted by permission.

Table 9.4 Differences of Practiced Sports Among Youngsters in the French-Speaking Community According to Age Group

Sport	Practiced by youngsters (in percentage)		
	Under 12 years	12 to 17 years	Over 17 years
Swimming	54	37	9
Soccer	41	51	7
Tennis	25	66.5	8.5
Martial arts	36	53	11
Cycling	35	57	8
Gymnastics	64	33	3
Dance	56	38	5
Basketball	35	53	12
Jogging	18	61	20
Horseback riding	26	64	9
Total sport population (N = 2,355)	38	52	10

Note. From *Sport: Les Jeunes et le Sport en Communauté Française* [Sport: Youth and Sport in the French Community] (p. 4), by D. Bodson, 1991, Brussels, Belgium: ADEPS. Copyright 1991 by ADEPS. Adapted by permission.

Participation in Organized Sport

A dense network of sport clubs, in a variety of types and sizes, is one of the typical features of Belgian sports. All these clubs offer sport programs for youth. For example, on average, 60.6% of Flemish boys aged 12-18 are members of at least one sport club. However, the participation rate in organized sports among Flemish youths decreases between 12 and 18 years, as indicated in Table 9.5.

Participation in sport clubs is remarkably popular among youngsters compared to participation in other sociocultural youth organizations. The average age to become a member of a sport club is 9.2 years. More than 50% of all youths become members before the age of 10. And 9 out of 10 members joined their first club before the age of 13. Multiple memberships in sport clubs often occur. Many young people change memberships from one club to another, or are members of different sport clubs at the same time.

Dropouts

According to a study conducted with Walloon youngsters, 17% have dropped out of sports (Bodson, 1991). The ages between 11 and 16 seem to be critical, because 67% of all dropouts occurred during that period.

A similar survey conducted in Flanders indicates that 38% of the youngsters dropped out of one or more sport clubs (Vanreusel & De Knop, 1992). The

Table 9.5   Age-Related Participation (in Percentage) in Organized Club Sports by Flemish Boys and Girls

Gender	Age							
	12	13	14	15	16	17	18	12-18
Boys (n = 1,518)	66	64	58	62	56	56	58	60.6
Girls (n = 1,551)	47	40	41	41	34	40	33	40.3

Note. From *Fysieke Fitheid en Sportbeoefening van de Vlaamse Jeugd: Vol. 4. Participatie en Dropout* [Physical Fitness and Sport Participation of Flemish Youth: Vol. 4. Participation and Dropout] (p. 6), by B. Vanreusel and P. De Knop, 1992, Brussels, Belgium: IOS. Copyright 1992 by IOS. Adapted by permission.

figures on the age categories during which most dropouts occur also point in the direction of a huge percentage of early dropouts, namely 49.7% between 11 and 13 years.

Both studies show that the level of dropout is higher among girls than among boys. However, the precise data on these gender differences differ slightly: the Walloon study indicates that one out of four girls leaves the club compared to only one out of six boys, while the Flemish data indicate that one out of three girls who started sport has left compared to only one out of five boys. The most important reasons for dropping out mentioned by participants in the two studies are: not interested anymore, too much school work, other leisure pursuits, too many injuries, and a "bad" atmosphere within the club.

Some of these reasons for dropping out of organized sports suggest that not enough attention is being paid to the special needs of children and youths in such programs, and this is corroborated by research. It is reported that 79% of the sport federations which are recognized by the Flemish sport administration have no specific training programs for youth coaching staff (De Knop et al., 1991). Moreover, in their content analysis of the (few) existing youth-guidance staff training programs of Flemish sport federations, De Knop et al. (1990) indicated that only a very small number deal with specific aspects of sport guidance related to youth.

Promotional Campaigns

As mentioned earlier, there are several organizations in Belgium that actively promote organized youth sport activities. Youth sports are promoted in a variety of ways, such as holiday sport camps, tournaments, initiation courses, special events, subsidization of activities, and awareness campaigns. Governmental as well as nongovernmental organizations are involved in these initiatives. Perhaps the most striking trend is that several sport federations are conducting promotional campaigns to attract more children to their sports.

The Sport Promotional Campaign of the Royal Belgian Soccer Federation

One of the most active sport federations in organizing youth promotional activities is the Royal Belgian Soccer Federation, which has, from 1989 on, undertaken several initiatives to promote soccer among children and youths. The most important initiatives are:

- *street soccer*, in cooperation with different municipal sport services and youth associations, directed toward underprivileged youths,
- *7 × 7 soccer*, in which the overall objective is to teach soccer in a "child-centered" way, on smaller fields, with moveable goals and without referees,
- *beach soccer*, which involves exhibitions and small tournaments on the beach during holiday periods, and
- the *soccer van*, by means of which, within a period of five years, two promotional teams of the Royal Belgian Soccer Federation are visiting 800 primary schools to promote soccer.

BLOSO Youth Sport Campaign 1992-1995

In 1992, BLOSO started a large-scale youth sport promotional campaign to encourage Flemish youngsters between 12 and 18 to take part in regular organized sports in sport clubs. This campaign used several initiatives to reach its objective. In general, two kinds of strategies could be distinguished. On the one hand, there was education of youngsters through a variety of activities organized to allow them to sample different sports, and made public through various media (e.g., television, radio, newspapers, magazines) in order to reach as many youngsters as possible. On the other hand, there was also a more structural approach that tried to prepare the sport technical and managerial staff members of sport federations and clubs to deal more appropriately with the needs and capacities of young sport participants. This was done by introducing specific youth themes (e.g., technical guidance for youth; organization of sideline activities; dealing with dropouts and parents) within BLOSO's regular staff training program.

Initiatives From the Belgian Olympic and Interfederal Committee (BOIC)

In recent years the BOIC has actively promoted organized youth sports in Belgium. With their Spring Games initiative, which started in 1985, they have introduced about a half million youngsters to a variety of sports and informed them about organized sport activities. In 1991, the BOIC published the *White Book on Physical Fitness*, in cooperation with the King Baudouin Foundation. This book provides detailed information on the alarmingly low physical fitness of Belgian youth. During that year they also hosted the first European Youth Olympic Days. Another initiative, *The Best 1000*, aims at the optimalization of the technical, medical, and psychological guidance of talented young athletes in cooperation with sport federations and the industry. In 1995 as part of the year theme "Olympism and Youth," the BOIC has given 13 "Olympic Youth Awards" to sport clubs which have made a special effort with regard to a specific youth sport policy.

Sport Campaign for Underprivileged Youth

In 1988, the King Baudouin Foundation started a campaign targeting underprivileged youth for sport involvement (De Knop & Walgrave, 1992). The basic idea of this campaign is to improve the problematic situation of these youth (poor education, bad housing, delinquency) by offering them sport opportunities, through which they can come in contact with youth welfare workers and teachers. In this way, sport is used as a means of social integration. Through this campaign, a number of successful initiatives have been organized within several domains (such as youth welfare work, education, organized sport, and local sport services).

Belgian Red Cross Youth Sport Injuries Prevention Campaign

In 1991 the Health Education Service of the Belgian Red Cross launched a 2-year campaign aimed at optimizing the prevention of sport injuries among 6- to 14-year-old Flemish children. This campaign, entitled *I Practice Sports Safely*, tries to make youngsters aware of their responsibility for their own health and for that of others by addressing them directly as well as indirectly (via youth sport coaches, physical education teachers, and parents). The campaign focuses on soccer, basketball, and volleyball, sports that are not only very popular among Belgian youth, but that also cause frequent sport injuries. There are three themes dealt with by the campaign: fair play, training, and appropriate sport equipment.

Conclusion

Sports appear to perform a significant role in the lives of many youngsters. The number of opportunities for participating in sport has risen substantially in the last decade. Today, young people can choose from a wide variety of activities and many organizational settings. Participation in organized or club sports is a dynamic process in which the involvement of young people is characterized by moving in and out of a wide range of activities with a considerable amount of experimentation.

However, a number of problems have arisen, such as the decline in participation with age even during the school years, a decline that accelerates in the middle and older ages. Together with the demographic changes taking place in Belgian society, this decrease of involvement among "older youths" in the sport clubs could mean a serious threat for organized youth sports in Belgium. Promotional campaigns in favor of sports and the development of programs for youth are attempts to reverse these trends. It should be stressed, however, that an overall youth sport policy has been lacking in the past and that only recently governmental organizations such as BLOSO have taken up this duty. The competition among the different sport federations to attract children at a very young age is the best example of this. In the beginning of this century, sport was an activity which started around the age of 15. Today, however, opportunities for involvement in organized sports begin at ages 5 and 6 in most team sports (such as soccer, basketball, and handball) and in many of the individual sports (such as gymnastics and swimming). This policy of attracting younger children to become involved in organized sport is not based on pedagogical objectives, but on objectives related to "survival." Sport clubs want to be on the market, that is, simply because their economic existence is threatened. Even the national sport promotional campaigns are not considering sport for children and youth as a goal in itself, a form of pure leisure, or a necessary pedagogical or developmental method. In this context, sport for children and youth is primarily promoted for reasons such as health and fitness, prestige, and integration.

Some municipalities have also understood that this competition does not favor children's development and have accordingly started so-called "sport academies." However, this can only be considered a starting point.

One of the main objectives of a future policy for youth sport should be to increase the quality from a pedagogical point of view. Such a policy needs to focus on the following topics: a cooperative approach to the provision of youth sport instead of a "competition" between the different organizations, pedagogical qualifications for youth sport coaches, setting up specific youth sport coaches' programs, trying to convince parents that informal play during childhood is of greater importance than formal sport participation, a promotion of sport for children and youth with emphasis on enjoyment and social motives, and a scientific evaluation of the effectiveness of sport promotional campaigns.

References

Bodson, D. (1991). *Sport. Les jeunes et le sport en communauté Française* [Sport. Youth and Sport in the French Community]. Brussels, Belgium: ADEPS.

De Knop, P., Bollaert, L., De Martelaer, K., Theeboom, M., Van Puymbroeck, L., & Wylleman, P. (1990). *Analyse van de jeugdsportbeoefening in Vlaanderen* [Analysis of youth sport participation in Flanders]. Brussels, Belgium: BLOSO.

De Knop, P., Laporte, W., Van Meerbeek, R., & Vanreusel, B. (1991). *Fysieke fitheid en sportbeoefening van de Vlaamse jeugd: Vol. 2. Analyse van de georganiseerde sport in Vlaanderen* [Physical fitness and sport participation of Flemish youth: Vol. 2. Analysis of organized sport in Flanders]. Brussels, Belgium: IOS.

De Knop, P., & Walgrave, L. (Eds.) (1992). *Sport als integratie: Kansen voor maatschappelijk kwetsbare jongeren* [Sport as integration: Chances for underprivileged youth]. Brussels, Belgium: Koning Boudewijnstichting.

Nationaal Instituut voor de Statistiek. (1993). *Perspectives démographiques 1992-2050* [Demographic perspectives 1992-2050]. Brussels, Belgium: Author.

Taks, M., Renson, R., & Vanreusel, B. (1991). *Hoe sportief is de Vlaming? Een terugblik op 20 jaar sportbeoefening 1969-1989* [How sport-active are the Flemish? Looking back at 20 years of sport participation 1969-1989]. Leuven, Belgium: SOCK.

Van Mulders, S. (1992). *Regulerende wetgeving* [Regulating legislation]. Brussels, Belgium: BLOSO.

Vanreusel, B., & De Knop, P. (1992). *Fysieke fitheid en sportbeoefening van de Vlaamse jeugd: Vol. 4. Participatie en drop out* [Physical fitness and sport participation of Flemish youth: Vol. 4. Participation and dropout]. Brussels, Belgium: IOS.

Chapter 10 Denmark

Bjarne Ibsen
Laila Ottesen

Denmark is a small country, with an area of 42,000 km², a population of 5.1 million, and a culturally homogeneous society (common ethnicity, history, language, and religion). Economically and politically, Denmark is a welfare state characterized by a large public sector, which spends more than half of the gross national product.

Twenty-one percent of the population are youngsters between 6 and 18. Danish children go to the unstreamed 'folkeskole' (the municipal primary and lower-secondary school) from about the age of 6 to the age of 17, precisely the age-group in question here. Normally, children are in school from 8:00 a.m. until 1:00, 2:00, or 3:00 p.m., depending on which class they are in, but when the school bell rings, the children scatter in all directions to various organized leisure-time options and activities.

The Organizational Network

The leisure-time sector for children and young people includes a predominantly local authority system (recreation centers, youth clubs, youth schools, and music schools), a system of association options (sport clubs, scout groups, etc.) and a commercial system (clothes, music, grill bars, films, magazines, etc.) (see Figure 10.1).

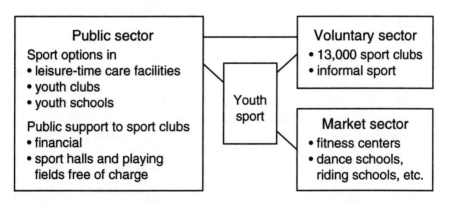

Figure 10.1   The organization of youth sport in Denmark.

After school, most of the younger pupils (up to the age of 10) go to recreation centers or leisure-time care facilities at schools, where they stay, under educational supervision, until their parents collect them after work. In Denmark, there is only a small amount of organized voluntary school sport (after school), and organized sport is very rarely offered at the "leisure-time care facilities at schools," nor is there room for sporting activities.

Children from 10 to 18 can go to recreation and youth clubs after school, where there is no educational supervision, that is, the children can come and go as they please (Andersen, 1989). The recreation clubs, for children between 10 and 14, are open from about 1:00 to 5:00 p.m., after which the youth clubs for the 14-to-18 age group take over and are open until 10 p.m. In most of the recreation and youth clubs, different sport activities are offered and there are also a small number of tournaments in which the club members can participate. In addition, half of the 14-to-18 age group go to youth school, which is a local-authority educational option with various school subjects and other subjects, of which sport only has a small part. Finally, about a quarter of the 12-to-13 age group and about half the 14-to-16 age group have paid employment after school and on the weekends.

When Danish children engage in sport, they go primarily to the voluntary clubs (Andersen, 1989). About 6 out of 10 children go to sport clubs and 9 out of 10 children have engaged in sport in a sport club at some time. Denmark has about 13,000 sport clubs—a sport club for every 400 people—closely spread all over the country, where children go to training once or twice a week, and play matches or take part in competitions or displays on the weekend.

Club Sport Programs

Clubs and associations are the predominant youth sport organization forms (Balle-Petersen, 1976). Despite the fact that both the market and the state have extended their activities to still more areas, the voluntary sector has also grown very rapidly, as has participation in these voluntary clubs and organizations. This growth is probably connected with the expansion of the welfare state. But a qualitative change in the association pattern has occurred. Clubs and organizations oriented toward values and social issues, aimed at groups outside the circle of members or at society as a whole, have declining support (political parties, religious associations, social aid organizations). But at the same time, more decentralized and autonomous interest associations and groups working for the members themselves have appeared in large numbers (sport clubs, hobby clubs, self-help groups). There has been a change from ideas, altruism, and solidarity to identity, self-determination, and fellowship (Ibsen, 1992).

The sport clubs are exponents of this trend. Since the mid-1960s, membership in sport clubs has exploded, with a doubling of both the number of clubs and the number of members in spite of the fact that a growing number of athletically active individuals in the same period have chosen to practice sport under commercially or municipally organized forms. This growth has changed sport clubs in a number of ways (Ibsen, 1992). Clubs have become larger, the composition of the membership has become more heterogeneous (greater age diversity, more equal sex distribution, and less socioeconomic selectivity), and expansion and differentiation of sport activities have occurred resulting in new clubs and sports. Members have a weaker link with the sport club than previously, sport clubs have become more exposed to competition, their importance for the local community has declined, and dependence on and contact with the public sector has increased. However, these developments and characteristics do not apply to all sport clubs to the same degree. It is possible to differentiate among three types of clubs (Ibsen, 1992).

The small sport club has relatively few members and is concerned with a narrow branch of sport. The club has a homogeneous membership with relatively many adult members. It is very *introverted and socially (fellowship) oriented* and the members have strong links with the club. Many clubs of this type were established, particularly in the 1970s and 1980s, and they constitute a growing share of the sport clubs in Denmark.

The ball club is a medium-sized club concerned with a ball game. The club consists predominantly of children and young people and puts a lot of emphasis on fellowship and sporting results. Since 1960, this type of club has constituted a declining share of both the clubs and club membership in Denmark.

The large exercise club, devoted to popular exercise sports like gymnastics, swimming, badminton, and tennis, is a large, hierarchical club with a heterogeneous membership. The members have a weak link with the club. From 1970 to 1980, the number of members in these clubs increased explosively. The growth has meant that the existing clubs have become larger while relatively few new clubs of that type have been established. These clubs' share of the total number of sport clubs has not changed since 1960.

The characteristic feature of clubs is that they have emerged ''from below'' and that the club and its members have a large degree of self-administration. The highest authority in the clubs is the annual general meeting, where members elect the executive committee and decide the budget. In most sport clubs, however, only members over 16 have the right to vote, meaning that children have little formal influence. Given the fact that they come to the club voluntarily, however, it could be said that they are able to show whether the club and its sport are in accordance with their interests and wishes.

In principle, the clubs are open to everyone who wants to participate, but a membership fee must be paid. The fee varies from sport to sport and from club to club, but on average, children and youth members pay 300 DKK (US $50) for a year, while adults on average pay 450 DKK (US $75).

Three Umbrella Organizations for Sport

Denmark has never had a unified sport organization, but two main organizations look after the general interests of the clubs, many of which are members of both of them. Both organizations, the Danish Sports Federation (DIF) and the Danish Gymnastics and Sports Associations (DGI) have roots in the last century, but their roots are completely different. Apart from these, there is a third organization, the Danish Companies' Sports Federation, which organizes sport clubs in companies.

DIF is an umbrella organization for specialized federations such as the Danish Soccer Union, which arranges soccer tournaments and has the right to establish national teams to represent Denmark in international tournaments. These specialized federations are also members of an international organization such as FIFA. DIF also has the right to select Danish participants for the Olympic Games. The specialized federations in Denmark are generally divided into 2 to 6 smaller regional federations. The competitive and tournament structure in DIF's specialized federations is local, regional, and national, depending on the qualification level. The competitions and tournaments for children and young people are, as a general rule, always divided into age groups (by year of birth, not school year) and by sex, within each discipline. DIF has its roots in Olympic amateur sport and in English ball games and water sport traditions.

The other main organization, DGI, has quite a different history. It originated in rural areas, with roots in Swedish gymnastics, the folk high school movement, and the national rifle-club movement. DGI, unlike DIF in which the majority of the clubs are also members of the specialized federations, does not consist of specialized federations, but instead includes 25 county associations. DGI competitions and tournaments are primarily played on the county level, but apart from these, there are displays and sport meetings, called national sport meetings and championships, where each county can be represented by a team. The competitive disciplines for children and young people are divided according to age and gender in DGI as in DIF.

Both organizations are directed toward the youths in the community. However, the strong growth in the sport participation of older age groups and the smaller numbers in the younger age groups have changed the composition of membership in the sport clubs. In the space of 20 years, from 1972 to 1992, the proportion of youth members has dropped from 48% to 40%. From having been *youth* clubs, sport clubs are increasingly becoming *adult* clubs, and new sport clubs—formed during the 1970s and 1980s—have relatively few children and youth members (Ibsen, 1992).

In reality, a fourth organization also exists since an act was passed in 1985 dealing with elite sport in Denmark, and an independent organization was set up to nurture the talented in the individual sport disciplines. This organization, Team Denmark, has resulted in greatly altered conditions for practicing elite sport in Denmark, even though it is still elite sport on an amateur level. In order to protect children, the act operates with a lower age limit of 15, when Team Denmark may subsidize talented sport players to start elite training. But as no age limits apply in the individual specialized federations, they can let their sport players practice top-level elite sport even though they are under 15.

Public Support for Sport Clubs

The national sport organizations get financial support from the profits on the soccer pools and lotto, and the allocation is determined by legislation. However, the organizations do not give grants to individual clubs, which are subsidized by the local authorities. This situation makes the clubs and members much more interested in local sport politics than in the politics of the main organizations. According to a special act on support for sport, culture, leisure-time, and adult education in voluntary organizations (the Act on Popular Education), the local authorities are obliged to support sport clubs. The support is given partly to subsidize the expenses of the club for premises and sport facilities and partly to subsidize club activities. However, the local authorities are only obliged to support activities for members under 25. Since the introduction of the Soccer Pools Act in 1948, Denmark has had a tradition of subsidizing sport activities for children and young people in voluntary clubs, and the state, through legislation, respects the self-administration of the clubs as much as possible. The local authorities have also subsidized sport by building halls and playing fields in the course of the 1960-1970s, and giving them free of charge to local sport clubs.

Today, there is a sport hall for every 4,000 people, swimming pools for every 12,000, and a soccer pitch for every 1,000. The extent and quality of the facilities in the Danish local authority areas are at a level that without doubt makes them among the best in Europe.

Sport Participation

Studies from the beginning and middle of the 1980s have consistently shown that 8 out of 10 children practice sport, 6 of these are members of sport clubs, and only 2 out of 10 practice sport outside a sport club (Andersen, 1989; Andersen & Schelin, 1988; Forchhammer & Petersen, 1980; Gallup Markedsanalyse A/S, 1985; Schultz Jørgensen, Gamst, & Andersen, 1986). A national investigation from 1985 into the life and activities of the 8-to-14 age group showed that 20% practiced sport daily and 58% weekly. The same investigation showed that 58% were members of a sport club (Gallup Markedsanalyse A/S, 1985).

The most recent large study of youth sport in Denmark, in 1987, investigated the living conditions and leisure-time pursuits of children and young people (Andersen, 1989) (see Table 10.1). The investigation showed that 4 out of 5 children between 7 and 15 years old go to organized activities in their free time, and by far the majority of these young people go to several activities or practice the same activity several times weekly. A few more girls than boys go to organized activities, mainly because girls 14 to 15 go more to organized activities than boys of the same age. On average, the children who go to organized activities spend just under four hours a week on organized leisure-time activities (weekend trips, competitions, etc., are not included).

For both boys and girls, sport and exercise are the predominant activities (see Table 10.1). Two-thirds of all children and young people between 7 and 15—boys and girls—practice some sort of organized sport in their free time (Andersen, 1989). On average, sport occupies about 75% of the time they spend on fixed leisure-time interests—particularly for boys, who spend about 90% of their time on sport, while girls spend roughly 60% of their time on sport activities. From

Table 10.1   Participation Percentages and Time Spent Weekly on Scheduled Leisure-time Interests Generally, and Sport/Exercise Specifically, for 7-to-15-Year-Olds in 1987 (N = 1,033)

Activity	Participation percentage			Time spent weekly* (in hours and minutes)	
	All	Boys	Girls	Boys	Girls
Organized leisure-time activity	81	79	83	3 hr 45 min	3 hr 57 min
Sport and exercise	65	65	64	3 hr 10 min	2 hr 33 min
Soccer	18	32	4	2 hr 30 min	2 hr 01 min
Gymnastics	14	5	21	1 hr 55 min	1 hr 33 min
Badminton	13	16	10	1 hr 43 min	1 hr 18 min
Swimming	13	13	13	1 hr 16 min	1 hr 16 min
Handball	11	7	14	1 hr 29 min	1 hr 28 min
Horseback riding	6	1	10	–	3 hr 43 min
Dancing	5	3	8	–	1 hr 33 min
Jazz ballet/dancing	2	0	4	–	1 hr 31 min
Other ball games	3	2	3	–	–
Table tennis	3	4	1	2 hr 19 min	–
Self-defense	3	4	1	–	–

*Where the average time spent is based on less than the participation of 20 children in the activity, the result is not listed.

Note. from *Skolebørns dagligdag* [School children's daily life] (p. 93), by D. Andersen, 1989, Copenhagen, Denmark: Socialforskningsinstituttet. Copyright 1989 by Socialforskningsinstituttet. Adapted by permission.

the beginning of the 1970s, when the first studies of the leisure-time and sport activities of children and young people were done (Frederiksen & Sørensen, 1977), until the beginning of the 1980s, the participation of children and young people in organized sports grew from about 50% to about 60% (Andersen, 1989). Since then, participation has stayed at the same level. The investigations reveal a tendency to a slight fall in boys' participation in organized sport, which, however, is compensated for by a slight increase in girls' participation, as well as a fall in participation in sport outside clubs (mainly unorganized sport), from 24% in 1981 to 17% in 1985 (Schultz Jørgensen et al., 1986).

The most popular sports are soccer, gymnastics, handball, badminton, swimming, horseback riding, and jazz ballet dance (see Table 10.1). For boys, the predominant sport is soccer, which is practiced by every third boy in this age group. For girls, the predominant activities are gymnastics, handball, and swimming. The sport interests of the children and young people are spread over even more sport disciplines than before, and a slow shift is occurring from ball games to more individual sports. In 1979, youth membership in the collective sport disciplines made up 52% of the children and youth members in the Danish Sports Federation. Ten years later, that share had fallen to 40%.

The proportion of children and young people who go to organized leisure-time activities varies only a little with the degree of urbanization, which, however, has a very significant impact on the activities they choose. For instance, 25% of the 7-to-15 age group living in small towns play soccer compared to just over 10% in the larger towns. Correspondingly, just under 20% play handball and 20% participate in gymnastics in less-urbanized areas, while only 1% play handball and 6% participate in gymnastics in and around Copenhagen.

Dropouts

As children and young people grow older, their leisure-time interests change, and many organized sport activities note a high dropout rate among young people 12 to 14. Conversely, other leisure-time activities note an increase in interest at that age. This means that there are relatively small differences in the proportion of children who go to organized leisure-time activities from the youngest, 7 to 9, to the oldest, 13 to 15 (see Table 10.2). Gradually, as children become older, they spend more and more time on organized leisure-time activities, but the proportion of boys who participate in these activities declines slightly. With regard to sport activity, interest peaks at the age of 10 to 12, when just over two-thirds of all the young people go to an organized sport activity. After that age, interest falls, and just over 60% of young people between 13 and 15 are involved.

Boys begin to specialize at the age of 13 to 15, and they spend a lot of time at what they are involved in. On the other hand, girls' choices of interests are broader. The greatest dropout for both sexes is in swimming and gymnastics. At the age of 7 to 9, every fifth child goes to swimming, but by the time they are 13 to 15, only every twentieth goes to organized swimming. Correspondingly, two-thirds of the children who went to gymnastics at the age of 7 to 9 have stopped by the age of 13 to 15. This dropout has worried both sport organizations and politicians, but the problem is more complex than is often stated. First, the dropout shown in investigations and membership of organizations conceals the fact that the dropout is in fact greater than the figures show, because it is partially offset by the intake of young people who have not previously practiced sport. Second, as a rule, dropping out may involve choosing among different activities. Children try several out, and then, during puberty, they choose one sport and concentrate on that. Third, the dropout rate is considered worrying by the authorities because their basic perspective is that participating in organized leisure-time activities will prevent social problems and crime. Their aim is to organize as many people as possible for as long as possible in some form of organized club activity. They focus on the children and young people who are ''club-free or club-less,'' whom they would like to have organized in a ''life-long club relationship.'' Of course, it must be termed generous when a society insists that there must be leisure-time and sport options to suit everybody. But, for one thing, not everyone wants that, and for another, there is no qualitative research about the

Table 10.2 Percentages of 7-to-15-Year-Olds Who Participated in Sport and Exercise, Classified According to Sex and Age, in 1987 ($N = 1,033$)

		Boys			Girls		
		7-9	10-12	13-15	7-9	10-12	13-15
Activity	Go to organized leisure-time activity	78	84	76	80	84	85
	Go to sport/ exercise	64	68	62	65	66	62
	Soccer	32	36	29	1	6	5
	Handball	4	8	8	13	14	16
	Badminton	13	19	15	7	14	10
	Swimming	19	13	7	23	12	5
	Gymnastics	6	5	4	34	17	12
	Horseback riding	0	1	0	5	16	10
Weekly time spent on organized free-time activities:	2 hrs $\leq$	44	32	12	39	30	15
	2 hrs $< \times \leq 4$ hrs	27	25	20	26	34	19
	4 hrs $< \times \leq 6$ hrs	7	16	16	13	12	23
	< 6 hrs	1	11	28	2	9	28

Note. From *Skolebørns Dagligdag* [School Children's Daily Life] (p. 98), by D. Andersen, 1989, Copenhagen, Denmark: Socialforskningsinstituttet. Copyright 1989 by Socialforskningsinstituttet. Adapted by permission.

type of meaningful leisure-time options that can be given to this group of "club-free or club-less" youths, or about how such options can be presented. The question of whether this is a task for the voluntary clubs at all should also be considered.

Unorganized Sport Activities

As described above, life for children and young people in Denmark is lived in a very fixed, organized setting, which does not leave much room for more unorganized, spontaneous, and self-organized activities—alone or with friends. The *time* and *space* for the children's and young people's self-organized activities have been reduced. Physical activity, nonetheless, still plays quite a large role in the self-organized activities of children and young people (see Table 10.3). Surprisingly small differences are apparent between the self-organized physical activities of boys and girls—unlike a number of other self-organized activities in leisure time—but the older the young people are, the less they participate in physical play like tag, roller-skating, and climbing trees. On the other hand, there is only a small fall in the proportion of those who sometimes play ball or go to

Table 10.3 Percentages of 7-to-15-Year-Olds Who Sometimes Participated in Different Forms of Unorganized Leisure-time Pursuits, Classified According to Age, in 1987 (*N* = 1,033)

Activity	Boys				Girls			
	7-9	10-11	12-13	14-15	7-9	10-11	12-13	14-15
Hide-and-seek and catching games	80	65	35	6	84	82	43	18
Roller-skating	35	45	33	10	70	73	50	15
Climbing trees/ building caves	81	68	45	12	65	58	27	8
Playing soccer in the garden, on the streets	86	83	89	74	44	58	51	43
Other ball games in the garden, on the streets	61	67	71	49	74	80	71	60
Go to swimming pool	57	68	73	59	57	83	74	61
Go to sport as spectator	34	40	44	45	21	12	19	31
Use computers	49	52	56	61	26	37	9	11
Go to the cinema with a friend	31	41	67	72	29	46	68	89

Note. From *Skolebørns Dagligdag* [School Children's Daily Life] (p. 137), by D. Andersen, 1989, Copenhagen, Denmark: Socialforskningsinstituttet. Copyright 1989 by Socialforskningsinstituttet. Adapted by permission.

the swimming pools—even though interest in these activities in organized forms diminishes greatly the older the youngsters become.

Promotional Campaigns

In spite of the fact that 6 out of 10 children and young people practice sport in a sport club, youth sport in Denmark has been subjected to criticism for many years. The criticism has focused in particular on the dropout rate among teenagers, the imitation of the norms of elite sport, and, especially, the strong specialization and selection in youth sport.

At the beginning of the 1980s, in reaction to this criticism, the DGI held the first courses in a completely new form of youth sport in which play and all-around movement training predominated at the expense of competition and learning specific sport disciplines. At the same time, special educational and inspirational material was developed, including ideas and suggestions for games and activities for children, and instructors for courses in the new youth sports were trained. Clubs that tried out the ideas could get financial help from the organization, and experiments were conducted with new forms of sport meetings and tournaments. Today, these special youth sport courses are held all over the country.

The other large national sport organization, Denmark's Sports Federation, has likewise taken a number of initiatives for the improvement of sport for children and young people, but the campaigns and ideas have not been as great a break with tradition as the efforts in DGI. The initiatives in DIF have been particularly aimed at getting the specialized federations to adapt their rules, equipment, and competitive forms to children's developmental stages. In the middle of the 1980s, DIF launched "sport's green card." The idea is that sport clubs, in cooperation with local authorities, inform all youngsters about the sport options in the local area, and invite them to try out the different sport disciplines and clubs for a period (usually a month), free of charge. About 15% of the local authority areas have implemented such a campaign. In 1989, DIF started a campaign under the motto, "fair play," in the hope that better behavior, joy of movement, play, and social contact with others could counteract result fixation, bad behavior, foul play, and ideals taken from elite sports. All the clubs received campaign material (stickers, posters, etc.) and during the year about 250 special fair play sport meetings were held, which focused on these values in youth sport. The most recent initiative in DIF is the "minisport" project, whereby the organization supports a number of sport clubs offering interdisciplinary sport that is not aimed at the skills of a definite discipline, for children up to 10.

Parallel with the sport organizations' efforts to renew and develop youth sport, a number of sport clubs received financial support in the 1980s from national experimental and developmental pools for experiments and new ideas. During the 1980s, the state granted very considerable sums for experimental and developmental programs in cultural, educational, and social fields. The overall idea behind these experimental programs was to make citizens get together in their local environments to implement innovative experimental projects within a broad central regulatory framework, for the purpose of readjustment and renewal. The efforts were not only aimed at the public sector, but also at building up a broad cooperation with and between clubs and local groups, in order to concentrate resources, revitalize local communities, and create unity, coordination, and fellowship instead of limited options and merely individual engagement in particular interests. Clubs were involved in many of these local experimental and developmental projects, among them many sport clubs, and some of these projects were aimed at youth sport (Hestbæk, 1992).

In this way, many sport clubs—with financial support from national experimental and development pools or from sport organizations, and inspired by the organizations' courses, material, and campaigns—have experimented with new youth sport, which differs from traditional sport, particularly in the following characteristics:

- *Interdisciplinary sport*: Play, ordinary movement training, and contact are emphasized more than specialized training in a definite sport discipline, and the activities are determined more by the children's motor, psychological, and social development than by the rules and norms of the sport discipline. Youth sports in general replace youth soccer, youth gymnastics, and youth athletics.

- *Family sport*: Many places have made an effort to avoid age and sex division by offering sport for the whole family.

- *Decreased emphasis on competition*: The competitive and tournament aspect is toned down by less use of competitions that segregate and separate the children and by greater participation in alternative forms of sport meetings.

- *Cooperation with municipal institutions*: Many experiments have established cooperation with municipal institutions (kindergartens, recreational centers, youth clubs, schools, the social services) or other clubs to give the children's daily life and the many local leisure-time options more coherence, to interest new target groups, and to integrate the activities in the local community.

- *Democratization and self-organization*: Finally, several clubs have also tried to involve the children and youth more and give them a feeling of responsibility and greater influence by initiating, for example, self-directing youth groups.

These many experiments have attracted a lot of attention and comment, and the experiences they have generated seem to be positive, but in reality only a very small section of the sport clubs have taken up these ideas. Only a few sport clubs applied for and got financial support from the national experimental and developmental pools for the development of youth sports (but youth's experiments made up only 5% of the projects that were given grants from the social development funds) and a study of the sport clubs from 1989 showed that only 4% of the sport clubs had such new youth sports in their programs (Ibsen, 1992).

Conclusion

This chapter gives a picture of youth sport in Denmark. It does not regard sport as an isolated phenomenon, but on the contrary tries to integrate sport in an everyday perspective. The quantitative studies referred to in parts of the chapter are most significant in giving an overview and in underlining differences, but perhaps particularly in comparing data. Furthermore, quantitative data also have the strong point that they can serve as the point of departure for further questions, for which many of the answers must be sought in more qualitative data. That is also the case with our knowledge of youth sport. We can show participation and organization patterns, but we know very little about the significance of these patterns for the everyday life of these children and young people. And we know even less about what significance they have for various distinct groups in the community.

Ever since the European Council framed the charter "Sport for All" in 1966, part of the Danish state's policy has been to get as many people as possible to practice sport throughout their lives. Sport was thereafter regarded as a welfare benefit, but also as a means of improving the health and social conditions of the population. The most important reason for supporting sport for youngsters is its socio-educational and health character, especially from a prophylactic perspective. Danish studies, however, have been unable to "prove" the alleged direct effect of sport on either the state of health or the level of delinquency in youth:

• A large Danish investigation of the physical profile and sport habits of schoolgoing young people can only show a weak connection between physical activity in leisure time and oxygen assimilation (cardiorespiratory efficiency), while other health objectives do not seem to be affected by it (Andersen & Schelin, 1988).

• Several Danish studies have been unable to show a link between participation in different forms of organized leisure-time activities and lower crime rates (Balvig & Kyvsgaard, 1990; Frederiksen & Sørensen, 1977). Thus it is doubtful whether the practice of sport in leisure time in itself reduces delinquency.

The character and level of leisure-time activities are symptoms, indicators, reflections, or effects of more basic aspects of young people's lives, especially relationships with family and school, as well as more general circumstances such as sex and age. And at the same time, these basic aspects of the life of young people are those that are significant for the character and extent of delinquency. The better integrated the young people are in family and school, the lower their level of delinquent behavior (Balvig & Kyvsgaard, 1990).

This does not mean that sport does not contribute prophylactically to the health and social aspects of the life of children and young people, but only that sport cannot be segregated as an isolated factor. We should, perhaps, ask other questions and supplement previous studies with qualitative investigatory methods, because, perhaps, the precise question is how one participates in sport and club life, and not simply whether one does it, and the question is what place sport and club life have in one's existence as a whole. On the basis of this outlook, cultural and social researchers have pointed to the psychosocial and cultural importance of sport for youngsters.

Great social changes in the last 30 years have created totally different conditions for the development of youth. The great value systems have been partially dissolved, traditions and norms have been changed, the social networks in the local districts have been weakened, the way families have been individualized has led to a looser authority structure and weaker formation of attitudes, and a number of commercial and educational adjustments have taken place. These changes have meant that the young people themselves must create their identities. These things put a grave obligation on institutions, including the institutions involved in leisure-time activities, to offer coherence and perspective as a background for the formation of identity, especially in young people. The time of youth has become a *waiting time* for the formation of a psychosocial identity (Schultz Jørgensen et al., 1986). In this work with identity, leisure-time—and especially sport because of its intensity—plays a major role.

A search can also be made for more cultural-analytic explanations for what makes sport significant in people's everyday lives, but that is not yet a particularly developed field of research. But that sport is significant in people's daily lives is clearly evident from the high voluntary participation, as previously mentioned. Sport and sport clubs can be used as the starting point for the formation of networks of various types, to give (leisure) lives a meaningful content, and to create coherence and wholeness in the everyday lives of the members (Ottesen, 1989, 1993).

Acknowledgments

We want to thank our colleagues Helle Rønholt and Mia Herskind for their good comments and suggestions for improvements of this chapter.

References

Andersen, D. (1989). *Skolebørns dagligdag* [School children's daily life]. Copenhagen, Denmark: Socialforskningsinstituttet.

Andersen, L., & Schelin, B. (1988). *Halvdelen dyrker idræt: 16-19 åriges skoleelevers idrætsudøvelse og indstilling til idræt* [16-to-19-year-old pupils' sport participation and attitude to sport]. Copenhagen, Denmark: Danmarks Højskole for Legemsøvelser.

Balle-Petersen, M. (1976). Foreningstiden [The association era]. In *Det forsø mte århundrede* (pp. 43-68). Copenhagen, Denmark: Dansk Kulturhistorisk Museumsforening.

Balvig, F., & Kyvsgaard, B. (1990). *Allerødderne og kriminalitet* [Youth and criminality]. Copenhagen, Denmark: Det kriminalpræventive Råd.

Forchhammer, J., & Petersen, J. (1980). *Kulturens børn* [Children of the culture]. Copenhagen, Denmark: Kulturministeriet.

Frederiksen, V., & Sørensen, P.M. (1977). *Ungdom, uddannelse og fritid* [Youth, education and leisure]. Copenhagen, Denmark: Munksgaard.

Gallup Markedsanalyse A/S. (1985). *Børn i Danmark: 8-14 år* [Children in Denmark: 8 to 14 years]. Copenhagen, Denmark: Author.

Hestbæk, A.D. (1992). *Børn og unges fritidsliv i forsøgsperspektiv* [Children and youth from an experimental perspective]. Copenhagen, Denmark: Socialforskningsinstituttet.

Ibsen, B. (1992). *Frivilligt arbejde i idrætsforeninger* [Voluntary work in sport clubs]. Copenhagen, Denmark: DHL/Systime.

Ottesen, L. (1989). Fodboldklub, familieliv og bytteøkonomi [Soccer club, family life, and the exchange economy]. In L.R. Christensen (Ed.), *Livstykker: 12 studier af livsformer og vilkår* (pp. 132-141). Copenhagen, Denmark: Kulturbøger.

Ottesen, L. (in press). The home-field as home. In *Stadion* (International Journal of the History of Sport). Academia Verlag, Sankt Augustin.

Schultz Jørgensen, P., Gamst, B., & Andersen, B. (1986). *Efter skoletid* [After school time]. Copenhagen, Denmark: Socialforskningsinstituttet.

Chapter 11 England

Anita White
Nicholas Rowe

The total population of England was 48,068,423 in 1991. The numbers in the preschool age group expanded by approximately 300,000 (10%) between 1988 and 1993 but the trend is projected to reverse after 1993. Over the last five years or so the numbers in the school-aged population declined by some 700,000, but a 12% increase in this age group is projected in the period to 2003 with resultant opportunities, stresses, and demands on all those concerned with providing for and promoting youth sport.

The Organizational Network

There is no unified scheme or program which provides opportunities for young people to participate in sport and develop their sporting potential. Provision is uneven and fragmented and much depends upon the locality in which young people live, their family circumstances (including income and social class), their gender, and their ability level. The complex nature of the institutional structures which impinge on young people's involvement in sport is shown in Figure 11.1. This diagram shows the major institutional influences affecting young people's involvement in sport. It is a simplified model which focuses on young people at the center. Moving out from the center one moves progressively up the organizational hierarchy from those institutions which have an influence on young people on an "everyday" and local basis to those institutions at the periphery which have a broader strategic influence. The institutions include a combination of public, commercial, and voluntary sectors. Each sector is located in close proximity to the two other sectors with which it is most closely associated and has the most interdependencies. The Sports Council and its 10 Regional Councils for Sport and Recreation fall under the aegis of the Department of National Heritage. With a responsibility to provide "sport for all" and excellence in sport the Sports Council attempts to coordinate and work with all different agencies referred to in Figure 11.1.

Within the education sector significant change is on the horizon, with a new national curriculum for physical education in schools being introduced for all children between 5 and 14, and a new national policy for Young People and Sport being developed and promoted by the Sports Council (Department of Education and Science, 1991; Sports Council, 1993). Within the school curriculum, physical education will for the first time become a statutory requirement with specified attainment targets and programs of study.

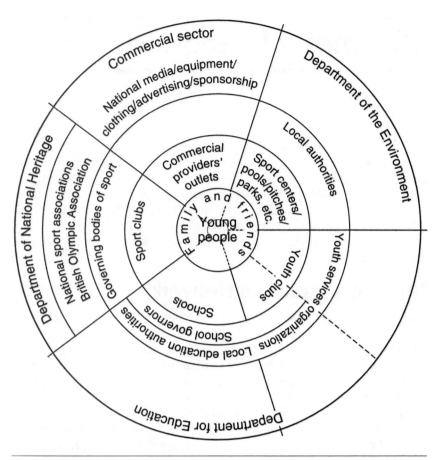

Figure 11.1   An institutional model of youth sport in England.

It is possible to identify four main types of organized provision for sport outside the school physical education curriculum: school sport, club sport, recreational programs of the local authorities, and youth groups. It should be noted, however, that young people's participation in sport is often in informal, unorganized, recreational settings, and indeed many young people express a preference for sport which is not organized and controlled by adults and adult agencies.

Club Sport Programs

As with school sport, there is great variability in the provision made in different clubs. Opportunities for young people depend largely on individual clubs and the attitude these clubs have toward junior membership. Some clubs have active junior sections, good links with local schools, coaching courses for beginners and improvers, and graded programs of competitive opportunities to enable youngsters to develop their sporting potential. Other clubs are run almost exclusively for the benefit of their adult members, consider their junior members a nuisance, and provide few coaching and competitive opportunities for young people. Most sport clubs in England are small, are oriented toward a single sport, and are financed from individual membership subscriptions with minimal contribution from government funds. Consequently, given the inability of children and youths to pay the same fees as adults and the limited external funding opportunities, there is little financial incentive to make special provision for young people.

Many young people, in fact, find sport clubs intimidating and unwelcoming places (Sports Council for Wales, 1993). Few clubs actively recruit junior members and many young people are only introduced to club sport through their parents, who may be members, or by a school teacher who is associated with a particular club. There is also evidence to suggest that young people from families in the upper socioeconomic groups are more likely to be members of a sport club than children with parents employed in manual occupations (Scottish Sports Council, 1988).

There is also inequality of provision and opportunity in sport clubs according to the gender and ability of young people. Boys have many more opportunities than girls (e.g., most communities run junior soccer teams for boys) and constraints surrounding travel and time away from home also affect girls' participation. There is also greater provision for those with sporting talent, and little provision for young people with disabilities, although there are clubs catering specifically to people with disabilities. Similarly, there are some clubs which cater specifically to people from particular ethnic minority groups.

School Sport Programs

Extracurricular school sport has traditionally been provided by teachers (of both physical education and other subjects) at lunch times, after school between 4:00 and 6:00 p.m., and sometimes on weekends. Teachers give their time voluntarily. Many teachers enjoy working with the most talented and enthusiastic youngsters after school hours, although there was a decline in the commitment of teachers to an area of work which fell outside their contract following teachers' industrial action in a protracted pay dispute in the mid-1980s.

Different schools have different traditions of providing extracurricular sport, and much depends on the interest and enthusiasm of individual teachers. Generally, boys' sport is better provided for than girls' sport, largely because more male teachers are interested in running teams for boys than female teachers in running teams for girls. Most extracurricular sport is organized around age-group competitions between local schools. In some sports there are national school organizations that provide graded competition at district, county, and area levels, with the most successful school teams going on to represent the country in international competition. A minority of extracurricular school club activities are more recreationally oriented and young people's involvement in them reflects their interest rather than ability. However, there is relatively little provision for children with disabilities, and opportunities have recently been further reduced with the introduction of mainstreaming.

Young people's participation in school sport is not only dependent on the ethos and tradition of the school, the goodwill of the teachers, and the young person's sporting ability, but also on home circumstances. The active cooperation, encouragement, and support of parents is needed, for example, to provide transport and to assist with the costs of equipment. Some teenagers, particularly girls, are expected to look after younger siblings and help with domestic duties in the home, and these expectations preclude many of them from participation in sport outside of school lessons. Many parents are also reluctant to allow their daughters to travel home from school after dark, another factor which limits girls' participation. Constraints associated with class and gender are compounded by cultural factors within some ethnic minority groups which do not have a tradition of involvement in certain sports or in physical activity generally (White & Coakley, 1992).

Recreational Programs of the Local Authorities

Provision for sport and recreation is a nonstatutory function for local authorities in England. However, nearly all local authorities own and manage public spaces such as parks and playing fields where sport is played, and most also own and manage indoor sport and leisure facilities. Many private clubs lease land or premises from local authorities and in this way, through subsidies, local authorities indirectly support club sport provision.

Some local authorities are proactive in promoting sport and active recreation opportunities within the community. The best of them have well-developed recreation strategies and *sport development* teams which aim to actively stimulate and facilitate participation. The focus of much of this sport development work in the 1980s was on ''outreach'' into the community, particularly to groups with low rates of participation (including women, people with disabilities, ethnic minorities, and the elderly).

Increasing numbers of local authority sport development teams are focusing on young people and looking to improve school and community links (Collins, 1992). Many local authorities run holiday and half-term play schemes for young people, offering coaching and organized activity by qualified personnel outside of the school or club networks.

Local authority sport provision is probably less exclusive and more available to all sectors of the population than school or club sport. However, opportunities vary from district to district, depending on the political priorities and values held by different local authorities and the extent to which they take a proactive role in providing recreation. Recent reforms in local government and education legislation, while providing opportunities for extending participation, may adversely affect sport opportunities for young people, a subject which is being carefully monitored by the national Sports Councils.

Sport Programs of Other Private Nonprofit Organizations

A network of youth clubs exists throughout England. Their origins date back to the Rational Recreation Movement of the early 1890s, when they were established to cater to the needs of young people (mostly boys) from disadvantaged backgrounds. They were, and still are, sustained largely through voluntary effort and much of the original ethos still remains, though they have changed with the times. It is estimated that approximately 1.5 million young people play sports at these clubs, although sport is usually seen as a vehicle for personal and social development rather than something that is done for its own sake.

Youth clubs cater to a somewhat different sector of the youth population than private sport clubs or school sports. Although increasing numbers of girls join youth clubs, the membership is still predominantly male. However, youth clubs do appeal to youngsters from low-income families in a way that private sport clubs do not. They provide an alternative outlet for many young people who otherwise would not participate in organized sport.

Sport Participation

Research on young people's involvement in sport in the United Kingdom has been characterized by a fragmented and ad hoc approach. With a few notable exceptions, most of which will be referred to in this chapter, previous studies have been based on small and often unrepresentative sample sizes providing isolated snapshots rather than consistent and reliable data over time. The definitions of activities and of participation have also varied considerably, making comparisons difficult. Even with these limitations, however, there is sufficient research evidence to piece together a broad picture of young people's involvement in sport.

General Information

Few data sources exist to enable assessment of participation rates by young people in England. Data from the Sports Council's National Demonstration projects conclude that young people's participation levels in sport are not lower compared with those of the rest of the population (Sports Council for Wales, 1993; Scottish Sports Council, 1988). Research on the Active Life Styles project (Sports Council, 1989) showed that 60% of young people 15 to 18 took part in sport regularly outside of the school curriculum.

A survey carried out on 9-to-15-year-olds by the Health Education Authority (1992) found that 88% of young people say they take exercise outside of school, and that among those who do, more time is spent on exercise outside school than on exercise during school hours. More than half (57%) exercise two or more hours a week outside of school, and 15% participate for more than 6 hours a week. The government's *General Household Survey* (Office of Population Censuses and Surveys, 1990), showed that 87% of 16-to-19-year-olds participated in at least one sport or recreational activity in the four weeks before the interview, the highest participation level of any age group.

These overall high participation levels mask, however, the important variations that occur among gender and age groups. For many years it was assumed that the major dropout from sport occurred when young people left school (Wolfenden Committee on Sport, 1960). The research evidence suggests, however, a more dynamic process whereby young people's involvement is characterized by moving in and out of a wide range of activities with a considerable amount of experimentation. More than 75% of the pupils surveyed as part of the Active Life Styles project (Sports Council, 1989) had taken part in at least 15 sports in their school careers and many who aspired to continue with their chosen school sport did so. All of the surveys were consistent, however, in finding that there is a decline in participation with age during the school years while other evidence indicates that the decline accelerates into middle and older age.

Participation Among Girls and Boys

Research carried out by Balding (1992) on more than 23,000 school pupils aged 12 to 16 across England showed a decline with age in participation (defined as participating at least once a week) outside of school time in most sports. For example, participation by girls in track and field declined from 11.4% to 5.8% between the ages of 12 to 16, and by boys of the same age from 14.4% to 6%. A similar picture was found in tennis, with figures of 17.7% to 14.2% for girls and 18.3% to 10.7% for boys. There were, however, some examples of activities which actually increased with age. The most notable of these is perhaps fitness and exercise activities among girls, where participation increased from 11.9% of 12-to-13-year-olds to 22.1% of 15-to-16-year-olds. Surveys in the UK are also consistent in identifying lower participation by girls compared with boys across all age groups. The Health Education Authority survey (1992) carried out in England found a marked difference between boys' and girls' participation in sport and exercise activity outside of school, with boys tending to increase their amount of exercise as they get older, whereas girls peak at 13 and then begin to tail off. By 15 years of age, 51% of boys are having at least 2 hours of sport and exercise a week ($M = 3.6$ hours), while only 43% of girls report a similar amount of exercise, with a lower weekly average of 2.4 hours.

Most Popular Sports

Swimming features as the most popular sporting activity among both boys and girls according to all the surveys. Research in Wales (Sports Council for Wales, 1993) found that 63% of girls and 48% of boys aged 11 to 16 years took part in swimming informally outside of the school curriculum. More specific details are provided by Balding's (1992) survey, which shows that 24% of boys and nearly 27% of girls swim on average at least once a week outside of the school curriculum. Other activities which feature prominently for boys are soccer, running/jogging, badminton, tennis, and snooker (billiards). For girls badminton also features, along with field hockey, tennis, gymnastics, keep-fit activities, and dance. Perhaps the most important finding, however, from the Active Life Styles project (Sports Council, 1989) is the wide array of over 40 sports that had been tried by at least some of the young people in their school careers. Within PE lessons alone an average of 15 different activities had been tried by each pupil.

Participation in Organized Sport

A minority of young people take part in sport as members of sport clubs, with boys much more likely to be members than girls. The Welsh study (Sports Council for Wales, 1993) found that just 47% of 11-to-16-year-olds belonged to youth organizations, with only half that number belonging to sport clubs. Among boys, 56% were members of sport clubs and youth organizations where they took part in sport, compared to only 38% of girls. Boys' membership in sport clubs in Wales was dominated by the two traditional team games of soccer and rugby, while girls' involvement included a broader range of activities. The Welsh report concluded, however, that

> this level of membership indicates that where community links do exist, the base for children's involvement appears to be very small and narrow. If continuity of participation is to be achieved when children leave school then the strengthening of children's section within clubs will be a necessary condition (p. 28).

The Welsh study also highlighted the importance of family connections, with a child more likely to be a member of a sport club if a sibling or parent is a member. The Active Life Styles project (Sports Council, 1989) in England identified snooker/pool, soccer, badminton, tennis, and field hockey as the leading club sports outside of school.

There is very limited information on young people's participation levels in extracurricular sport. The research that has been carried out has tended to focus on the time and types of activities available rather than on how many children take part.

Recent research by the Secondary Heads Association (1990) examined 1,275 state secondary schools across England. Results showed a significant decline in the opportunities available for children to take part in extracurricular sport. Sixty-two percent of those schools surveyed said that provision during the school week had decreased over the previous 10 years, with 70% expressing a similar sentiment about the time available on weekends. When asked why this was the case, 83% said that it was related to increased workloads for teachers, 80% referred to the requirements for Saturday jobs, and 63% said it resulted from restrictions linked to teachers' employment contracts. In Wales, 40% of the young people surveyed (Sports Council for Wales, 1993) said that there were activities that they would like to do in extracurricular time which they were unable to do at the moment because these activities were not offered by the school.

Reasons for Participation in Sport

Enjoyment was identified as a major motivating factor in the Active Life Styles project (Sports Council, 1989), and was consistently reported as a much more important factor than competition or success. Eighty-six percent of the children who took part in Wales said they did so "for fun or to keep fit." This conclusion has been reinforced by recent qualitative research by Lee and Cockman (1991), who examined young people's values and motivations for taking part in tennis and soccer. Within the UK, parents have been identified as playing a crucial role in socializing children into sport, with peer group influence also growing in importance with age (Rowley, 1992a, 1992b, 1992c).

The Active Life Styles project (Sports Council, 1989) clearly demonstrated other aspects of children's lifestyles which are increasingly placing competing demands on their time. For example, 44% of children in the study had part-time employment of some kind. Of those who did not take part in sports 25% said they did not have the time, with an additional 5% saying that they had too much school work. The impact of increasing demands of school work was also identified in the Sports Council's Training of Young Athletes Study as an important reason for dropout from elite levels of sporting involvement (Rowley, 1992b). The evidence suggests, however, that for many "not having the time" represents a choice to do other, often physically inactive pastimes. The Active Life Styles project (Sports Council, 1989) found that one third of young people spend five or more evenings a week at home and 86% spent their Saturdays "going around the shops."

These simple measures of the constraints on participation expressed through large-scale surveys hide, however, a more complex interaction of sociocultural factors that influence involvement. Qualitative research carried out by White and Coakley (1992) on 34 young men and 26 young women aged 13 to 23 years showed that "sports participation was not a separate experience in young people's lives; the decision to participate was integrally tied to the way young people viewed themselves and their connection to the social world in which they lived" (p. 32).

The interview data indicated that the decisions young people made about sport participation reflected the following:

- A consideration of the future, especially the transition to adulthood
- A desire to display and extend personal competence and autonomy
- Constraints related to money, parents, and opposite-sex friends
- Support and encouragement from parents, relatives, peers, or all three
- Past experiences in school sports and physical education

Results of the qualitative evaluation showed that young people's involvement and commitment to sport and leisure shifted over time, with many seeing sport skills and sport participation as peripheral to other issues and concerns.

Promotional Campaigns

A number of different agencies at local, regional, and national levels have run schemes, programs, and campaigns designed to increase young people's participation in sport. Most of these have attempted to bridge the gap between physical education in the curriculum and sport outside school. The most successful programs have been those in which different agencies have worked in partnership to make better provision of sporting opportunities for young people.

National Programs

Young people (13 to 24) were identified as a target group by the Sports Council in 1982. In 1986, the Sports Council ran a national publicity campaign, "Ever Thought of Sport?" aimed at preventing dropout from sport among those leaving school. This campaign was implemented regionally through local initiatives that brought together local authorities, schools, and sport clubs. In 1987, a School Sport Forum was established by the Sports Council at the request of the two government departments with an interest in young people and sport: the Department of Education and Science and the Department of the Environment. Its report "Sport and Young People: Partnership and Action" (School Sport Forum, 1988), made 69 recommendations for better provision for young people and sport focusing on the child, improved leadership, and partnership between different sectors and agencies.

During the 1980s the Sports Council also set up a number of action research programs, known as National Demonstration Projects. The most significant of these was the Active Life Styles project cited earlier. This project, established in Coventry in 1984, addressed sport development issues both within and outside the curriculum. In particular it sought to establish a new structure for youth sport in Coventry, to develop sport leadership in the community, to foster pupil-run clubs, to promote equal opportunities for participation in sport, and to establish a sport information network. The Active Life Styles project has provided a blueprint for the development of sport for young people in other localities. Another National Demonstration Project, "Everybody Active" (Sports Council and Sunderland Polytechnic, 1991), established with Sunderland Polytechnic in 1987, focused on young people with sensory and physical disabilities, seeking to increase their involvement in sport as participants, coaches, officials, and organizers within and outside of school. Again, important lessons were learned from this project that are being widely disseminated. Through introducing a wider choice of activities, fostering independence, and assisting integration, this scheme has helped young people to pursue their own personal programs of activities. This support has concentrated on overcoming the social constraints that are often more important than any disability itself.

Local Authority Programs

A number of local authorities have established schemes to increase sporting opportunities for young people and improve school/community links. For example, the Nottinghamshire County Council runs a network of sport training centers at leisure centers, youth and community centers, and schools where qualified coaches give expert instruction. The scheme is designed not only to increase participation but also to develop sporting talent. The Ipswich Borough Council runs a project with the Eastern region of the Sports Council known as

Ipswich Sport 2000. Like the Nottingham County Council scheme it is designed to develop pathways for young people to progress and develop their sport potential. The coordination of local agencies and the education of coaches are central elements of this scheme.

Sport-Specific Programs

The schemes described above all include a number of sports, but some national sport organizations have also developed schemes designed to attract young people to their sports. As with programs described earlier the focus has been on good school/community linkages. Two examples of such schemes are the Rugby Union Youth Development Scheme and the Netball Youth Development Programme, both established in the late 1980s. Rugby Union has established a network of 30 youth development officers operating at county levels who promote and market rugby in clubs, schools, and youth agencies. The whole initiative is coordinated by a National Youth Development Officer. Similarly, the All England Netball Association, with sponsorship from the National Westminster Bank, has established a youth development officer to prepare a youth development plan. The objectives include encouraging school teachers to promote netball; improving links with teacher-training colleges; raising the quality of coaching; encouraging clubs to provide facilities, coaching, and competitive opportunities; and encouraging local authorities and sport center managers to run holiday programs.

Conclusion

Although there are many imaginative and innovative schemes for promoting youth sport in England, provision is variable and the development of sport for young people has been hampered by a lack of shared vision and poor coordination between different agencies.

However, it is clear that young people are high on the agenda of sport organizations and providers at local, regional, and national levels. Following a period of consultation, the Great Britain Sports Council has recently published a national policy for young people and sport (Sports Council, 1993). This sets out aims and objectives and includes *frameworks for action* for different agencies. It is hoped that this will assist the creation of better-coordinated structures at the local level to enable all young people to participate in sport and to realize their full potential.

Research on young people's participation has been as patchy as the provision of sport. To rectify this, the Great Britain Sports Council has recently commissioned a large-scale survey of young people's involvement in sport, which will provide baseline information against which the success of its policies and those of its partners can be measured.

These developments, coupled with the new national curriculum in physical education, point to better planned, organized, and researched sport opportunities for young people in England as we move toward the year 2000.

References

Balding, J. (1992). *Young people in 1991*. Schools Health Education Unit, Exeter, England: University.

Collins, M. (1992). *Local authority sports development officers*. Unpublished report to the Sports Council, London, England.

Department of Education and Science and the Welsh Office (1991). *Physical education for ages 5 to 16: Proposals of the Secretary of State for Education and Science and the Secretary of State for Wales*. London: DES and Central Office for Information.

Health Education Authority. (1992). *Tomorrow's young adults*. London: Author.

Lee, M., & Cockman, M. (1991). *Ethical issues in sport III: Emergent values among young football and tennis players*. Unpublished report to the Sports Council, London, England.

Office of Population Censuses and Surveys. (1990). *General household survey*. London: HMSO.

Rowley, S. (1992a). *Training of young athletes study: TOYA and lifestyle*. London: Sports Council.

Rowley, S. (1992b). *Training of young athletes study: TOYA and retirement*. London: Sports Council.

Rowley, S. (1992c). *Training of young athletes study: TOYA and identification of talent*. London: Sports Council.

School Sport Forum. (1988). *Sport and young people: Partnership and action*. London: Sports Council.

Scottish Sports Council. (1988). *School aged sport in Scotland: Report on a research programme*. Edinburgh, Scotland: Author.

Secondary Heads Association. (1990). *Enquiry into the provision of physical education in secondary schools*. Leicester, England: Author.

Sports Council. (1989). *Active Life Styles, an evaluation of the project's work*. London: Author.

Sports Council. (1993). *Young people and sport: Policy and framework for action*. London: Author.

Sports Council and Sunderland Polytechnic. (1991). *"Everybody Active" project. Phase 2 monitoring report: Implementing the schemes*. London: Author.

Sports Council for Wales. (1993). *Children's sports participation 1991–1992*. Cardiff, Wales: Author.

White, A., & Coakley, J. (1992). Making decisions: gender and sports participation among British adolescents. *Sociology of Sport Journal*, **9**(1), 20-35.

Wolfenden Committee on Sport. (1960). *Sport and the community*. London: Central Council of Physical Recreation.

Chapter 12 Finland

Lauri Laakso
Risto Telama
Xiaolin Yang

Finland is a country with 5 million inhabitants, of whom 25% (1.3 million) are under 19. The total area of the country measures 337,000 km^2. Finland is sparsely populated; however, there is a considerable amount of variation in the concentration of population in different parts of the country. Similarly, there are also differing climates throughout Finland.

The Organizational Network

The focus of Finnish sport organization is its voluntary associations. The greater part of organized free-time sport for young people takes place in sport clubs, all of which belong to one of four central organizations. Three of them, the Finnish Central Sport Federation (SVUL), the Finnish Workers' Sport Federation (TUL), and the Swedish Central Sport Federation (CIF) of Finland, offer large programs with numerous sports, and they are divided into specialized leagues and sections, according to the type of sport. The fourth central organization, the Football Association of Finland (SPL), is a specialized independent union for soccer. All central organizations have their own district networks, which are responsible for sport activities at the district level.

The organization of sport is currently undergoing a period of change in Finland. Through the establishment of a new sport organization (the Finnish Sports Federation, or SLU), an attempt has been made to solve economic problems and streamline overlapping activities.

Leisure-time physical activity and sport competitions have never been organized on any large scale by schools in Finland. It is possible for the schools to arrange activities, including sports, outside the regular class hours, but such school sports are of less importance than the activities organized by sport clubs. In addition to sport clubs and schools, physical activity is also arranged by some other youth organizations and scout groups, but only 3 to 5% of youths take part in it regularly.

Some 40 to 50% of youths participate in some form of organized physical activity at least once a week. The proportion among boys is somewhat higher than among girls, and for both sexes the rate of participation decreases considerably with age (see Figures 12.1 and 12.2).

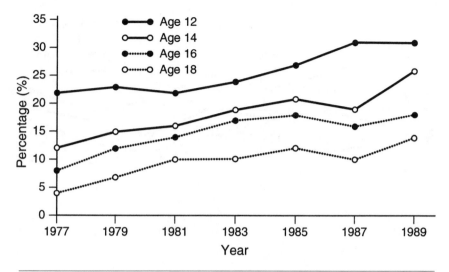

Figure 12.1   Participation in sport club activities among Finnish girls (at least once a week).

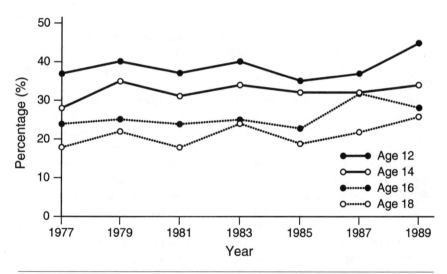

Figure 12.2   Participation in sport club activities among Finnish boys (at least once a week).

Participation in nonorganized physical activity also lessens with age, but the difference between boys and girls is very small (see Figures 12.3 and 12.4). Yet the number of young people who take part in independent physical activity is larger than of those who are involved in organized activity. The differences between different types of sport are considerable. The most popular fitness sports,

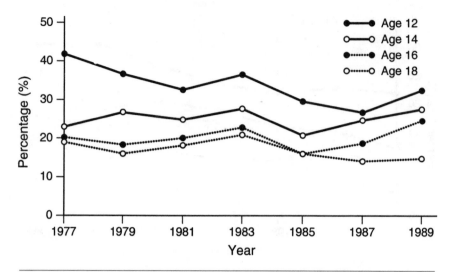

Figure 12.3   Participation in nonorganized physical activity among Finnish girls (at least twice a week).
Note. Data from the project, "Cardiovascular Risks in Young Finns."

such as cycling, swimming, jogging, and downhill skiing, remain for the most part outside organized groups, whereas sport clubs attract most of the young people who are interested in team sports and martial arts (wrestling, boxing, and judo).

The greater part of sport club activities has traditionally been centered on coaching and competitions. All sports run their own systems of competition for the young in different age groups, which culminate in national championships. The major objective of this system has obviously been an attempt to find all the children who would have a chance to be competitively successful in some type of sport (Vilhu, 1989). This activity is not, however, centralized in the sense that every type of sport has its own competitions, and the age categories also vary from sport to sport. The best-known competitions for different age groups are the Hopeasompa competition in skiing; the Sisulisä, Vetoapu, and Kyvyt esiin competitions in track and field; the Siniviitta swimming competition; the Young Jukola relay competition in orienteering; and the Pesis camps for Finnish baseball.

Young people have their own competitive divisions in each ball game at the local, district, and national levels. In addition, a recent phenomenon is the organization, during weekends for instance, of various kinds of tournaments in which junior teams can participate. The best known is the Helsinki Cup, which is an annual international event in soccer for boys and girls. In 1992, the number of teams participating in the event was 659, with a total of about 13,000 team members.

In addition to regular activities for young people, some sport organizations are also involved in competitive sports in the schools. This is a link between

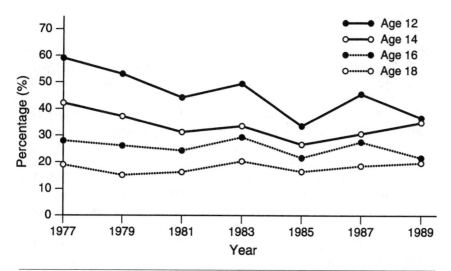

Figure 12.4   Participation in nonorganized physical activity among Finnish boys (at least twice a week).
Note. Data from the project, "Cardiovascular Risks in Young Finns."

junior sport organized by sport clubs and school free-time activities. These competitions often start within schools and are continued between schools first locally, then within districts, and finally nationally. Many of these competitions are focused on a certain school grade. The best-known competitions that are arranged by sport organizations in the schools include Terveet Ympyrät in basketball, the Maitokannu and Staffetkarneval competitions in track and field, the school tennis championships, and the Jumppakärpänen and Jumppasirkus competitions in gymnastics.

Schools in Finland are less important than in many other countries as organizers of free-time physical activities for young people, but the number of competitions in different sports between schools is quite high regionally and nationally. These competitions are organized by the Finnish School Sport Federation, but the number of participants is clearly smaller than in sport club competitions. Competitions are also arranged for teachers in some sports.

Sport Participation

The data used for the present report come primarily from two national-level research programs, which are the "Juvenile Health Habit Study" and the study called "Cardiovascular Risks in Young Finns." If no specific reference is given, the research results reported are derived from these two studies. The Juvenile Health Habit Study (NTTT) has been concerned with health habits among young Finns and also with the ways in which they take part in organized or nonorganized physical activity. The measurements were made in the course of two years, the latest in 1993. The sample was gathered from the national demographic register from among 12-, 14-, 16-, and 18-year-olds born on a certain day, and the sample (*N* = circa 3,000-4,000) represents Finnish youth quite well (Rimpelä et al., 1987). The 1993 data have been used for the consideration of different types of sport only, and all the results are preliminary, because at the time this report was written the results had not yet been checked.

The program called "Cardiovascular Risks in Young Finns" has been concerned with the participation of young Finns in physical activity in general, the intensity of the activities they are involved in, and their involvement in organized sport. The material for the longitudinal study comes from six age cohorts, which were, at the beginning of the study, 3-, 6-, 9-, 12-, 15-, and 18-year-olds. The measurements were done in 1983, 1986, and 1989. Physical activity among the 3- and 6-year-olds was measured in a different way, and they were not included in the data of the present report before they were 9 years old. After the data collection period of 9 years the materials consists of data for 9-to-27-year-olds (Telama et al., 1985).

A number of studies have been made of physical activity among Finnish youth. Yet it is rather difficult to tell what proportion of young people participates in physical activity. It has been estimated that 82% of Finns are involved in some kind of physical exercise (Pehkonen, 1991). The percentage, however, is cut to one half of that, if the criterion is "exercise at least twice a week" (Laakso, 1986).

Participation Among Girls and Boys

A little more than 20% of Finnish girls and 30% of Finnish boys are involved in nonorganized physical activity at least twice a week. The percentages of those who take part in organized club activities at least once a week are 30% for girls and 45% for boys.

However, figures cannot be calculated over the whole groups because participation is strongly reduced with age. While 34% of 12-year-old boys are involved in nonorganized physical activity, the corresponding figure for 18-year-olds is only 16%. The corresponding figures among girls are 27% and 17%. This means that the reduction is smaller among girls, and that at the age of 18 there is no difference between boys and girls in participation in nonorganized physical activity. The above proportions correspond to those for adults in that in the last few years no difference has been found to exist between men and women in the rate of participation in leisure-time physical activity.

However, it has been found that men (and boys) spend more time on physical exercise than women (and girls) do. The reduction with age of physical activity is also clearly seen in how much time is spent on physical activity. While 10-to-14-year-olds spend an average of 85 minutes a day on physical activity, for 15-to-19-year-olds the figure is only 38 minutes (Herva & Vuolle, 1991).

The intensity of physical activity is the only indicator of the total involvement in physical exercise that is not reduced linearly with age. Many studies indicate that the number of those, particularly young people, who practice physical activity up to the stage at which they sweat and lose their breath increases with age. This is true for boys in particular. An increase can also be found among girls until the age of 18.

A combination of the intensity and frequency of physical activity brings to mind the ''heavy activists'' who often reach the level of sweating and breathlessness in their physical exercise. A comparison of different age groups implies that the proportion of these activists does not become smaller with age. Heavy exercise seems to become even more popular among boys with age.

This implies that interest in physical activity becomes clearly differentiated during adolescence: the number of those who are not involved in physical exercise increases with age, while the number of those who practice sport gets smaller accordingly. At the same time, the group of ''heavy activists'' is more clearly distinguished from the others, and their number increases somewhat as people get older.

Participation in Sport Club Activities

Although no difference can be seen between boys and girls in the total amount of physical activity, even today boys are more active participants in sport club activities in all age groups. With age, active participation is reduced, however, for both boys and girls. As many as 54% of 12-year-old boys participate once a week in training sessions and competitions organized by sport clubs, but among 18-year-olds the number is only 34%. For girls the numbers are 41% (12-year-olds) and 16% (18-year-olds).

However, not all of those who participate in club activities take part in competitions. About one fifth of 12- and 15-year-old boys and almost the same proportion of girls in the same age groups participate in competitions at the district level. It is obvious that participation in national competitions is more rare (see Figure 12.5).

At the age of 12, when participation is at its highest, about one third of the boys and one fifth of the girls say that they are being coached for competitions. The proportion of those who are being coached declines rapidly after the age of 15. It may be rather difficult to define what it means to be coached as opposed to participating in training offered by sport clubs. The figures in the table are only slightly smaller than the numbers of those who take part in training sessions organized weekly by sport clubs. It seems that young people who regularly take part in training sessions regard themselves as being coached. The most common sports in which boys are coached are soccer and ice hockey. For girls they are gymnastics, track and field, and volleyball.

The most common sports among young people are familiar ones such as cycling, swimming, walking, and jogging. These same sports also remain popular with both boys and girls as they grow older. For girls, gymnastics competes in popularity with the basic sports, and for boys, the same is true for the most popular ball games, soccer, and ice hockey, up to the age of 16. After that the popularity of such sports declines rapidly. The popularity of skiing, however, declines much earlier, and it is one of the most popular types of sport only among 12-year-old boys and girls.

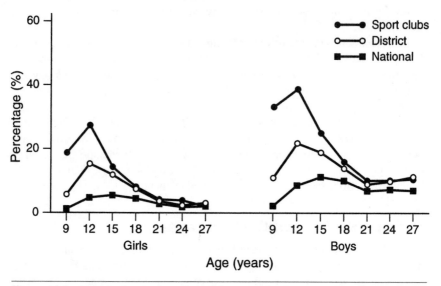

Figure 12.5   Participation in three levels of competition by age and gender.

Different studies have given slightly different results for the proportions of participation depending on the way in which the inquiry has been carried out. Yet there is no difference as concerns the popularity of the most important types of sport: they retain their position in all studies.

Further down in the order of priority there may be some variations because the percentages for participation are relatively low. Soccer and ice hockey are popular also among girls, and the same goes for gymnastics among boys. These sports are followed by badminton, downhill skiing, various forms of exercise to build up strength, Finnish baseball, skating (mainly for girls), tennis, basketball, indoor bandy, karate, and track and field. An interesting type of sport belonging to this group is horseback riding, which comes after the most popular sports among girls, but which is not practiced to any marked extent by boys.

Dropout

Although one of the most important objectives of physical education is the establishment of habitual physical activity, very little is actually known about the degree to which physical activity remains habitual from one period to another. The habitual character of physical activity as measured by means of five variables is not very pronounced in the youngest age groups even at 3-year intervals, but is stepped up after puberty. Physical activity at the age of 9, for example, is a poor predictor of the level of activity 9 years later, but the habitual character of physical activity seems to be stabilized after the age of 18. It is slightly better for boys than it is for girls. Among the individual variables, participation in sport club activities has the highest degree of habitualness.

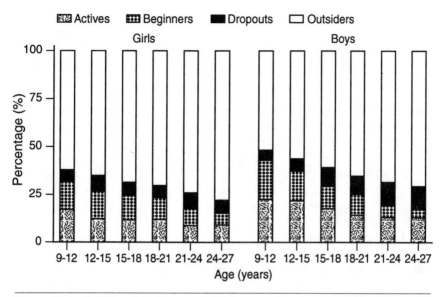

Figure 12.6   Stability of the 3-year training in sport clubs by age and gender.

Figure 12.6 shows the degree to which, at different ages, young people join sport club activities, stay on, and drop out. The criterion used is participation about once a week. The data are available for young people from the age of 9 to the age of 27. About 5% of girls and 20% of boys have become members of sport clubs by the age of 9. Joining sport clubs is common from the age of 9 to the age of 12, which results in highly increased membership, but it is at this age that dropping out also begins. Drop out rates increase clearly with girls from the age of 12 to the age of 15 and with boys from the age of 15 to the age of 18. Membership in sport clubs declines with age, but many still join clubs between 18 and 21 years of age. The number of those who remain as members does not change very much with age. This covers 10-15% of the girls and 15-20% of the boys. All in all, the turnover is very quick in club activities.

Both membership in sport clubs and dropout rates are related to the degree of physical activity and the residential environment of the family. Children of fathers who themselves are involved in physical activity join sport club activities more often and drop out less often than children of passive fathers. In sparsely populated areas, participation in sport club activity is more rare than it is elsewhere, and the dropout rate is higher.

Changes in Physical Activity

In connection with a research program concerned with health-related behavior among youths, it has been possible to observe trends in physical activity among young people at 2-year intervals since 1977. Results based on the 1991 and 1993 data are not exactly comparable and therefore are not included here. The results (see Figures 12.1 to 12.4) imply that nonorganized physical activity has declined to a degree among the youngest, that is, the 12-year-olds, for both boys and girls. Among boys, a declining trend in participation is also seen for the 14-year-olds and the 16-year-olds. Among girls in the same age groups, physical activity seems rather to have increased during the past 12 years. Among 18-year-olds, there seems to have been no real change: both boys and girls participate in nonorganized physical activity as much as they did in 1977. The intensity of physical activity has slightly increased from 1980 to 1989.

Young people take part in training organized by sport clubs more than they did at the end of the 1970s. With girls the trend is clearly upward in all age groups, while with boys it is not as linear but nonetheless clear. The greatest changes in the past 12 years have taken place among the 12-year-olds and the 18-year-olds. The increase in organized sport participation can be seen at all levels of participation.

Taking part in competitions also became slightly more common from 1980 to 1989 in the age groups of 12 and 15 years. The percentage of youths who say that they are being coached for competitions has similarly increased. There are also changes in time use, in that young people spent more time on physical activity in 1987 than they had 8 years earlier. Among youth under 15 nonorganized physical activity has also increased, so the total time used for physical activity was greater in 1987 than in 1979, in spite of the fact that the time used for outdoor recreation was clearly smaller than in 1979.

Among 15-to-19-year-olds rate of participation in nonorganized exercise seems quite stable. However, because the time spent on outdoor recreation had declined among this group in 8 years, the total time spent on physical activity was even smaller in 1987 than in 1979 (Herva & Vuolle, 1991).

Promotional Campaigns

Toward the end of the 1980s, sport organizations launched activities to promote sport among young people, for a number of reasons: the high dropout rates in sport for the young, increased interest in sport for young people among themselves and their parents, and the willingness of sport clubs to enhance their own social importance as an educational environment for the young. Here only the two largest programs, the "Young Finland" program founded by the former SVUL and the "LETE" program of the TUL, will be briefly described.

The Young Finland program, sponsored by a number of large national companies and the National Board of Medicine, has both sport and educational objectives. The sport objective is to offer young people multifarious opportunities to take part in sport activities. Training for top athletics is still one of the ways in which physical activity for young people is organized, but sport clubs also make it possible for young people to take part in activity for physical fitness and in less strenuous competitive activities. One of the most important goals is, accordingly, to organize competitions for those who are not necessarily interested in coping with the anxiety relating to the need to succeed, for example, or who want to take part in games without having to wait for their turns in reserve. The sport objectives also comprise the attempt to help young people adopt training programs which open channels to several sports.

The educational objectives of the Young Finland program are concerned with the development of young people into balanced individuals as sportspersons and human beings who have a positive image of themselves. This means the development of, for instance, independence and social skills and the availability of positive experiences. The educational goals also comprise health education and the introduction of healthy ways of living. In addition to various kinds of opportunities relating to sport, the program also includes training which is necessary for the continued recruitment of new instructors from among the young. The program began in 1987 among the youngest school-aged adolescents, and was continued later among the older ones. The latest introduction in the program has been a program for the pre-school group.

The most important activities in the Young Finland program have been the organization of training, the production of materials, and marketing. Thousands of instructors have been trained in general or sport-type-related courses. In addition, new diploma examinations have been created for coaches for children and adolescents. The program has also been responsible for the production of a large quantity of literary and audiovisual material. The most important materials are the guides for instructors in different types of sport and workbooks designed for the use of the young athletes themselves, that is, so-called passes. These passes are designed to give instructions for sport and to encourage young people to observe their own development and to pay attention also to other kinds of behavior.

The program run by the TUL (the Finnish Workers' Sports Federation) is called LETE. The acronym is based on the first letters of a number of Finnish words: "L" refers to physical education, "E" to positive experience, "T" to know-how, and the second "E" to empathy. The most important objective of the program is to give educational information to instructors and coaches who work with young people. Social education and problems of health education figure very high in the priorities of this program, in addition to competitive and interest-related activities. An important objective is to enhance adoption of healthy ways of living and to offer alternatives that would help solve problems among young people in Finland.

The LETE program makes an attempt to offer activities geared to the abilities and wishes of young people, which may result in many types of activity, from fitness sports to competitive sports. The need to offer positive experiences encourages many-sided activities, where young people can derive the experiences from their own growth and their own development.

Involvement in know-how means, in addition to knowing how to be physically active, knowing about physical activity and the human being as well as various factors having an impact on them. Empathy training aims at socioethical objectives and at teaching young people to be attentive to others and adopt cooperative practices.

The objectives and contents of the LETE program are similar to those of the Young Finland program, but there are also some differences. The LETE program is concerned, for instance, with various types of cultural activities to a larger extent than is the Young Finland program. The LETE program also calls attention to the importance of young people's deciding on their own activities and environment. One of its slogans refers to educating people to be the heroes of their own lives.

The LETE program has produced several sets of materials. In addition to theoretical information, the materials also give concrete practical instructions by means of training cards for the maintenance of many-sided physical activity. A totally new approach to materials related to physical activity is represented by a number of LETE books, which discuss nature, health, and early childhood. The LETE program has been sponsored by a number of large national corporations and the National Board of Social Affairs and Health.

Conclusion

There has been a great deal of discussion about the decline of physical activity among young people. Statements have also been made to the effect that sport has lost some of its importance among young people and their physical fitness has declined. There is not much evidence from research either to back up or to disprove such arguments. It seems obvious that sport no longer holds a position of undivided popularity similar to the one that it had among young people in the previous decades. It has been replaced by some other values.

However, the present discussion has also implied that the change in values has not yet been reflected in physical activity among young people. Nonorganized physical activity involving games and play has declined to a degree, but at the same time participation in organized sport activities has increased. Thus the total amount of physical activity has not decreased among young people. It is known, moreover, that among adults physical activity has almost doubled in the 1970s and 1980s. The increase has been particularly pronounced among women.

It can be concluded that the changes that have taken place do not show in the total amount of activity. In addition to the increased degree of organization of physical activity, the most important change perhaps has been its differentiation. The menacing pictures of physically inactive youngsters are correct in that a certain proportion of young people drop out from physical activity during adolescence. It is possible that the passivity of this group has become greater. On the basis of demographic research, however, it is difficult to establish this, because at the same time the activity has been stepped up at the other end of the scale. Physical activity seems to be differentiated very clearly in the way that among young people the two extremes are becoming more clearly distinct.

The observations that have been made of the physical fitness of young people in Finland are indicative of the same development (Nupponen, Halonen, Mäkinen, & Pehkonen, 1991). Better physical fitness for those who are fit does not result in a higher average level of fitness among young people because at the same time the fitness of those whose physical fitness is low is getting even lower.

It could be asked whether the added organization of physical activity among young people is a positive or a negative development. Many parents regard it as positive. Organized activity means that children are kept "off the streets" in a controlled environment. It also means that part of the responsibility for children's education can be transferred to persons who have accepted the task voluntarily. It is quite common, too, that a child's interest in physical activity involves one or both of the parents. There are many duties relating to the management, maintenance, practical arrangements, and financing of sport teams that require assistance from the parents. In this way, organized sport can be a factor that keeps the family together.

Moreover, the expertise housed in sport clubs is obviously an advantage to people who participate in sport activities. This includes coaching and guidance, venues, equipment and other facilities, and different kinds of safety measures.

However, it is sometimes thought that excessive organization of physical activity will result in a decrease in nonorganized activity among children and, thereby, also in a lack of independence among people in general. In the same way, it has been maintained that the decline in independent game and play activity among children will cause problems in ethical growth and result in the development of extrinsic morals. For families, the problem may be a narrower range of activities and a total concentration on the child's physical activity.

The greatest problems, however, relate to excessive competitiveness and damaging early coaching. This overemphasis on competition has been seen in the behavior of both children and parents, and it has resulted in premature dropout in many cases. The campaigns for the promotion of sport among young people have therefore started from the idea of decreasing competitive activity and of creating more alternatives to competition. At the same time, an attempt has been made to enhance independent activity among young people and to further the importance of sport as a means of social education.

References

Herva, H., & Vuolle, P. (1991). *The use of time in Finland*. Jyväskylä, Finland: Foundation for Promotion of Physical Culture and Health Report 79.

Laakso, L. (1986). Leisuretime physical activity among Finnish adults. In P. Vuolle, R. Telama, & L. Laakso (Eds.), *So move the Finns* (pp. 87-99). Helsinki, Finland: State Press Center.

Nupponen, H., Halonen, L., Mäkinen, H., & Pehkonen, M. (1991). *Research on increased efficiency in physical education in school*. Turku, Finland: University of Turku, Department of Teacher Training in Rauma.

Pehkonen, J. (1991). *Physical and sport activities in Finland 1991: Part I. Physical activity research reports 1/1991*. Helsinki, Finland: Finnish Central Sports Federation: Developing Services.

Rimpelä, M., Rimpelä, A., Karvonen, S., Siivola, M., Rahkola, O., & Kontula, O. (1987). *Change in health habits of young people in Finland in 1977-1987.* Health Education Series, Report 7. Helsinki, Finland: National Board of Health.

Telama, R., Viikari, J., Välimäki, I., Siren-Tiusanen, H., Akerblom, H., Uhari, M., Dahl, M., Pesonen, E., Lähde, P.-L., Pietikäinen, M., & Suoninen, P. (1985). Atherosclerosis precursors in Finnish children and adolescents. Leisure-time physical activity. *Acta Paediatrica Scandinavica,* **74** (Suppl. 318), 169-180.

Vilhu, J. (1989). Children's sport organizations in Finland. In T. Pyykkönen, R. Telama, & J. Juppi (Eds.), *Moving children* (pp. 103-113). Helsinki, Finland: State Press Center.

Chapter 13 Germany

Wolf-Dietrich Brettschneider
Hans-Gerhard Sack

In 1994, 4 years after the unification of Germany, there were about 81 million Germans. Among them there were 9.5 million young people between 6 and 18 years old, about 56% of whom were actively involved in organized sport. The demographic development of the population shows a dramatic decrease of young people, whereas the number of elderly people is projected to increase during the next decade. The implication for organized sports is obvious: the sport clubs and the sport federations will have to care more and more about the elderly, as the young people become a minority. Organized sport will no longer be a privilege for young people only, but a matter for all people.

In the course of rapid social and cultural change in Germany during the 1980s and 1990s, traditional concepts of youth sport have lost their validity. Apparently the dynamic changes in the fields of youth and sport have followed the same patterns of social development. We are witnessing a process of mutual adaptation and differentiation underlying the changes presently affecting the sport culture as well as the youth culture in Germany. Sporting activities, sporting orientation, and sport stylization have become important elements within the pluralization of youth cultures. And vice versa: the great variety in adolescent sport culture today is unmistakably a reflection of trends connected with present changes in Germans' experience of adolescence.

Youth in the Context of Social Change

The gap between the generations is narrowing. The older generation is losing its monopoly on introducing adolescents to life. The growing importance of technological developments is diminishing the adult privilege of being the keepers of the key to wisdom. In the field of leisure—especially in fashion, music, and sport—the enhanced status of health and fitness, and the omnipresence of youth in commercials, have had the effect of changing the power balance between the generations. Adolescents have become trendsetters for adults in many fields of everyday life. Adults who do body building or who jog, who try to keep up a youthful and sporty appearance at work and in their spare time, are sufficient evidence of such a trend. At the same time, adolescents in Germany have had to face the fact that they can no longer rely on secure traditional ties such as family, neighborhood, religion, and nation for their identities. Adolescents of today are, unlike their parents' generation, called upon to be the producers of their own biographies. As this is hardly possible at school, the motor of individualization runs on "high revs" in leisure time (Beck, 1986). Sport profits from this development.

Sport Participation

These social changes in childhood and youth are well reflected in the field of adolescent sport. In the last 30 years the number of young people who participate in sport has increased enormously, to a point at which sport has a top position among the favorite leisure-time activities of adolescents. It is safe to say that sport, both informal and organized, has a strong appeal to *all* groups of adolescents. With regard to sex, age, and socioeconomic status and their relevance to participation in sport, we are confronted with a rather recent phenomenon. In the course of the last 30 years, we have witnessed a process that could be described as a gradual *social leveling* in sport.

As a result of expanding education, adolescents generally have more leisure time at their disposal than did previous generations. German adolescents are willing to invest in informal and organized sport activities approximately 8 to 10 hours per week. Within the last 30 years the number of sport activities youths participate in has doubled. At the same time, traditional kinds of sport have lost much of their former popularity. In Germany this trend is most obvious in gymnastics, athletics, handball, and soccer, whereas hall games such as tennis, volleyball, badminton, and squash; new individual sports such as body building, jogging, biking, and surfing; and Eastern movement forms and the different forms of aerobic dancing have become more and more attractive. Another change is that whereas formerly the decision to join a sport club or to go in for a certain kind of sport was often a commitment for life, today there is a greater willingness to try out various kinds of sports.

Sport settings are also becoming more differentiated. Alongside "classic" places such as school, sport clubs, or families, sport is also practiced in commercial settings such as fitness studios or in tourism. Attitudes have also changed. Adolescents know exactly what they are looking for in sport: competition and performance improvement in clubs, social contact in their peer groups and on vacation, and fitness and consciousness of their own bodies when they are alone. Fun and achievement—although the emphasis will depend on situation and context—are central. They have to be regarded not as alternatives, but as two sides of the same coin. All in all, the youths' understanding of sport has changed. Forms of sport and movement, such as walking, skateboarding, cycling, and trekking, which a few years ago would not have been, are today seen as sports. We are presently witnessing a cultural redefinition of sport. Adolescents no longer accept the institutional meaning of sport, but attach great importance to their subjective understandings of it.

These changes clearly reflect recent tendencies in our society. It is no coincidence that the direction adolescent sport culture has taken corresponds to a trend which sociology has termed *individualization*. During the past several decades, the German people experienced the dissolution of secure traditional ties, which were provided by affiliation with a rank or class in society, by family or neighborhood, or by a generally accepted system of virtues. This dissolution has contributed to the establishment of a social norm prescribing individual responsibility for the organization of one's own life. The trend not to stick to one particular sport, but to participate in various kinds of sport that exhibit a high degree of individualism, can be seen as a symbol of the new demands with which the younger generation is confronted in Germany.

On the brighter side, the trend toward individualization results in a pluralization of lifestyles and a growing spectrum of life options for adolescents. On the darker side, this trend is also a burden on young people, leading to insecurities about how to build up an identity and find a specific and individual style of life.

Sport and Lifestyle

Lifestyle expresses the fact that an individual as a member of a society is able to organize his or her life in a specific and therefore distinctive way. It is a kind of link between two requirements: on the one hand, it is a means of securing one's individuality. On the other hand, lifestyle is also a means of signaling one's wish to belong to a certain social and cultural group, which wants to be different from other groups. The main function of lifestyle is the preservation of one's personal and social identity, since it both allows the development of everyday routines and a stable subjective identity and presents one's private sphere to others. These two demands on lifestyles manifest themselves mainly in leisure time. Therefore, sport activities, body concept and orientation toward fitness and health, the wish to look good and feel great, and the longing for youthfulness can all be seen as elements and symbols of lifestyles. In their study on more than 4,000 13-to-21-year-olds Brettschneider and Bräutigam (1990) found that sociostructural variables such as gender, age, and social stratum, and variables of the sport-and-body-concept, were combined with variables referring to the adolescents' personalities, their relationships with their parents, their preferences in pastimes, their views on health issues, and their general political and social orientations. The purpose was to draw up a typology with the help of factor and cluster analyses. Groups should be found which differentiate individuals according to the patterns of their attitudes, considering the aspect of maximum potential homogeneity within each group and maximum potential separation among the groups. Distinctive profiles become apparent:

Type 1.   There is a small group of adolescents whose appreciation of sport is limited. They are interested in computers, in music, or in other leisure-time activities. Their (slightly overweight) bodies do not epitomize the actual body ideal, but they have no problems with their physical appearance. Their social network is intact, and relations with friends and parents are equally harmonious. Five percent of the population belong to this group, which may be called the "no-sport group."

Type 2.   We find another small group of adolescents for whom sport activities are instrumentalized and for whom specific sports are the means of image promotion (4%). Adolescent males, for instance, are very much interested in body-maintenance activities as a means to enhance and display masculine virility. For both male and female members of this group, their concept of life does not indicate clear plans for the future. They meet adults in a very reserved manner. Not parents, but peer groups and pals are their major reference groups in everyday life. We may say that action and motion are the elements that characterize the lifestyle of this group.

Type 3.   Almost one fifth of our sample belongs to a group whose lifestyle is influenced by a negative body concept (17%). Their well-being is impaired by delicate health and a general feeling of physical discomfort. There is a strong longing for a slim and athletic figure, which is thought to enhance personal attractiveness. Again, there is a complex interaction between the sport concept, body image, and self-concept and attitudes toward social and political affairs in the framework of adolescent lifestyles.

Type 4.   Our next group (13%) is absorbed in a constant search for individuality and self-expression, always trying to promote the stylization of life, in fashion, leisure, and music as well as in sport, the latter based on fun and good atmosphere rather than on training and performance. These adolescents are hoping to maintain or produce a fit and slim body; they are disposed toward a health-oriented hedonism. They do not care much about their future and their relationship to adults and their parents. It is style and individualism that are of top priority in this group.

Type 5.   Sixty-one percent of the population have a profile the contours of which reflect the normal adolescent biography. In this surprisingly large group of inconspicuous adolescents, we find boys and girls in whose lives the sport concept as well as the other facets of lifestyle are well balanced. Achievement and fun, competition and spontaneous activities are not seen as alternatives, but as two sides of the same coin. In such an interpretation, sport in all its variety is a commonly accepted element in adolescents' mainstream lifestyles. These adolescents are satisfied with their body images and with their physical and facial attractiveness. They do not pay much attention to weight control and they do not describe any health problems. They live on good terms with their parents and their peers. They have a positive outlook on life.

This five-cluster typology clearly shows the connection between sport and lifestyle, between adolescents' general perspectives toward life, their attitude toward parents, adults, and peers on the one hand, and their sport concepts, their body images, and their health evaluations on the other hand. As far as the stability of these clusters, that is, the degree to which they might change in the course of adolescence, the findings do not tell us anything. Therefore, it is safe to say that their value has primarily to be seen as heuristic (Brettschneider, 1992).

Participation in Organized Sport

Before we refer to exact empirical findings on children's and adolescents' participation rates in organized sports, a few data shall help us to understand better the structure of youth sport in Germany.

The umbrella organization for youth sport is the German Sport Federation (DSB) and its divisions, which deliver general guidelines for promoting youth sports. This body and its various sport associations and federations such as the track and field association or the volleyball federation are responsible for establishing competitive systems and for organizing nationwide sport events. However, the full responsibility for attracting girls and boys to organized sport and keeping them in this system is in the hands of the local sport clubs, which are autonomous in what sports they offer and in the way they arrange and present them.

The membership rates in sport clubs are extremely high in Germany, though varying by gender and age. One third of the overall population are members of sport clubs. In 1989, 20 million people out of 60 million were organized in about 65,000 sport clubs. In the 7-to-14-year-old group every second girl was a member of a sport club. Among boys the rate was even higher: 64% of the boys were sport club members. Among 15-to-18-year-olds 70% of the male and 46% of the female adolescents were active members in sport clubs.

Despite these impressive figures, it must be stated that the absolute numbers of boys and girls have been declining in the last decade. Yet these curves must not lead to misinterpretations. In the same period of time, a tremendous decline has taken place among the age groups in question. Generally, it can be said that the rate of organization among the girls is still increasing, whereas among the boys the growth in sport membership has come to an end. The curves in Figure 13.1 refer to the number of sport club members without setting them into relation to this demographic development. The dramatic increase of members in 1991 results from the unification of the two German states.

In the autumn of 1992, a representative sample consisting of 3,630 students 8 to 18 in all types of public schools was asked about their sport club memberships (Kurz, Sack, & Brinkhoff, in press). This survey was conducted in the German state of North-Rhine-Westphalia (NRW) using standardized questionnaires, and found that 40.7% of the students declared themselves to be members of sport clubs. In 1988, Brettschneider and Bräutigam (1990) found, in a survey of 4,200 students 13 to 21, an organization rate of 45.5%. When interpreting the findings of the latest study (1992) and comparing them with those of Brettschneider and Bräutigam, we have to consider the fact that the ages of the two populations differ. Therefore, we might assume two different explanations for the differences in the results: sample error and a general decrease in organizational binding.

The findings of Brettschneider and Bräutigam (1990) and Kurz, Sack, and Brinkhoff (in press) differ from those figures we got by using the calculation, in which memberships in sport clubs (taken from the different sport associations)

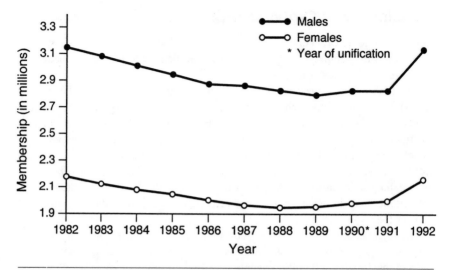

Figure 13.1   Development of sport club membership between 1982 and 1992 among 6-to-18-year-old females and males.

were set into relation to the overall population in the state of NRW (taken from the official census in 1987). The percentage of young people in sport organizations lies between 54.4% and 63.5%. Because the figures relating to organized sport derive from statistics calculated by the sport associations (e.g., basketball, soccer, and athletics), we assume that a considerable percentage of sport club members are members in a second or even third sport club (multiple membership). The data show that this is especially true for boys. We might conclude that about every second sport club member belongs to more than one sport club, which means that he or she is interested in different sports. The rate of organization among youngsters depends strongly on age, sex, structure of settlement, and school career (see Figures 13.2 to 13.5).

The rate of organization increases between the ages of 8 and 10, but decreases considerably in late adolescence (from 14 to 18). Boys are found more often in sport clubs than girls. Children living in suburban and rural areas are more likely to belong to sport clubs than youngsters from metropolitan areas, and students from schools with a higher social status (high schools) are more likely to belong to sport clubs than youths who go to schools with a lower social status (*Hauptschule*).

These results, which show the influence of social determinants for sport club commitment, are almost identical to those found by Sack (1980) and Brett-schneider and Bräutigam (1990). Therefore, we conclude that the social structure in organized sport has not been strongly affected by the social changes in the last 15 years.

Admission.   In comparison with the 1970s, youngsters seek sport club membership at a much earlier age. The average age of admission to the first sport club

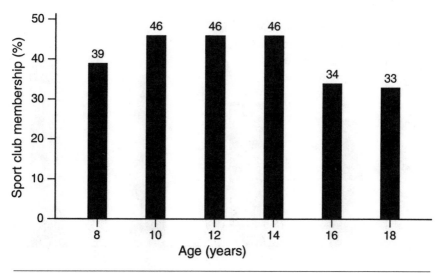

Figure 13.2   Sport club membership in relation to age.

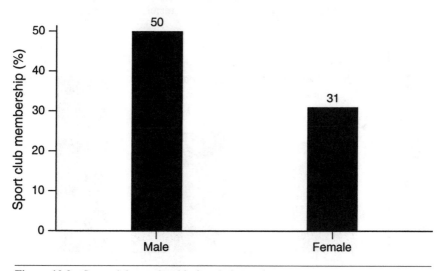

Figure 13.3   Sport club membership in relation to sex.

is 8.2 years (± 3.0 years), or, in other words, 50% of youngsters enter their first sport club shortly after their seventh birthday. This is a dramatic change compared to the seventies, when the 50% mark was not reached before the age of 10. Admission age depends on the type of sport. Entrance into a sport club and commitment to sport club membership are also strongly influenced by social factors, which can be divided into two main groups: social reasons such as friends, family tradition, and peer groups, and sport-related reasons such as excellent training conditions, qualified coaches, and so forth (see Table 13.1).

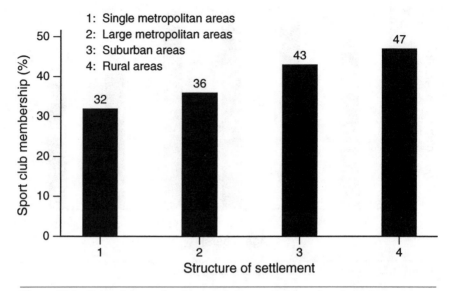

Figure 13.4   Sport club membership in relation to structure of settlement.

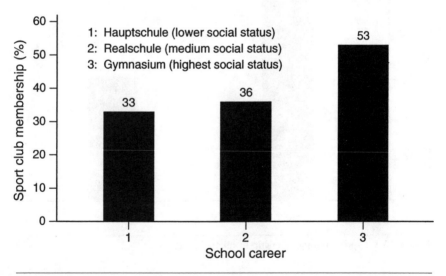

Figure 13.5   Sport club membership in relation to the level of education (school career).

However, both influences are equally strong. The question whether the sport clubs profit more from the youth culture or from the mass culture cannot be answered in a satisfying way.

Commitment.   There are various factors which promote commitment to a sport club.

Table 13.1   Subjectively Perceived Reasons for Membership in the First Sport Club by 8-to-18-Year-Olds

	Members	
Reasons (ranked)	Present	Former
Because I knew some people there	52%	47%
Because my friends went there	50%	58%
Because it was important for me to get promotion/support	50%	28%
Because I thought it was the best sport club for me	38%	29%
Because it was expected to offer the best training conditions	36%	18%
Because the specific sport was important for me	31%	23%
Because the best coach was there	23%	9%
Because the club was within easy reach of my home	16%	13%
Because my parents were members there too	14%	6%
Because my parents wanted me to go there	11%	17%
I don't know anymore	8%	11%
Because my physical education teacher gave me the idea to go there	6%	9%
Because my physician recommended sports	4%	7%

First of all, intensive engagement in sport activities (characterized by frequent training, competitive sport activities, team membership, success in sports, involvement in leadership functions) prevents the influence of alternative leisure attractions to a certain degree.

Second, young people seem to stay in clubs if they feel integrated into a training group that includes both social and sport activities.

Third, the sport club career is stabilized if parents are interested in the sport activities of their children (showing support and recognition of sport performance).

Fourth, young people stay in sport clubs if the social structure of the club meets their personal requirements such as social, emotional, or achievement motivation.

Fluctuation.   Fluctuation is the opposite of commitment. Fluctuation is common in sport clubs. Just about every member of a sport club has either changed to another sport club or to a different sport at some point. The percentage of dropouts increases with growing age: 16% at the age of 8, 24% at the age of 10, and 47% at the age of 18. The influences responsible for dropping out might be various. The reasons stated by the former sport club members are presented in Table 13.2.

The most influential factor has to be seen in the shift of leisure interests. This can be observed in many findings on adolescent development. The second complex of reasons refers to the social interaction between the young athletes and their coaches.

Whereas this type of fluctuation ends up with young people leaving the sport organization for a shorter or longer time (about 65% think about reentering),

Table 13.2   Reasons for Dropout From Sport Clubs (Ranked)

Reasons	
General lack of interest in sports	19%
Lack of time for sports	17%
Dissatisfaction with the coach	8%
Poor social climate in the sport group	6%
Problems at school/at the job	4%
Sport injuries	3%
Accidents	3%
No opportunity for training	2%
Authoritarian coach	2%
New hobbies	2%
Lack of leisure time	2%
Miscellaneous	4%

there is another type of fluctuation: leaving one club and entering another. Most sport club members change training groups or sport clubs at least once in the course of their sport careers. In most cases, change in club membership is accompanied (or caused) by a change of sports (from track and field to soccer or from gymnastics to volleyball, etc.). There are only a few members who change from one sport club to another in order to seek better training conditions in their sport.

Youth and Sport in the Eastern States of Germany

In October 1990, the two German states—the Federal Republic of Germany (West Germany) and the German Democratic Republic (East Germany)—merged to become one state. What is the significance of this date for youth sports in Germany? Four years have passed since the Unification Act. In what situation does youth sports find itself today? Did the Unification Act automatically produce a sport fusion? In order to answer this question, we concentrate on some findings of a comparative study on the sport cultures of children and youths in West and East Germany. Some information on how sport was experienced by the youths of the former GDR may help to understand the present situation better.

Elite sport and recreational sport in the former GDR.   The successful international sport program of the GDR, which helped to divert the attention of the people away from their existence under the socialist state, was a complex structure and was known for seeking out and screening talents. This screening included all children in the GDR and began as early as the first school year, sometimes as early as kindergarten. It was repeated again in the third and sixth years. The children underwent anthropometric measuring and motor tests that were supposed to predict their athletic ability at maturation. The judgments of sport instructors and trainers complemented the data. These results formed the basis of decisions about who should be supported in what kind of sport. The selected children were sent to local sport centers for extensive basic training, concentrated on specific sports which acted as "feeder" systems to the 25 elite sport schools. These special schools served as the nucleus for promoting sport talents in the GDR. About 10,000 children lived, trained, and were educated here. They formed the pool from which potential Olympic champions emerged. These schools were formally under control of the Ministry of Education, but in fact they were controlled by the sport federation, the daily regime and the curriculum being dependent on the development and the individual performance of the children and the demands of the training and competition cycle. These schools provided optimal conditions for learning, training, and living in promised social security for their student athletes.

Less attention was paid to the sporting needs of the majority of GDR youths. Nevertheless, sport was an important element in the lives of most of them. Playing games and sports were included in the programs of the 6 kindergartens and youth organizations, which appealed to more than 90% of the young populations. Of great importance were the sport societies supported by the schools or by the National Sports Federation. In the GDR, 5,222 out of 5,369 schools were directly linked to those sport societies, where qualified sport instructors, teachers, parents, and alumni taught, most often, the traditional sports such as athletics, handball, soccer, volleyball, and gymnastics. Outdoor activities imported from the United States, such as skateboarding, surfing, and mountain biking, or the various Eastern forms of movement, so popular in West Germany, hardly existed in the East. Either ideological barriers or lack of equipment hindered their development.

Differences and similarities between youth sport in East and West after unification.   The interesting question now is whether the characteristics of the GDR sport system have left their traces, as far as the sport involvement and sport concepts of young people are concerned. Two representative analyses— comparing East and West German youth—form the basis for answering these questions (Behnken & Zinnecker, 1991; EMNID, 1991). Behnken and Zinnecker's 1991 findings refer to 14-to-19-year-old boys and girls, that is, to the age group that will determine the direction and speed of sport development in a decisive way. Because in the GDR almost everything was organized, informal sport activities such as jogging, aerobics, or table tennis are still more popular among Western than Eastern youth. These findings regarding informal activities mark a total contrast to the situation in organized sports. Here, the level of participation of the East German youth in sports such as athletics, handball, and gymnastics is two to three times higher than it is in the West. The attention paid to sports among West German youths is far less than it is in the East. Two thirds of the East German youth attach great importance to sports, compared to only half of the West German youth (EMNID, 1991). This result is reversed when considering active sport participation during leisure time. Here only 67% of East

German youths include sport as part of their leisure-time activities, compared to 80% in the West (EMNID, 1991). Similar differences occur over the question of what the youths are actually seeking in sport. Gratifications and motives such as performance, effort, and competition find much more approval with East German youths than with their peers in the West. On the other hand, West German youth put more emphasis on well-being, relaxation, and enjoyment.

There is a clear difference between what sport means for East and West German youth. For East German youth, sport is above all a summation of the different forms of institutionalized sport. Their sport activity demonstrates a pattern that is strongly oriented toward performance and competitive sports. However, they tend to a more hedonistic individualized value system, which is also characteristic of other areas of social life. Their concept of sport thus shows those characteristics typical of West Germany in the sixties and seventies. Presumably there will be a swift adjustment in sport, as in leisure and in recreation in general, between East and West.

Conclusion

Sport in the Eastern states of Germany is no longer under the control of the Communist Party. The structures of the old GDR that made top-level sport dominant no longer exist. The political organizations that had supported mass sports have dissolved and are now in a process of reestablishing themselves. Sport is now playing a more subordinate role.

As to top-level sport, we may say that the efficient nationwide program for screening and promoting talents of the former GDR does not exist any more. The promotion of talent is no longer the result of exact analyzing and planning, but, as in the former FRG, left to personal choice. The most important training centers have disappeared. The elite sport schools still exist on paper, but are now integrated into the normal school system, losing their special status.

These conditions apply to mass sport as well. The former organizational structure was an indispensable authority for socializing the GDR youth. Membership in one of these sport organizations was not voluntary but obligatory. After unification and the cancelation of all government subsidies, many of these organizations ceased to exist, causing a dramatic exodus from sport clubs by 6-to-18-year-olds. The reasons for this exodus are above all economic. Club membership means paying fees, and youths need this money in order to satisfy needs that are more important than sports.

The present loss of social security and the lack of orientation among the East German youth, caused by the dramatic social changes and the new challenges confronting them, have initiated a strong promotional campaign focused on youth sport in the Eastern states of Germany. Sport is presented as a meaningful leisure-time activity and a kind of social catalyst among young people. This campaign is supported by the different sport federations and associations, by the local sport clubs, and by various governmental bodies, whose support is mostly concentrated on establishing and reestablishing a sufficient infrastructure for sport activities.

In West Germany there is no need for sport facilities. But there is a need to stop the constantly growing rate of young people dropping out of organized sport. Various sport associations and federations have recognized this problem and put a great deal of emphasis on campaigns to keep children and youths in the sport clubs and, in addition, to attract those girls and boys who are fond of sports and who are involved in sports, but who have never been sport club members.

References

Beck, U. (1986). *Risikogesellschaft* [Society at risk]. Frankfurt, Germany: Suhrkamp.

Behnken, I., & Zinnecker, J. (1991). *Schülerstudie '90: Jugendliche im Prozeβ der Vereinigung* [Pupils' study '90. Youth in the reunification process]. München, Germany: Juventa.

Brettschneider, W.-D., & Bräutigam, M. (1990). *Sport in der Alltagswelt von Jugendlichen* [Sport in the everyday life of youngsters]. Frechen, Germany: Rittersbach.

Brettschneider, W.-D. (1992). Adolescents, leisure, sport and life-style. In T. Williams, L. Almond, & A. Sparkes (Eds.), *Sport and physical activity* (pp. 536-550). London: Spon.

EMNID. (1991). Sport- und Freizeitverhalten: Ein Ost-West-Vergleich [Sport and leisure behavior: An East-West comparison]. Bielefeld, Germany: Author.

Kurz, D., Sack, H.-G., & Brinkhoff, K.-P. (in press). *Kindheit, Jugend, Freizeit und Sport* [Childhood, youth, leisure, and sport]. Manuscript Bielefeld.

Sack, H.-G. (1980). *Die fluktuation Jugendlicher im Sportverein: Teil 1 und 2.* [Fluctuation among youngsters in sport clubs: Part 1 and 2]. Frankfurt, Germany: Deutscher Sportbund.

Chapter 14 The Netherlands

Albert Buisman
Jo M.H. Lucassen

The Netherlands is a small country with a surface of 33,803 km². By car it takes an hour and a half from the North Sea Coast on the west to the German border on the east, and about four hours from north to south. In 1980 there were 14,092,614 inhabitants (415 per km²) and in 1992, 15,129,150 (446 per km²) (Centraal Bureau voor Statistiek, 1993).

In the Netherlands the term ''youth'' is generally used to describe someone under 25 years of age. Since 1980, the age of entry into adulthood as defined by several laws has been reduced from 21 to 18 (ter Bogt & van Praag, 1992; Diekstra, 1992; Meeus & 't Hart, 1993). In sports, the group youth generally targets sport participants from 4 to 18 years of age, although the entry and exit ages in organized sport differ somewhat from sport to sport. In the last decades, the age of entry has been lowered substantially by most sport associations. There is also a tendency to reduce the exit age for youth from 18 to 16 years.

In this brief picture already several questions arise. What, for example, is the attitude toward the recent development of younger children participating in organized sport? (See, for example, Martens, 1978.) Elsewhere (Buisman, 1993), we tried to outline a pedagogical theory which can serve as a basis for a discussion of these questions.

> We should[,] however, thoroughly consider the position of children and adolescents in sport and develop policies for them. They are physically and mentally vulnerable and thus need special care in sport as well as everywhere else. They are still maturing and therefore need to be educated and taught to gradually assume responsibility for themselves. Education, including sports, has to enable them to do so (p. 210).

When Grupe (cited in Malina, 1988) presented a discussion about top-level sport for children, he was much more specific in his criteria, suggesting, for example, that (a) the interest in top achievement must be geared toward the total development of the child, (b) premature and one-sided specialization in sports is to be avoided, and (c) sport should not be the only leisure activity of the child (pp. 223-224).

The Organizational Network

In this chapter we will describe the development of organized sport for youths who participate in sport clubs at the local level. These sport clubs are primarily led by volunteers and are highly autonomous. The role of the government is more to stimulate than to supervise. It provides (limited) financial support, mostly by providing facilities and paying the costs of trainer/coach education.

The sport associations are also fairly autonomous. They hold membership in the National Sport Federation and the Dutch Olympic Committee (these organizations recently fused), who have both an advising and a policy-making role. We have observed that the sport organizations on the national and regional levels are slowly professionalizing, and are thus able to do a better job in meeting the needs of youth sports.

We cannot neglect to mention that our discussion here has its foundation, in part, in several important articles written by Dutch colleagues. Kamphorst and Giljam (1989) have described in detail sport trends in the Netherlands, mentioning general sport participation as well. In this chapter we also borrowed from the thoughts of Crum (1992, 1993) concerning *sportification* and *desportification* in sport and society. Although government and sport try to base their sport policy on papers such as these, articles of this kind pay relatively little attention to youth sport.

Sport Participation

In the next decades, the percentage of youths as part of the total Dutch population will decrease substantially (see Table 14.1), a demographic development that will be found in other Western European countries as well.

Crum (1993) interpreted the graying of Dutch society as a threat for the sport clubs. "The low birth rate and the fact that the clubs no longer have a monopoly on the sport market reduces their growth from the bottom up. In the long run

Table 14.1   Percentage of Population of the Netherlands in Various Age Groups

Age group	Year				
	1980	1985	1990	1991	1992
0-9 years	31.5	28.3	27.5	25.2	24.9
10-39 years	31.5	33.2	33.0	33.0	33.0
40-64 years	25.6	26.6	28.6	28.9	29.1
65-79 years	9.3	9.4	9.9	10.0	10.0
80 years and over	2.2	2.2	2.6	2.9	2.9
Total Population (in millions)	14.1	14.5	14.9	15.0	15.1
Inhabitants per km^2	415	426	439	442	446

Note. From *Statistisch Jaarboek 1993* [Statistical Yearbook 1993] (p. 35), by Centraal Bureau voor de Statistiek, 1993, The Hague, The Netherlands: SDU. Copyright 1993 by Centraal Bureau voor de Statistiek. Adapted by permission.

this could be fatal for the survival of the sport clubs'' (p. 3). It is difficult, moreover, for the sport associations to develop comprehensive strategies to promote youth sport, because of intense competition between the sport clubs.

Participation in sports among the total population 6 years of age and older has increased since 1979, as Figure 14.1 indicates. This figure depicts a maximal estimation of sport participation based on answers to a broadly based conceptual question. All facets of sport and recreational sport were included. Included also were one-time participants in swimming, cycling, and jogging.

Obviously, recreational sport is no longer an exclusive privilege of youth. In the 1980s the participation in sport by those between 35 and 54 years old has increased. This means that those who were teenagers in the 1960s and 1970s and started a sport at that time have continued to participate (Social and Cultural Planning Office, 1992).

More information about sport participation in the Netherlands can be found in the research reports of Manders and Kropman (1982, 1987). Kamphorst and Giljam (1989) provided a useful summary of the results:

> . . . although, measured over a six-year period, there has been a remarkable increase in sport activity in Holland of about 12 percent, large differences [among the age-groups] persisted. In 1978 the difference in [nonparticipation] between the youngest and the oldest age categor[ies] was 35 percent, [whereas] in 1984 this was 32 percent. Furthermore, age seems to be retaining its importance in explaining differences in sport participation (p. 289).

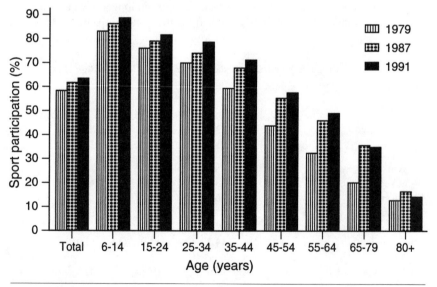

Figure 14.1   Sport participation by age (in percent).
Note. From *Sociaal en Cultureel Rapport 1992* [Social and Cultural Report 1992] (p. 299), by Social and Cultural Planning Office, 1992, Rijswijk, The Netherlands: Author. Copyright 1992 by Social and Cultural Planning Office. Reprinted by permission.

Crum (1993) noticed other trends in sport participation. In his opinion, ''until the middle sixties sport was pre-eminently a matter of competition, of gain and loss, of league tables and records, of 'citius, altius, fortius''' (p. 2). Of course, there were other motives, but they were overshadowed by the achievement motive. Crum (1993) further stated:

During the past decades the movement-cultural landscape has drastically changed. The changes went along two lines. The first could be called ''the line of sportifica-tion.'' ''Sportification'' stands for the process in which the competition and achieve-ment orientations of the traditional sport are radicalized. This process has been highly stimulated by the political role of sport during the Cold War and also by the medicalization, the commercialization, the professionalization and the scientif-ication of sport. . . . The second line, a contrastive one, could be labelled as the ''line of desportification.'' Due to factors such as ''the rediscovery of the body,'' the upgrading of health as an important value in modern life, the rise of hedonism and narcissism, the cultural process of individualization and the proliferation of the ''sport for all'' idea, the traditional characteristics of sport (competition and achievement maximization) vanished to the background and new motives—such as fun, fitness, lust, adventure and bodyshape—began to colour the landscape of sports. The ''desportification of sport'' resulted in an erosion of the familiar concepts of sport and of its traditional organizational structure. Nowadays the ''non-sportive'' sport has [many] more participants than the ''real'' sport (p. 2).

Some of the types of sport activities in which the Dutch are involved can be found in the reports of the *Social and Cultural Planning Office* of the Dutch government (see Table 14.2).

This list seems to support the pronouncements that Crum made. It illustrates the large differences between participation rates in organized sport and in nonorga-nized activities. Participants in such activities as swimming, cycling, walking, and badminton do so mostly on their own time and in their own places. Team sports like soccer, volleyball, field hockey, and handball are still mostly practiced in organized competition.

We suspect that tennis has a high organization level because of the social contacts it provides. The high percentage of members of the (two) gymnastic associations could be accounted for by the large number of children sent to a club by the parents for health reasons. Unfortunately, this table is not detailed for different age-groups. If we had this kind of information, we probably could have seen that Crum's desportification theory is more applicable to adults than to children. We could also then take into consideration the process of desportification within a sport club. However, the number of memberships in sport associations is only one of the factors indicating sportification or desportification.

The level of sport participation of Dutch youth is fairly high. About 90% of the young Dutch between 8 and 12 are active in sport in some way, 85% as members of sport clubs. These figures decrease to about 80% active participation and 70% membership at the age of 18. The main motives mentioned by young people for participating are ''pleasure in sport as such'' (85%), ''gaining health'' (65%), ''for company'' (45%), ''to achieve'' (20%). The third motive is men-tioned significantly more by girls, the fourth more by boys (Lucassen, 1984a, 1984b).

Table 14.2   Participation in Sport (Percentage of Dutch Population of 6 to 79 Years of Age)

Sport	Participation rate in %		Members of associations in %		Users of facilities in %	
	1979	1991	1979	1991	1979	1991
Swimming	31	33	11	10	89	88
Cycling (recreational and competitive)	25	14	3	5	8	8
Walking	22	8	3	6	8	6
Skating	14	13	3	5	28	25
Soccer	12	10	61	67	77	82
Tennis	8	10	59	65	84	88
Jogging	8	11	14	8	31	14
Gymnastics	9	7	65	59	94	90
Sailing, rowing, canoeing	6	7	12	10	12	9
Badminton	8	7	18	36	40	62
Volleyball	5	6	50	49	89	88
Table tennis	7	3	13	20	47	47
Indoor soccer	3	4	49	49	99	95
Horseback riding	3	3	40	43	29	36
Martial arts/self-defense	2	2	84	79	97	93
Basketball	2	1	33	36	85	75
Hockey	1	2	72	80	87	93
Handball	2	1	64	73	92	94
Korfball	1	1	75	81	95	95
Athletics	1	1	40	57	71	83
Motor sport	1	1	32	27	19	24
Golf	–	1	–	38	–	87
Baseball	–	1	–	43	–	74
Fitness	–	9	–	61	–	88
Other sports	5	10	53	51	74	65

Note. From Sociaal en Cultureel Rapport 1992 [*Social and Cultural Report 1992*] (p. 300), by Social and Cultural Planning Office, 1992, Rijswijk, The Netherlands: Author. Copyright 1992 by Social and Cultural Planning Office. Adapted by permission.

In the last 30 years the Dutch government has invested a great deal in the building of public pools, playgrounds, ice-skating tracks, and gymnasiums. Without this support many sport activities, including indoor activities during the wintertime, could not have grown so rapidly. We realize that this investment in facilities can only be realized in a country that became prosperous during the sixties and the seventies.

Table 14.3 focuses on the participants of organized sport. A distinction is made in this table between youth members and adult members. The Netherlands

Table 14.3   Members of Sport Associations of the Netherlands Sport Confederation in 1992

Organization	Boys	Girls	Youths	Men	Women	Seniors	Total	Clubs
Athletics	13,571	9,586	23,157	33,988	16,496	50,484	73,641	265
Aquatics sport			12,137			82,016	94,153	375
Badminton	10,359	11,008	21,367	36,776	30,476	67,252	88,619	831
Baseball/softball	8,318	3,009	11,327	11,728	6,563	18,291	29,618	227
Basketball	15,850	6,795	22,645	14,745	7,275	22,020	44,665	475
Billiards	1,042	85	1,127	32,125	1,910	34,035	35,162	1,925
Bridge		101			88,219		88,320	930
Chess	5,822	813	6,635	21,557	609	22,166	28,801	627
Cycling	532	56	588	26,631	2,815	29,446	30,034	413
Christian Gymn. Assoc.	9,090	39,414	48,504	2,111	16,714	18,825	67,329	279
Equestrian sport(s)	7,336	23,204	30,540	20,341	20,008	40,349	70,889	2,375
Field hockey	31,402	34,150	65,552	35,915	25,497	61,412	126,964	326
Gymnastics	31,776	136,509	168,285	15,121	88,863	103,984	272,269	1,134
Handball	9,635	23,849	33,484	16,579	17,801	34,380	67,864	575
Hiking			11,454			15,490	26,944	400
Ice skating			33,015			111,792	144,807	746
Judo			40,216			16,138	56,354	719
Korfball	16,584	20,309	36,893	24,766	21,782	46,548	83,441	552
Lifeguarding	9,754	9,178	18,932	6,113	5,503	11,616	30,548	181
Skiing							161,405	38
Soccer			361,062			638,537	999,599	5,798
Student sport						62,988	62,988	16
Swimming	52,304	55,655	107,959	27,787	27,584	55,371	163,330	510
Table tennis	8,721	2,688	11,409	26,529	5,648	32,177	43,586	871
Tennis	82,050	71,416	153,466	239,276	275,212	514,488	667,954	1,750
Volleyball	16,623	30,112	46,735	56,098	55,481	111,579	158,314	1,779

Note. From *Ledental N.S.F. per 1 Jan. 1993* [List of Members Jan. 1, 1993] (appendix 1), by Nederlandse Sport Federatie, 1993, Arnhem, The Netherlands: Author. Copyright 1993 by Nederlandse Sport Federatie. Adapted by permission.

Sport Confederation had a number of problems gathering these statistics over the years. Most of the sport associations do not have the organization, the expertise, or the money to register these data automatically. The sport associations do differentiate by age but do so in differing ways. This diversity makes a national overview almost impossible. It is striking that some associations, including large associations such as soccer, badminton, bridge, and judo, have not even made tabulations by gender.

Such tabulation has just begun in soccer (ten Pas, 1993). The Royal Dutch Soccer Association has roughly 24,000 senior women and 12,000 girls (6-18 years old) among its soccer players. Added up this makes 36,000 females out of a total number of nearly a million. This is not much, but it puts soccer in the top ten of women's sports. A number of (autonomous) regions of the soccer association do not give a high priority to women's soccer. While in some regions 60% of the clubs include women's soccer, other regions do not exceed 28% (ten Pas, 1993). In addition, young girls under 14 have the opportunity to play soccer with and against boys. This policy is strongly stimulated by the soccer association. We expect that a greater number of girls will find their way to the soccer clubs partly because of the overall increase of girls in sport. However, in part this growth may come at cost of other sports.

At present, we can distinguish the following as the main institutional frameworks in which young people are active in sports:

- Sport clubs
- Schools and universities (Faber, 1989)
- Clubs for children and youth (e.g., scouting, Catholic countryside youth clubs)
- Sport and fitness studios
- Recreational organizations and travel companies (e.g., camping, leisure parks, sport camps)
- Families

All these institutions differ with respect to the intensity, continuity, and regularity of their sport programs, the goals they (hope to) achieve, and the specific parts of the youth population they attract (target group) (see Table 14.4).

School Sport Programs

The relationship between physical education and organized sport in the Netherlands has been characterized by certain tensions and has repeatedly been described as a love-hate relationship. Historically, the development of Dutch sport has had two roots: German/Swedish gymnastics and English sports. For more than a century there has been an ongoing debate between proponents and opponents of sports-oriented physical education and of close cooperation between organized sports and physical education. In the last two decades, a growing comprehension of and interest in physical education in sport and vice versa has begun. Several factors are responsible for this development:

- Sport participation has grown extensively and since 1960 explosively: sport and movement culture have become more nearly identical. Many physical education teachers have acknowledged this development and have introduced more sport activities in their curricula.

- Sport has become more youth-oriented because of the growing participation of children, the following of a more educational approach, and the introduction of minisports.

- Although to some extent differences in responsibility, purpose, and approach exist, the aims and tasks of physical education in schools and of youth sport in

Table 14.4 The Most Important Formal Social Settings in Which Dutch Youths Participate in Sport Activities

Sport program features	Sport settings Sport clubs	Youth clubs	Schools	Community programs
Volume	±25,000 clubs, continuous or seasonal programs	±3,000 organizations, series of activities	±8,500 primary ±2,300 secondary P.E. and extracurricular sport	250 communities with series of single activities
	1.7 million members	100,000 participants weekly	2.3 million pupils	50,000 participants weekly
Goals	Mainly recreational sport as goal in itself	Recreational, but also aiming at social contact, personal development, and social aid	Educational development	Mainly recreational
Target groups	Youth attending school, middle and upper class	Working-class youth, less educated, socially deprived	All youth, compulsory	Mainly working-class youth
Organization	Voluntary work, competitive	Strongly professionalized	Totally professionalized	Strongly professionalized
Type of activities	Rule-governed activities, one branch of sports	Short, demand-oriented popular activites, rule-adaptation, experiments	Broad introduction to movement culture	Open house, introductory courses

sport clubs have become more alike: primarily to introduce children into (a part of) movement culture, to stimulate their enjoyment in practicing sports, and to prepare them for lifelong participation.

Sport Clubs' Systems for Qualifying Youth Sport Leaders, Coaches, and Tutors

Four streams can be distinguished in the education of coaches:

• Voluntary courses for youth sport coaches and tutors. About 50% of Dutch sport associations sponsor courses for these jobs. These courses require about

30-60 hours of schooling. About 300 of these courses are organized per year involving about 4,500 students.

• Courses for recreational sport. These courses, about 30 a year, are mainly organized by local governments.

• Professional sport coach schools. There are five of these schools in the Netherlands, educating about 500 professional sport leaders yearly.

• Schools for teachers in physical education (PE). They graduate about 400 physical education teachers per year, and many of their graduates work part-time as sport coaches.

Approximately 70% of all youth leaders followed some kind of specific education as sport officials. About 45% were educated one way or another as youth coaches. Another 15% were educated to become members of the boards of sport clubs and organizations. Most training courses for youth coaches are open to those 17 years of age and older. Their participation is often financially supported by clubs and communities.

Special Sport Club Services for Young People With Physical, Mental, or Social Disabilities

At the moment such special services are not very widespread in the Netherlands. There have been extensive programs to stimulate sport participation among different groups of disabled people, youth included. In general a two-track approach is followed with respect to these groups:

• Facilitating the creation of separate sport activities and organizations. From this have emerged special clubs for youths with disabilities, immigrant, and delinquent youths.

• Stimulating the integration of these groups into other sport clubs. Although there have been some promising experiments, most of the clubs are hesitant and reactive in this respect.

The adaptation of sport facilities for participants with disabilities has been subsidized by the government. The development of sport programs has been stimulated by subsidies for facilities, qualified sport coaches, materials, professional advice for program development, and promotional activities.

Originally there were several organizations for sport for participants with disabilities. These were organized around specific disabilities (hearing, visual, or mental impairment, etc.). Currently they have been brought together in two large, federation-like organizations which together have about 28,000 members: the Netherlands Sports Organization for people with mental disabilities (NSG), and the Netherlands Association for adapted sports, for those with physical disabilities (NBAS).

Sport in a Multicultural World

The Netherlands has 640,000 inhabitants who have a foreign nationality (Stichting voor Economisch Onderzoek, 1988, 1989). About a third are youngsters between 5 and 25 years old (25,000 from Suriname, 29,000 from Turkey, and 35,000 from Morocco). Second-generation inhabitants number about 1 million; generally, their parents are German, Indonesian, Surinamese, Turkish, or Moroccan. This ensures cultural diversity within a total population of 15 million inhabitants.

Intolerance toward immigrants and discrimination, including resistance against the participation of immigrants in sport clubs and associations, is growing markedly stronger among some youth groups. This resistance becomes especially obvious with respect to the implementation of projects and measures to promote multiracial participation.

Yet many sport clubs are successfully integrated at a multicultural level. Famous soccer players such as Gullit, Rijkaard, and Menzo, of the Dutch national soccer team, are role models for a lot of Dutch youngsters. Sometimes it has been necessary to establish special sport clubs for players from Turkey, Morocco, Indonesia, and Suriname. These players had such negative experiences with Dutch sport clubs that the Dutch sport administration had to allow such clubs. But this interpretation of cultural diversity is not the official policy!

Youth Culture

Young people (especially those between 10 and 25 years of age) have developed more or less distinct lifestyles, which are expressed most markedly through different opinions, leisure activities (informal groups, going out), and cultural orientations (nonconformism, clothing, music) (ter Bogt & van Praag, 1992; Diekstra, 1992; Meeus & 't Hart, 1993). Sport clubs and organizations seem to find it increasingly problematic to create sport practices congruent with the cultural preferences of young people. Activities in which more and more adults and elderly people are taking part and are in charge may lose their attractiveness to young people.

Some sport associations have recognized these problems and have tried to develop youngster-oriented sport. Minisports for children have been created in soccer, volleyball, and basketball, and a special social lifestyle has been developed around the club, with disco, summer camp, and sport courses. Unfortunately, there are sport associations and clubs where youth sport is a nonissue. Baar (1991) found in his research on dropouts in gymnastic clubs that the main reason for dropping out was the social life inside the club. Other contributing factors were the leadership style of the trainer, the negative influence of the peer group, and an out-of-date sport market (Vanreusel, 1992).

These developments call for an adapted approach for sport education for young people:

- A broad orientation and introduction to sport activities.
- The development of knowledge of how to choose critically out of many possibilities in accordance with personal preferences.

- Opportunities to try several sports.
- The development of a variety of offers in accordance with differences in motives and needs in organized sport.

Promotional Campaigns

The promotion of youth sport in the Netherlands takes place in different ways. Since the Netherlands Sport Confederation has taken on a stronger coordinating role in the last few years, the promotion actions are organized by separate sport associations.

Projects on the Association Level

Several sport associations have developed important projects to attract young participants, including those involved in soccer, field hockey, water polo, handball, and gymnastics.

The 4 × 4 youth soccer plan of the Royal Dutch Soccer Association. The overall objective of this new game for children ages 6 to 12 was to teach soccer in a friendly way, with small fields, moveable goals, and no referees. The game was presented to the children as a whole. This meant that participating youngsters received no specific skill, tactical, or fitness training but learned to score goals, to defend, and to change quickly between offense and defense through playing. The small team size allows each child to have a great deal of ball contact, which avoided the repetition and long waiting lines which are the norm in drills. Goals can be scored from any position, there is no goalkeeper, and no calling offside. The playing time is restricted to 15 minutes. That the enthusiasm for this game is growing is evident by the fact that hundreds of clubs have already introduced it.

Field hockey, an example of an explicit youth policy. The hockey association has initiated an explicit youth policy. Most of the Dutch sport organizations do not go this far (yet). The coherent youth policy developed for hockey has the following goals: (a) to teach kids to play hockey well and have lots of fun doing it, (b) to adjust teaching to a child's development phase, (c) to teach kids a fair play mentality, and (d) to uphold the quality and quantity of the people who coach and train the youth (Nederlandse Sport Federatie, 1992).

The fair play goal is remarkable. Almost no other sport organization has the courage to make this a policy goal. To help achieve this goal, activities have been initiated whereby children can follow a skill progression and gain a diploma, and the clubs are sent information so they can make a teaching plan to set up minihockey games. A referee project has also been instituted to make youths more "whistle-minded." The project initiators want to convey that whistling the game is just as normal as playing it, in order to lessen hostility between players and referees and the poor attitudes that such hostility can foster.

Youth sport and fair play. This project was carried out from 1985-1987 and consisted of three innovative practices. The purpose of this project was to stimulate fair play in youth sports, specifically in water polo, handball, and gymnastics.

A new game of water polo for participants aged 10 to 13 was developed so that they played a smaller area, five against five, girls and boys together, with unlimited substitution and a prohibition against underwater pushing. A rule book for children and one for coaches, and a manual for teaching practice, were written.

The handball experiment involved youngsters aged 14 to 18. They were taught to defend by using offensive strategies that raised the activity level of the game and that could reduce roughness. The youngsters also watched themselves on videotapes to learn more about the physical nature of the game and the way responsibility for rough play rests with everyone.

In gymnastics the project was focused on providing more opportunities for children aged 10 to 13 to engage in physical movement, such as balancing, juggling, swinging, and playing. The purpose was to counteract the current emphasis on elite competition geared to the few very gifted youngsters. Children were given checklists with progressions so they could monitor their own progress.

Both the participating youngsters and coaches gave positive evaluations to the games and the practices described above. However, innovators experienced great difficulty in their attempts to institutionalize these concepts and ideas within each association (Buisman, 1987, 1988/1989).

Projects on the Federation Level

Three projects were initiated at the national level of the Netherlands Sport Confederation.

The youth and sport club project.   This project was carried out as a joint venture of the Netherlands Sport Confederation and the Faculty of Education of the State University of Utrecht from 1982 to 1986 (Buisman, 1984). Its overarching objective was to make youth sport more child-friendly by raising the awareness of those in leadership positions about youth sport. First, attempts were made to stimulate discussions among youth sport leaders about critical youth sport issues. Second, the participating sport clubs were asked to categorize the nature of their clubs, that is, were they oriented toward performance or toward leisure? Were they oriented toward children or adults?

The concept of child-friendliness thoroughly marked the discussions and the manuals in the project. This meant that attention was paid to different psychological phases of development, to individual differences, to physical differences among children, including disabling conditions, and to the different meanings given to body experiences (Buisman & Zwezerijnen, 1982; Lucassen, Ooyen, & van Maanen, 1982).

Sports, well chosen, for kids 10 to 12 years old.   The Netherlands Sport Confederation has developed a sport information kit for primary schools, entitled "Sports, Well Chosen." The development of this kit grew out of the growing interest of national sport bodies in promoting sports at school. But all were working at separate initiatives, which irritated school teachers. Hence a coordinated approach was needed and the sport information kit was created.

The overall aim of the information kit is to support children aged 10 to 12 years in the process of choosing a sport which is most suited to their preferences and possibilities. Apart from a short video, the kit contains workbooks for children, a set of sport selection cards, a software program, information cards on 55 types of sport, and a teacher's guide (Lucassen, 1992).

Prevention of injuries in youth sports (National Institute for Sports and Health).   At the end of August 1989, a 3-year education campaign was started, aimed at reducing the number of sport injuries in the Netherlands (van Mechelen & Hlobil, 1987). The campaign, named "Injuries, Master Them" consisted of a general part and a sport-oriented part. A mass media approach was chosen for the general part, and an interpersonal approach for the sport-oriented part. To measure the efficiency of the campaign, specific elements were submitted to an evaluation.

The most important aim of the mass media portion was to highlight the problem of sport injuries to sportsmen and sportswomen aged 10 to 25. The campaign also encouraged them to increase their knowledge of this problem and to change their attitude toward it. To handle this a multimedia approach was chosen. In highlighting the sport injuries problem, the campaign was reasonably successful, and in increasing knowledge of the sport injuries problem, the campaign was partly successful. A slight change was observed in the thinking of sportsmen and sportswomen about the risks they run of receiving sport injuries, but the change was only temporary (Joossen & de Geus, 1991).

Conclusions on Youth Sport Promotion

Although the several projects we have discussed are not completely representative of the Dutch youth sport situation, we can draw some conclusions:

• Most of these programs are *child-oriented*. The resistance toward this kind of thinking in a traditional sport culture tends to be underestimated or overlooked.

• Most strategies developed to influence the sport world are aimed at trainers/ coaches and officials. The structure of sport has received little attention.

• Attractive material such as videos, brochures, and posters have been created in conjunction with these projects. However, because most projects lacked an implementation phase, the colorful materials were often left on the shelf.

• The use of volunteers to carry out these projects was a factor the importance and the limitations of which were often underestimated.

Youth Sport Policy

Only a few policy papers have been written on youth sport on the national level in the Netherlands. Two policy papers concerning sports in the future, "Sport as an Inspiration for Our Society" and "A New Setup," were presented from the perspective of organized sport in 1992 (Nederlands Olympisch Comité & Nederlandse Sport Federatie, 1992; Nederlandse Sport Federatie & Ministerie van Welzijn, Volksgezondheid en Cultuur, 1992). Both of these papers gave a great deal of attention to top-level sport and its position in society. But the issue of youth sport itself had no specific place in either, which we found very disappointing. On the other hand, we have to mention that a lot of attention was given to specific groups such as people with disabilities, girls and women, and cultural minorities. Under these headings explicit attention was paid to children and youngsters.

We noticed that many instrumental functions were ascribed to sport (sport as means) in both of the 1992 policy papers. These functions included sport for health reasons, for teaching team spirit, and for developing perseverance. These functions can also, however, be ascribed to playing in a band or orchestra. In the thinking about the functions of sport, little attention was paid to factors such as the sport experience, the making of rules for competition, and physicality (sport as a goal). According to Steenbergen, de Vos, and Tamboer (1992), the double character of sports (sport as a means as well as a goal) is therefore out of balance.

Fortunately, the different sport associations are not sitting still. For example, the soccer association is busy with the development of youth soccer (the 4 × 4 game for young children), the volleyball association has developed a model for training that makes allowance for child development, and the hockey association has its fair play program. These policy ideas were implemented instead of remaining only ideas.

Teacher/Coach Education in Youth Sport

The contents of the teacher and coach education courses vary greatly in quality. These differences can easily be detected. Sometimes the textbooks are theoretically sound but do not translate theory into practice. This can be very disappointing to participants in the courses, who are primarily volunteers who use their leisure time to coach and who have very practical reasons for taking coaching education courses. There are also textbooks which work the other way, offering a lot of practical situations and no theoretical depth. Only a few courses pay attention to the minisports. When we question this omission, we run up against a great deal of misunderstanding. We are confronted with questions such as: ''Isn't it important to teach the total sport at the youngest age possible?'' and ''Isn't the total sport experience a good preparation for (sport)life?''

Most of the sport associations have difficulty in writing an integrated and coherent text. Often, a variety of articles are used to create a reader and the users of the text, that is, the students of the coaching education course, have to integrate the ideas themselves. Also, the articles are often written at various levels, which creates incongruities. For example, one book contained a nice chapter about the psychological development stages of the child and yet paid no attention to these stages when the theme was the teaching and training of children.

Unlike the policy papers mentioned before, most of the textbooks have a wide scope with respect to sport. Attention is not only given to elite youth sport but also to the various recreational sports. Achievement is also defined in a pluralistic way. Beside the competitive meaning (winning from someone else) most of the textbooks of the sport associations also mention the individual meaning, that is, using self-comparison to define achievement.

Most of the textbooks, however, present a rather rigid concept of health. Health is usually defined in the context of the biological structure of the human body. A dynamic concept of health such as that used by the World Health Organization is often missing. This organization defines health as "well-being," which is a subjective meaning of health with respect to sport.

Thus we found overall that the textbooks used in the courses display more encouraging developments than the national policy papers, in part because the contents of the texts are often much more concrete. The textbooks can be seen as the calling cards from the sport associations. One limitation of our analysis, however, was that we only analyzed the textbooks and not the lessons of the courses themselves.

Conclusion

The foregoing discussions enable us to make predictions about youth sport development in the Netherlands in the beginning of the new century.

• The total numbers of participating children and youngsters in organized sport will—also as a result of the graying of the population—decrease in absolute numbers. However, it is possible that the decrease will be limited by immigration, and by the increase of participation in sport by girls.

• A great deal of the development of youth sport will depend on the flexibility of organized sport. We outlined two directions (Crum, 1991). One direction leads to a stronger development of competitive sport and the technology which comes with it: tracking down youth talents, training of (still younger) children, and permanent selections (sportification). The other direction is desportification, also in organized sports. This includes a greater freedom for the youth: more choice and flexibility about when and how much to participate, greater individualization in sport, and more cooperative than competitive games. If the sport clubs succeed in combining both directions they could create a strong foundation for the future of youth sport. This will require a lot of flexibility of sport clubs and sport associations!

• Ideally the sport associations, together with the Netherlands Sport Confederation, will manage to develop a joint strategy to improve the quality of youth sport. Today separate efforts are the rule: every association for itself and rivalry when it comes to youth sport. A good start could be the new project of the Netherlands Sport Confederation mentioned earlier (Sports, Well Chosen), which encourages children to make their own sport choices at school from information provided by a number of sport clubs.

• The cooperation between organized sports and schools will continue to be problematic for a long time, not so much because of the differences between objectives and goals but because of the great cultural differences between the two areas. Successful collaboration requires the school to be more sport-friendly and the sport clubs to take a more pedagogical approach to those with and without an abundance of talent in sport. Unfortunately we do not expect any initiatives from the Dutch government that could give sports and physical education a higher priority in the education programs.

• Youth sport in the Netherlands will gradually become more professionalized. The clubs will hire professionals who will act as coordinators of the sport activities, who will take care of the continuity of the club, and who will be responsible for the education and coaching of the volunteers. In spite of this professionalization, however, the mainstay of the clubs will still be the volunteer trainers, coaches, and board members.

• The sport federations and associations (on a national level) will also be professionalized. Therein lies the possibility of building a bridge between the culture of sport and the youth culture. Different sport associations already have gained valuable experience in developing a specific youth sport culture. These experiences could be used by other sport organizations. The foregoing discussions illustrate that the developments in youth sport manifest themselves in various ways and reflect not only the heterogeneity of the Netherlands but also dominant principles such as the autonomy of the sport clubs and the sport associations, the influence of top-level sport, and a top-down youth sport policy.

References

Baar, P.L.M. (1991). *Sportuitval bij het jongensturnen* [Young male dropouts in gymnastics]. Unpublished doctoral dissertation, Utrecht University, The Netherlands.

Buisman, A.J. (1984). Pedagogische concepten van sportclubs [Educational concepts of sport clubs], *Jeugd en Samenleving*, **6/7**, 375-391.

Buisman, A.J. (1987). *Jeugdsport en fair-play* [Youth sports and fair play]. Haarlem, The Netherlands: De Vrieseborch.

Buisman, A.J. (1988/1989). Youth sports and fair play: A report of experiments in handball, waterpolo and gymnastics. In *Synopsis of the VI ISCPES conference proceedings in Hong Kong* (pp. 67-73). Hong Kong: The Chinese University.

Buisman, A.J. (1993). Contents and implementation of a youth sports policy. In W. Duquet, P. De Knop, & L. Bollaert (Eds.), *Youth sport: A social approach* (pp. 206-222). Brussels, Belgium: VUBpress.

Buisman, A.J., & Zwezerijnen, G. (1982). *Jeugd en sportvereniging: Deel I. Opvattingen over jeugdsport* [Youth and sport clubs: Part I. Opinions about youth sports]. Baarn, The Netherlands: Nelissen.

Centraal Bureau voor de Statistiek. (1993). *Statistisch jaarboek 1993* [Statistical yearbook 1993]. The Hague, The Netherlands: SDU.

Crum, B.J. (1992). *Over versporting van de samenleving* [Sportification of the society]. Haarlem, The Netherlands: De Vrieseborch.

Crum, B.J. (1993, April). *The bond of Dutch youth with the sport club*. Paper presented at the FIEP World Congress, "Physical Activity in the Lifecycle," Wingate Institute, Israel.

Diekstra, R.F.W. (Ed.) (1992). *Jeugd in ontwikkeling: Wetenschappelijke inzichten en overheidsbeleid* [Youth in development: Scientific opinions and government policy]. The Hague, The Netherlands: Wetenschappelijke Raad voor het Regeringsbeleid/SDU Uitgeverij.

Faber, K. (1989). *Bewegingsonderwijs op maat* [Physical education to measure]. Baarn, The Netherlands: Bekadidakt.

Grupe, O. (1985). Top-level sports for children from an educational viewpoint. *International Journal of Physical Education*, 1, 9-15.

Joossen, J.J.J., & de Geus, G.H. (1991). *Voorlichting over sportblessures* [Information about sport injuries]. Amsterdam, The Netherlands: Stichting Consument en Veiligheid.

Kamphorst, T.G., & Giljam, M. (1989). Trends in sports in the Netherlands. In T.J. Kamphorst & K. Roberts (Eds.), *Trends in sports: A multinational perspective* (pp. 277-304). Culemborg, The Netherlands: Giordano Bruno.

Lucassen, J. (1984a). *Jeugdsportleiders over hun funktie* [Youth sport coaches about their tasks]. The Hague, The Netherlands: Nederlandse Sport Federatie.

Lucassen, J. (1984b). Het normatieve spektrum van de jeugdsport [Normative aspects of youth sports]. *Actor*, 3(1), 56-65.

Lucassen, J. (1992). Kinderen introduceren in de sport [Introducing children to sports]. *Lichamelijke Opvoeding*, 11, 493-496.

Lucassen, J., Ooyen, D.H.P., & van Maanen, E.P. (1982). *Jeugd en sportvereniging: Deel II. Op zoek naar een eigen werkwijze* [Youth and sport clubs: Part II. Looking for an own method]. Baarn, The Netherlands: Nelissen.

Malina, R.M. (1988). Biological maturity status of young athletes. In R.M. Malina (Ed.), *Young athletes: Biological, psychological, and educational perspectives* (pp. 121-140). Champaign, IL: Human Kinetics.

Manders, T., & Kropman, J. (1982). *Sportbeoefening, drempels en stimulansen* [Sporting, thresholds, and stimuli). Nijmegen, The Netherlands: Instituut Toegepaste Sociologie.

Manders, T., & Kropman, J. (1987). *Sport: Ontwikkelingen en kosten* [Sport: Developments and costs]. Nijmegen, The Netherlands: Instituut voor Toegepaste Sociologie.

Manders, T., & Kropman, J. (1992). *Sportdeelname in Nederland* [Sport participation in the Netherlands]. Nijmegen, The Netherlands: Instituut voor Toegepaste Sociologie.

Martens, R. (1978). *Joy and sadness in children's sports*. Champaign, IL: Human Kinetics.

Meeus, W., & 't Hart, H. (Eds.) (1993). *Jongeren in Nederland* [Youth in the Netherlands]. Amersfoort, The Netherlands: Academische Uitgeverij.

Nederlands Olympisch Comité & Nederlandse Sport Federatie. (1992). *Sport als bron van inspiratie voor onze samenleving* [Sport as an inspiration for our society]. Amsterdam, The Netherlands: A.T. Kearney.

Nederlandse Sport Federatie. (1993). *Ledental N.S.F. per 1 jan. 1993* [List of members Jan. 1st 1993]. Arnhem, The Netherlands: Author.

Nederlandse Sport Federatie & Ministerie van Welzijn, Volksgezondheid en Cultuur. (1992). *Een nieuwe opstelling* [A new setup]. Arnhem, The Netherlands: Nederlandse Sport Federatie.

Social and Cultural Planning Office. (1992). *Sociaal en Cultureel Rapport 1992* [Social and Cultural Report 1992]. Rijswijk, The Netherlands: Author.

Steenbergen, J., de Vos, N.R., & Tamboer, J.W.I. (1992). Het dubbelkarakter van sport. *Lichamelijke Opvoeding, 14*, 638-641.

Stichting voor Economisch Onderzoek. (1988). *De Macro-economische betekenis van de sport in Nederland* [The macroeconomic meaning of sports in the Netherlands]. Amsterdam, The Netherlands: Stichting voor Economisch Onderzoek, Universiteit van Amsterdam.

Stichting voor Economisch Onderzoek. (1989). *Sport en gezondheid, economisch bezien* [Sports and health, from an economic point of view]. Amsterdam, The Netherlands: Stichting voor Economisch Onderzoek, Universiteit van Amsterdam.

ten Pas, P. (1993). *Waar zijn voetballende meisjes en dames in Nederland verstopt?* [Where are the girls and women in Dutch soccer?]. Zeist, The Netherlands: Koninklijke Nederlandse Voetbal Bond.

ter Bogt, T.F.M., & van Praag, C.S. (1992). *Jongeren op de drempel van de jaren negentig* [Youth on the threshold of the nineties]. The Hague, The Netherlands: Sociaal en Cultureel Planbureau/VUGA.

van Mechelen, W., & Hlobil, H. (1987). *How can sport injuries be prevented?* Oosterbeek, The Netherlands: Nationaal Instituut voor de Sportgezondheidszorg.

Vanreusel, B. (1992). *Sociale betekenis van sportdeelname* [Social meaning of sport participation]. Leuven, Belgium: Universiteit.

Chapter 15 Norway

Mari-Kristin Sisjord
Berit Skirstad

Norway is a vast land and yet it is the most sparsely populated country in Europe, with a population of 4.2 million inhabitants. The majority of its people (75%) live in small towns or sparsely populated areas: a not altogether surprising situation considering that over one third of the country is situated above the Arctic Circle.

The topography consists of fjords, mountains, narrow valleys, and large unpopulated areas. There are great regional differences in Norway, for example, in terms of language, climate, and economy. There are two official written languages in Norway, *bokmål* and *nynorsk*, and numerous local dialects. An ethnic group known as the Sami people, constituting 1% of the population, has its own culture and language.

The Organizational Network

The Sport Department of the Ministry of Cultural Affairs is responsible for matters relating to sport. Indeed, its main aim is to provide the entire population with opportunities for sport and physical activities (Kulturdepartementet, 1992).

Norway is divided into 19 counties and 439 municipalities for administrative purposes, and each region is served by a local cultural affairs department, whose responsibility it is to build and run the facilities within the municipality (see Figure 15.1).

Another body that is influential in sport matters is the Norwegian Confederation of Sports (NIF), which is the largest voluntary organization in Norway, with a membership of 1,710,459 (NIF, 1992b). It is the country's predominant popular movement, involving almost 40% of the Norwegian population.

The Norwegian Confederation of Sports is an umbrella organization comprising 45 sport federations. The main aim of the organization is to give everyone the chance to engage in sport activities irrespective of their activity level or degree of ability. The different sport federations are self-governing, and each is responsible for the development, organization, and activities in its sport. This can cause a situation which leads to irregularities in the provision of sports to particular target groups. For example, 12 out of the 45 federations have no activities for children and varying age minimums of 12 to 15 years (NIF, 1992a).

The highest authority for sport in the nongovernmental structure is the General Assembly of Sports, which is held every 4 years. Altogether, 131 representatives

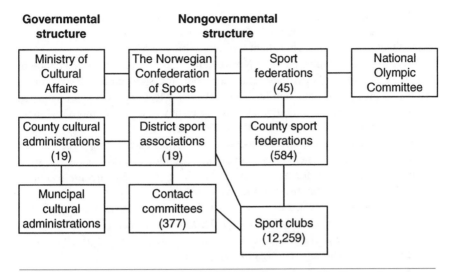

Figure 15.1   Governmental and nongovernmental structures of the Norwegian sport organization.

have voting power: 11 from the Executive Board, 60 from the 19 districts, and 60 from the 45 federations. In addition, the employees have 6 nonvoting representatives, who have the right to speak and forward proposals.

In 1992 a National Youth Assembly for Sport was created, the result of an initiative taken by young people themselves. The aims of this general assembly are to represent the interests of young people between the ages of 15 and 25, and to provide sporting opportunities which they perceive to be important and relevant. They call themselves "engaged youth." Their plan of action for the period 1992-98 includes the following aims (although this list is not exhaustive):

- There should be a youth consultant post at the Norwegian Confederation of Sports by 1993.
- Half of all the sport federations and district associations should have staff working with youth issues by 1995.
- Ten out of the 19 district associations should organize a Youth General Assembly of Sports in the period 1993-94.
- Youth should be represented on executive boards, in committees and groups within the Norwegian Confederation of Sports, and in district associations and sport federations.
- The second Youth General Assembly of Sports was organized in March 1994 prior to the mother organization's assembly; the third Assembly will be in 1996, the fourth in 1998, and then every fourth year.
- At least two youth representatives should be admitted as observers at the General Assembly of Sports.
- Youth workshops for coaches and leaders should be held. (NIF, 1992c)

NIF's Central Administration has a Department for Education and Development, where youth sport belongs. Out of a total of 15 to 18 employees in this department, there is one consultant working with youth sport.

There are 12,259 sport clubs in Norway, and these represent the backbone of Norwegian sport; 5,686 of these clubs are company sport clubs. The members are the employees or their families (NIF, 1992b). Most sport clubs are engaged in more than one sport, although there is a tendency to establish more and more specialist sport clubs concerned with only one activity.

The country is divided into 19 district associations, each with a large number of local associations. The Ministry urges the counties to make plans for sport facilities and provision for outdoor pursuits. These plans also include responsibility for larger sport facilities in the municipalities.

Eleven voluntary organizations are involved in outdoor activities under an umbrella organization called *Friluftslivets Fellesorganisasjon* (FRIFO). In addition, the scouts, the church, welfare organizations, and political, agricultural, and homemakers' associations all organize activities.

Guidelines for Youth Sport

As early as 1976, the general assembly published the document "Foundations and Guidelines for Sport Work with Children," and further guidelines concerning youth sport in 1982. The focus of these documents was the importance of encouraging the development of all-around athletes among children, and the adaptation of adult competition rules to the needs of children. After further input from the sport federations, particularly with regard to sport for the under-10s, a plan of action with guidelines for youth sport was finally agreed upon in 1987. Clearly, youth sport has been given a high priority in the period 1982-1987, although it has to be acknowledged that only 8 out of the 45 federations have a majority of youth members (under 17 years of age), and that the work has mainly been carried on at the central and district administrative levels.

As far as the 1987 guidelines for youth sport are concerned, the main aims of the Norwegian Confederation of Sports were as follows: "To stimulate children's physical, psychological, and social development, and to provide an educational introduction to a wide range of sporting activities" (NIF, 1987b, p. 8). Three categories were determined, each with a specific administrative objective: for children 5 to 7 years old, the objective was to engage them in play and all-round activities; for those 8 to 10 years old, to teach them a wide range of sports; and for those 11 to 12 years old, to embark upon more specialized training in one or more sports (NIF, 1987a, 1991a). In 1991 a final copy of guidelines for youth sport was published, which summarized the past 20 years of development in this area.

Courses for Children

Courses covering a wide range of sporting activities have been prioritized for children 5 to 12. These courses are taught by accredited leaders and a sensitive child development philosophy has been adopted. Wherever possible local playgrounds meant as sport facilities have been used. At the end of 1991, 47,000 children were participating in courses arranged by 663 "sport schools," in which approximately 7,300 instructors were engaged (NIF, 1992b). It is hoped that the number of participants will increase in the future. With regard to funding, NIF receives a share of the revenue from the national lottery which is earmarked for supporting the sport schools. In addition, further state monies are used annually to provide sporting activities for socially disadvantaged young people from the cities.

School-Based Leisure

Starting from 1994 all 7-to-10-year-olds in Norway have the opportunity to participate in after-school leisure activities. This age group's school day finishes early, and this initiative from the government is an attempt to overcome the problems posed by working parents. Instead of hoards of latchkey children being left to their own devices, it is hoped that parents will enroll their children in structured activity.

NIF has some reservations, however, concerning the initiative, namely, the fear of cheap unqualified labor being employed (older pupils, students, the unemployed, and pensioners), and the fear that a loss of membership from local sport clubs would have serious financial consequences for their running costs. This situation poses a challenge for NIF during the next few years, but it is hoped that, through close cooperation with the sport federations, these problems can be solved. The initiative can strengthen the provision of sport for children in Norway (NIF, 1992d).

Sport Participation

During the past decades, there has been a tremendous increase in the number of young people taking part in organized sport. The annual reports from the Norwegian Confederation of Sports show that in the age group up to 17 years, the number of memberships has increased more than threefold between the mid-1960s and the early 1980s (annual reports from the Norwegian Confederation of Sports present the number of memberships in three categories: 0-12 years, 13-16 years, and older. Up to 1990, two categories were used, divided at the age of 17 years). The reports show that among boys the peak year was in 1983, with 306,000 memberships, and among girls it was 1986, with 234,000 memberships. Since then the number of memberships has undergone a minor decrease, which can partly be explained by lower birth rates. The decrease among girls during the last few years is lower than among boys. The annual report from 1992 shows that memberships among girls are 223,000, compared to 284,000 among boys. These figures show that more than 50% of young people in the age group up to 17 years are involved in organized sport.

Types of Sports

The annual reports demonstrate a considerable dispersion of memberships among the different sports, from more than 300 up to almost 300,000 (NIF, 1992b).

The most common sports among young people correspond to those federations with the highest number of memberships. For many years, soccer in particular, European handball, skiing, track and field, and gymnastics have been the most popular activities. However, some changes have taken place during the last few years. Among the traditional sports, some are losing memberships, and there seems to be a move from individual sports toward team sports. The decrease in overall membership might indicate an increase in participation in nonorganized activities, or, on the other hand, it could be a sign of less physical activity during leisure time.

These recent trends are illustrated in Figures 15.2 and 15.3, which represent sports with a membership of more than 5,000 boys or girls.

The histogram shows that the most popular sports for girls are soccer, skiing, track and field, handball, gymnastics, swimming, volleyball, and horseback riding (see Figure 15.2). An increase in team sports during this five-year period can be noticed. Traditionally, European handball has been the girls' number one team sport in Norway, and this trend continues. As in other countries, soccer is a relatively new sport for girls; however, it has grown to be the second most popular in terms of memberships. Interest in volleyball is increasing too, though to a lesser extent. Until a few years ago, gymnastics had a leading position among the girls, but this activity is decreasing year by year. Skiing and track and field as well have been decreasing during the last few years. Participation in swimming is fairly stable, while horseback riding is increasing. In 1986 orienteering held the eighth place in popularity, but since then horseback riding has overtaken it and orienteering is back down at nine.

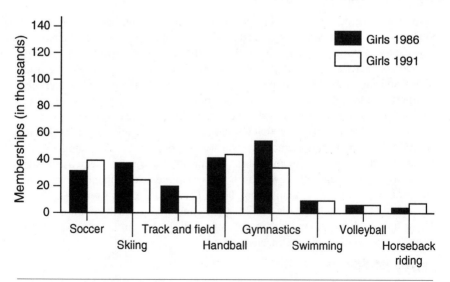

Figure 15.2 Number of memberships in the eight largest sport federations among girls in 1986 and 1991.

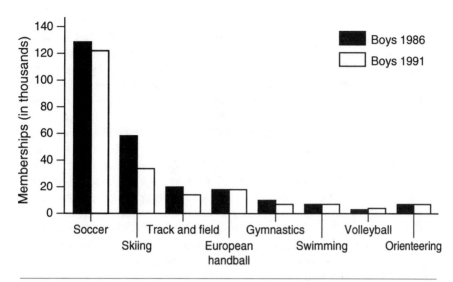

Figure 15.3   Number of memberships in the eight largest sport federations among boys in 1986 and 1991.

The histogram for boys shows a still more biased distribution of memberships, as soccer alone has more members than the other seven sports together (see Figure 15.3). Besides that, the changes among boys show patterns similar to Figure 15.2, as European handball and volleyball are increasing in popularity, while skiing, gymnastics, and track and field are decreasing. Swimming and orienteering show minor changes, though orienteering has lost memberships during this period.

Age group differences show similar tendencies to the distribution among girls with regard to gymnastics, skiing, European handball, and track and field. Both volleyball and orienteering have almost twice the memberships in the age group 13 to 16 years compared to 0 to 12 years, whereas in soccer there are 50% more in the youngest age group.

Altogether, the figures indicate that youth participation in organized sport is concentrated within relatively few sports. This trend appears to be general, irrespective of geographical location, although the range of choice available in extremely rural areas is somewhat limited. The trend of a decrease in interest for more traditional activities can be explained by a number of reasons. A decrease in participation in skiing may be accounted for by a lack of snow in the past five years, a preference for jazz ballet or aerobics may explain a decline in gymnastics, and activities such as snowboard and telemark skiing have attracted would-be downhill skiers.

Studies of participation in leisure-time activities show that sport, however, is still the most popular activity among youths. A nationwide survey found patterns of participation similar to those found in the annual reports from the Norwegian

Confederation of Sports. Among youths 14 to 16, team sports seem to be most favored. As many as 50% of the boys responded that they participate in soccer, and 24% listed some other kind of team sport. Corresponding percentages among the girls were 20% and 40%. Concerning individual sports, 9% listed cross-country skiing, 6% track and field, and 2% swimming, regardless of sex. The percentages for alpine skiing were 4% for boys and 2% for girls. Other sports had less than 2% participation (Grue, 1985).

In a study of youths aged 8 to 24 (MMI, 1991), the respondents were asked about their main sport activities, and about which activities they took part in on at least a monthly basis. The result confirmed the studies mentioned earlier, although it also reports other main activities, such as cycling, dancing, aerobics, and jazz ballet for girls, and cycling for boys. Monthly activities seem to include a wider range of activities and higher participation rates than the annual reports indicate. Correlated to membership in sport clubs, it becomes obvious that a considerable part of those activities take place outside the organized sport system. In particular this holds for cross-country and downhill skiing, swimming, cycling, aerobics, jazz ballet, and strength and fitness training. The results point to the fact that activities outside the sport system either refer to the outdoor recreation tradition like skiing, cycling, and swimming, or to activities run on a more commercial basis. The latter is probably most common among the oldest respondents in the sample (up to 24 years old), as the same trends are still more distinct in the adult part of the population (Dølvik, Danielsen, & Hernes, 1988).

Frequency of Participation in Sport

From the same study, questions about the frequency of sport participation show that most Norwegian youths are involved with physical activity on a regular basis (2 to 3 times a week) (MMI, 1991). However, the question could have been interpreted to include physical education classes as well as leisure-time activities. Another study with a national sample states that 78% of youths take part in sport activities at least once a week (Wold & Aarø, 1987). Similar trends are found in a survey which reports participation rates in sports, play, and recreational activities. With regard to gender, the same number of girls and boys report participating in sports at least weekly. However, boys report more frequent exercise, as measured by the number of times and hours per week (Wold, 1989). Among those active in organized sport, the largest number said they trained 2 to 3 times a week, although a significant number also listed higher frequencies as well (Sundet, 1983). There seems to be a tendency toward more frequent training with increased age (Sisjord, 1993; Wold, 1989).

During adolescence more frequent training may indicate growing seriousness about sport, however, the percentage of youths participating in competitive sports actually decreases with increasing age. The level of competition is heightened from 14 to 16 years, but there are fewer competitions at the club level, and the proportion of youths participating in sport on a recreational basis and just for fun decreases (Grue, 1985). However, gender differences are recognized, as higher rates of boys than girls are competing in sport (Grue, 1985; MMI, 1991; Wold, 1989).

Motivations

Studies about motivation for participating and questions concerning the personal benefits to be gained from sport show that the main reasons for participation in organized sport are fun and enjoyment, social aspects, and health benefits (Fasting, 1987; Hustad, 1985; Stensaasen, 1976). The aspect of competition is also a frequent answer in one of the studies (Hustad, 1985). Reasons like "My parents like me to do it" or "My friends are interested" are less frequently mentioned.

The social class profile of young sport participants reflects the makeup of the population at large (Grue, 1985). However, distributions of dropouts from organized sport versus sport participants indicate that children from less privileged social classes tend to drop out from sport at an earlier stage than children from more privileged classes (Lippe, 1979; Railo, 1980; Sisjord, 1993). Results from a nationwide study (Grue, 1985) show that youths from more privileged groups participate to a greater extent in competitions on higher levels than do youths from less privileged backgrounds. The latter indicates that increasing competitiveness and seriousness in sport leads to dropout, and that this most likely happens to those who are less competition-oriented or less successful in sport. Accordingly, studies show that dropouts answer that they would like to continue in sport on a noncompetitive basis (Sisjord, 1993).

Dropout

A nationwide survey showed that as many as 85% of young people are involved in organized sport during childhood or adolescence (Grue, 1987). This holds true for girls as well as for boys. However, by the age of 14 the percentages of youth memberships in sport clubs have dropped to 59% for girls and 63% for boys. The corresponding percentages at the age of 16 are 54% and 58%, suggesting that sport participation is relatively stable from 14 to 16 years, which is the age when youth are terminating elementary school. Although most young people continue to participate in sport in high school, this involves a shift in class settings and to some extent in friendship groups. That factor may contribute to an explanation for the increasing dropout over the following two years, as the percentages at the age of 18 years are 29% for girls and 34% for boys (Grue, 1987). Other studies also report dropout at an earlier age among girls than among boys (Railo & Ommundsen, 1983; Wold, 1989).

A recent study (Sisjord, 1993) including a wider age span showed similar trends with regard to sport participation and dropout. Among the 15-year-olds the participation rate is 58%, at 16 years 51%, at 17 years 46%, at 18 years 33%, and at 19 years 31%. The same study showed participation rates between 50% and 60 % from 8 to 14 years, except for the age of 13 years, which is reporting 65% participation in sport (MMI, 1991). The peak in the participation rate is comparable to those in other countries. However, dropout in Norway seems to occur at a later stage than reported in other studies, and also than reported in studies conducted previously in Norway.

There is a considerable body of literature dealing with dropout from sport, and the phenomenon has received several explanations. Some studies have focused upon dropout from one particular sport, while others have examined withdrawal from organized sport in general. Most studies have been retrospective, approaching dropout as a termination of the sport career. However, it appears that sport adherence and dropout are complex phenomena, which include a variety of activities, levels, and age groups. Empirical findings show that some youngsters briefly explore sports when they are trying out different achievement domains, while others may withdraw from one sport only to enter a new one (Fasting, 1987; Patriksson 1987). This has led scholars to elaborate the conceptual framework, and some have suggested a classification system for dropout, distinguishing between transitions between individual sports and dropout from sport in general.

Among youths, studies show that sport participation may be connected to one or more activities, but usually the number of activities decreases as the youngsters grow older. The greater levels of training required as one continues to pursue a sport make it difficult to combine several activities, and the youngsters have to make a choice.

A major part of the literature questions why people discontinue sport involvement. In empirical research, there has been a tendency to consider dropout in terms of an occurring event, and then examining reasons behind dropout. Among the most frequent reasons given to explain dropout from youth sport are "too time-consuming," "conflicts with other leisure interests," "not fun anymore" (Fasting, 1987; Olsen, 1979; Railo & Ommundsen, 1983; Rudaa, 1974; Sisjord, 1993). Factors related to trainers, teams, negative experiences, competition, or achievement are also reasons for quitting sport, but to a lesser extent. One study reported lack of support from parents as well as from trainers as being a more frequent reason for dropout than competition stress (Railo & Ommundsen, 1983). Empirical findings, however, show that decisions about quitting sport are multifactorial. Even if one single factor seems to cause dropout, in general, there are a number of underlying factors (Sisjord, 1992).

Quite often experiences from sport are evaluated against paid effort, and against other leisure activities and leisure styles in youths' daily lives. Even if sport is experienced positively, dropout may occur if the youngsters' friends withdraw from sport. During adolescence, friendship may be more important than success in sport (Skard & Vaglum, 1984). On the other hand, sport participation may continue when athletes are doing well socially, even if their sport performance is less highly valued (Sisjord, 1993).

Problems in Youth Sport

Sport clubs within the Norwegian Confederation of Sports are run on a voluntary basis to a certain extent. Sport on lower levels and youth sport are often coached by unpaid individuals who have an interest in sport but lack formal training. From the sport organizations' point of view, it is difficult to recruit enough qualified trainers, and this factor is considered to have a restraining influence on developing youth sport. Among trainers, there is a tendency to think in terms of the outcome of the game, rather than of the process of sport as part of a child's socialization. On the other hand, however, there are many leaders and trainers in sport who consciously try to do what is most beneficial for children's development and for youth sport in general.

Traditionally, the individual sport federations have offered programs for training and developing skills within their particular sports. The move toward the establishment of sport schools has caused organizational problems. It seems that opinions about the promotion of youth sport differ from one sport federation to another, and that at the local level some sport leaders find it difficult to cooperate in developing joint programs in youth sport. However, in general, sport schools seem to be more and more accepted among sport leaders, and among parents as well.

Another problem in youth sport is connected to competition among various federations. Since the decisions about youth sport were agreed upon (NIF, 1987b), some sport leaders have had difficulties with, or refused to lead, the new system.

It still remains, though, that a great deal of sport provided for children is arranged within specific sport federations. As the youngsters grow older, they experience ever-increasing demands on them in terms of the frequency and the intensity of training sessions, a situation which results in their being forced to drop certain activities in order to give priority to one single sport. In short, it is exceedingly difficult to be active in a broad range of sports, a fact which, according to Ingvaldsen (1986) can have serious implications for dropout rates. Indeed, as sport clubs raise their expectations of young participants, demanding a high level of skill competency and positive results in competition, dropout rates also increase.

Given the fact that more than eight out of ten Norwegian children (for shorter or longer periods) are involved with sport, this certainly poses a challenge to the sport leaders concerning program development. With increasing age, organized sport becomes even more serious. One important question arises, that of which groups should be given priority. Or is it possible to differentiate between those who are participating on a recreational basis and those aspiring to higher levels? Leaders in the sport clubs have to cope with these problems if the slogan "sport for all" is to come true. However, it seems difficult to develop appropriate programs at all levels, and to avoid dropout from youth sport, particularly in team sports, where noncompeting groups are rare since the teams belong to a league system.

As far as dropout rates are concerned, one could be tempted to ask whether it is realistic to pursue the goal of keeping as many young people as possible engaged in some kind of organized sport, and one could also ask whether it is indeed desirable to encourage youngsters to join an environment that is adult-dominated. Does such an organizational structure prevent them from developing certain skills, such as decision making and leadership qualities? According to Ingebrigtsen (1988), young participants would prefer to have more autonomy.

So it will be interesting to see the pattern of future development in youth sport programs.

Most young people who are motivated to compete in sport at higher levels run into the problem of how to combine sport with education. As they reach high school age, schoolwork and sport place greater demands on them. For some athletes this means a choice between school or sport, if they want to attain the grades required to enter college or university. Some of the sport federations have tried to solve this problem by setting up special training programs which form a part of the normal school day, either by establishing special schools or by special agreement with existing schools. Furthermore, special study units have been developed for those whose training and traveling commitments do not allow them to attend one of the special school programs.

Promotional Campaigns

A campaign called "Basic Values in Sport," launched in February 1993, has been given a high priority for the period 1993 to 1998. The main aim for the Norwegian Confederation of Sports is to ensure that sport survives as a positive creator of values for individuals and for the society (NIF, s.d.). The campaign aims to define a common set of values for sport in Norway and to stimulate the realization of these values in practical sporting behavior. This is necessary to try to counteract negative trends such as drug abuse, increasing commercialization, and violence in sport. The first step in the campaign is to have a debate in the sport clubs. Campaigns are used as door-openers in order to convey a message.

In 1988 and 1989 an anti-doping campaign was directed toward young athletes and in 1990 and 1991 toward coaches and leaders. In the anti-doping work there has always been cooperation with public authorities, the private sector, and other organizations. The school system proved to be a much better agent in changing attitudes and knowledge on doping than the sport clubs (NIF, 1991b).

Other campaigns have been implemented, including a project to encourage immigrant participation in sport. A national fitness project leading up to the Winter Olympic Games at Lillehammer in 1994 was another initiative, implemented jointly by the Ministry of Health and Social Affairs and the Ministry of Cultural Affairs.

Conclusion

Sport is a popular activity among youths in Norway. Aside from physical education in school, most organized sport activities take place in sport clubs organized by the NIF. The most common sports among young people are soccer, European handball, skiing, track and field, gymnastics, swimming, volleyball, orienteering, and horseback riding. The percentage of youths participating in organized sport, however, decreases with increasing age. Studies show that the athletes' reasons for quitting sport are connected to experiences in sport settings, or to the priority they give to other leisure activities or school work.

Hence, new strategies and new measures are needed in Norway. Currently, traditional sports, as offered via the NIF, are being challenged on a number of fronts—by new activities, such as aerobics, rafting, and fitness studios; by demographic changes, particularly in terms of immigration; and by economic cutbacks—and a range of initiatives has been launched recently in an attempt to meet these challenges.

References

Dølvik, J.E., Danielsen, Ø., & Hernes, G. (1988). *Kluss i vekslinga: Fritid, idrett og organisering* [Leisure, sport, and organization]. Oslo, Norway: Fagbevegelsens senter for forskning.

Fasting, K. (1987). Youth sport: Too boring—restrictive—competitive? *12th ICSSPE Sport and Leisure Seminar. 10th Trim and Fitness Congress* (pp. 56-63). Norway: NIF.

Grue, L. (1985). *Bedre enn sitt rykte: En undersøkelse av ungdoms fritidsbruk. Fase 2 av Foreningsundersøkelsen* [Better than their reputation. A study about youth and leisure. Part 2]. Oslo, Norway: Kultur-og Vitenskapsdepartementet.

Grue, L. (1987). *Ungdom uten opprør?* [Youth without revolt?]. Oslo, Norway: Kultur-og vitenskapsdepartementet, Ungdoms-og Idrettsavdelingen (STUI).

Hustad, O. (1985). *Fysisk aktivitet i fritiden hos 15-åringer: En undersøkelse i kommunene Levanger og Høylandet høsten 1984* [Physical activity during leisure time among 15-year-olds: A study from Levanger and Høylandet, autumn 1984]. Levanger, Norway: Levanger Lærerhøgskole.

Ingebrigtsen, J.E. (1988). *Kampen om den vellykkede ungdom!? Rapport nr. 3 fra prosjektet: "Sosialisering til og i idrett"* [The contest for the successful youth]. Norway: NAVF senter for barneforskning, Idrettsforskningsgruppa, Universitetet i Trondheim.

Ingvaldsen, R.P. (1986). Konkurranseorientert barneidrett—en negativ faktor for utvikling av toppidrett [Competition-oriented youth sport—a negative factor for the development of top-level sport]. In *Barn og idrett*. Proceedings from a research seminar at Sole Turisthotell (pp. 89-98). Oslo, Norway: Norsk Forening for Idrettsforskning.

Kulturdepartementet. (1992). *St. meld. nr. 41 (1991-92) om idretten: Folkebevegelse og folkeforlystelse* [Whitepaper on sport]. Oslo, Norway: Author.

Lippe, G. vd. (1979). *Frafallsproblemer i kvinneidretten: En empirisk undersøkelse av jenteklassen 1956-59 i Tyrvinglekene 1972. Del 1 og 2* [Dropout among women in sport: A study among girls born 1956-59 participating in the Tyrving games in 1972. Parts 1 and 2]. Oslo, Norway: Norges Idrettsforbund.

MMI (Markeds-og Mediainstituttet). (1991). *Barn og ungdomsundersøkelse 8-24 år* [Study of children and youths 8-24 years]. Oslo, Norway: Author.

NIF (Norges Idrettsforbund). (1987a). *Saksliste idrettstinget Sheraton Hotel, Sandvika 7.-10.mai 1987* [Agenda]. Oslo, Norway: Author.

NIF (Norges Idrettsforbund). (1987b). *Bestemmelser om barneidrett vedtatt på idrettstinget 1987* [Guidelines for children's sport]. Oslo, Norway: Author.

NIF (Norges Idrettsforbund). (1991a). *Bestemmelser om barneidrett med utfyllende kommentarer* [Guidelines for children's sport, with comments]. Oslo, Norway: Author.

NIF (Norges Idrettsforbund). (1991b). *Report of the Third Permanent World Conference on Anti-Doping in Sport.* September 23-26, 1991. Bergen, Norway: Author.

NIF (Norges Idrettsforbund). (1992a). *Barneidrettsbestemmelsene. En oppfølging av særforbundenes konkurransepraksis* [Guidelines for children's sport: An overview of the individual sport associations' use of competition]. Oslo, Norway: Author.

NIF (Norges Idrettsforbund). (1992b) *Årsrapport 1991* [Annual report 1991]. Oslo, Norway: Author.

NIF (Norges Idrettsforbund). (1992c). *Rapport fra ungdommens 1. idrettsting* [Minutes from the first youth sport parliament meeting]. Oslo, Norway: Author.

NIF (Norges Idrettsforbund). (1992d). *Idrett og skolefritidsordninger: Status, erfaringer, anbefalinger og fremtid* [Sport and after-school activities: Status, experiences, recommendations, and the future]. Oslo, Norway: Author.

NIF (Norges Idrettsforbund). (s.d.). *Sport for a better society.* Oslo, Norway: Author.

Nilsen, B. (1988). *Idrettsskoler* [Sport schools]. Oslo, Norway: Norges Idrettsforbund/Universitetsforlaget.

Olsen, A.M. (1979). *Frafall blant gode skøyteløpere i alderen 10-15 år.* [Dropout among competitive speed skaters 10 to 15-years old]. Oslo, Norway: Norges Idrettshøgskole.

Patriksson, G. (1987). *Idrottens barn: Idrottsvanor—stress— ''utslagning''* [Children in sport: Sport habits—stress—dropout]. Stockholm, Sweden: Friskvårdscentrum.

Railo, W.S. (1980). Barne-og ungdomsidretten sett i relasjon til psykososial helse [Child and youth sport seen in relation to psychosocial health]. *Tidsskrift for den Norske Lægeforening,* **12B**, 799-806.

Railo, W., & Ommundsen, Y. (1983). *Idrett, oppvekstmiljø og frafall* [Sport, social environment, and dropout]. Oslo, Norway: Norges Idrettshøgskole.

Rudaa, S. (1974). *Nordisk undersøkelse om ungdom og idrett.* [A Nordic investigation into youth and sport]. Oslo, Norway: S.I.

Sisjord, M.K. (1992, November). *Rethinking youth sport concerning participation and dropout.* Paper presented at North American Society for the Sociology of Sport Conference, Toledo, OH.

Sisjord, M.K. (1993). *Idrett og ungdomskultur* [Sport and youth culture]. Published doctoral dissertation, the Norwegian University of Sport and Physical Education, Oslo.

Skard, O., & Vaglum, P. (1984). Barn i risiko for atferdsforstyrrelser: Rekruttering til og trivsel i fotball [Children at risk of deviant behavior: Recruitment to and enjoyment of soccer. Sport and social environment]. In *Idrett og oppvekstvilkår*. Proceedings seminar Orkanger. Oslo, Norway: Norsk Forening for Idrettsforskning.

Stensaasen, S. (1976). *Idrettspedagogiske problem: Project leisure and sport. NORA nr. 39* [Pedagogical problems in sport]. Oslo, Norway: Norges Idrettshøgskole.

Sundet, J.M. (1983). *Barn, ungdom og idrett: Rapport fra en spørreskjemaundersø kelse blant barn og ungdom (12-15 år) om idrettsrelaterte aktiviteter samt deres holdninger og motivasjon for idrett og konkurranser* [Children, youth, and sport: A survey report on sports-related activities among children and youth, including their attitudes and motivation toward sport and competition]. Oslo, Norway: Psykologisk Institutt, Universitetet i Oslo.

Wold, B. (1989). *Lifestyles and physical activity: A theoretical and empirical analysis of socialization among children and adolescents.* Unpublished doctoral dissertation, Faculty of Psychology, University of Bergen, Norway.

Wold, B., & Aarø, L.E. (1987). Developing healthy lifestyles. In *Growing into the modern world*. Proceedings from the International Conference on the Life and Development of Children in Modern Society: Vol. II (pp. 815-825). Trondheim, Norway.

Chapter 16 Poland

Seweryn Jerzy Sulisz

The Republic of Poland is situated on the North European Plain between the Baltic Sea and the Carpathian Mountains. Its area is 312,683 km², and it has a population of 38,365,000. The Polish language belongs to the West Slavic group. Public schools of all types are free, the system of schooling is standardized, and attendance through the eight-year primary school course and supplementary study until the age of 18 are required.

Prominent universities include the University of Warsaw (1818), the Jagiellonian University (1364) in Krakow, and the Catholic University of Lublin (1918). The largest Polish academy preparing persons qualified in physical culture is the Academy of Physical Education in Warsaw, founded in 1929. The highest academic institution is the Polish Academy of Sciences.

The concept of Sport for All, although creating an appropriate framework for organizational and methodological solutions, is so far only a statement of principle at this moment in Poland.

The creation of a uniform model for the functioning of sport is not an easy matter, nor is it possible in the near future, because sport is not a unitary phenomenon that allows itself to be treated uniformly across all its aspects. The variety of disciplines entering into the composition of sport and their territorial reach, as well as the preparation, behaviors, interests, and expectations of people connected with it all need to be taken in consideration.

Therefore, the variety of functional conceptions, objectives, and intentions that arise in regard to youth sport should not surprise us. A serious shortcoming, for example, which hinders the participation of youths in sport is the current inefficiency of the organizational system. There is a lack of coordination between the sport system connected with schools, and the system of performance sport—in which the leading role is fulfilled by clubs and the sponsorship system, sport federations, and the bureaucratized structures directing sport.

The unexpressed differences in the objectives pursued by these different systems result also from the lack of a national physical culture system, a lack which will also be difficult to remedy given the country's current economic problems. In the new sociopolitical situation in Poland, however, a plan for the creation of such a system was offered by the draft of the Physical Culture Act from 16 April 1993, which was sent to the Polish Parliament.

The Organizational Network

Within the framework of the existing organizational structure, children and youths may realize their sport aspirations primarily in schools and in extracurricular sport clubs. The former, being the basic links in the School Sport Federation, are integrally connected with the Ministry of National Education. Sport clubs, on the other hand, associated with individual sport federations, pursue the aims of performance sport and concentrate exclusively on the advancement of competitors toward the goals of success in competitions.

Club Sport Programs

Statistical data from the last two years (Sawinski, 1992) does not confirm the current opinions that the sport organizations, in quantitative measure, are experiencing a crisis, for the number of sport clubs had increased from 1,846 in 1990 to 2,040 in 1991. This tendency is connected mainly with the rise of unisectional or sport-specific clubs, for it is easier for such clubs to find sponsors with adequate funds at their disposal.

During this period, the number of club sections increased from 5,052 to 5,288. In 1990, 283,000 athletes trained in all clubs. During the following year, the number of active sport club members increased to 296,000.

Young athletes, those who are not counted in the seniors category in a given sport discipline, made up a decided majority of the active members. In 1990, there were 186,000 of them, while in 1991, there were 207,000. More specific data in this area have been assembled in Table 16.1, which concerns the state of activity in selected sport disciplines.

From the list, it appears that there are sport disciplines in Poland in which young athletes constitute the majority of members, and these are not exclusively disciplines where high performances are achieved at a young age. The highest percentages of young athletes in relation to the total practicing a particular discipline are noted in artistic gymnastics, fencing, sport gymnastics, modern pentathlon, and classical-style wrestling.

The fewest young athletes in 1991 were observed in such disciplines as skiing, sport acrobatics, sailing, judo, soccer, and table tennis.

During this last period, an annual system of competitions for athletes in individual age categories was accepted by the Polish Sport Federations.

School Sport Programs

The School Sport Federation (SZS) has been active for more than 35 years. Many well-known Polish athletes took their first steps in this organization. The main statutory objectives of the Federation are the promulgation of physical culture among school youths, the development of youth sport interests, improvement of the physical fitness of students, and the creation of conditions for developing sport mastery. Taking into consideration the varied interests of students and the need to prepare the entire population for lifelong physical activity, SZS established a hierarchy of activities which place sport for everyone at the top, then sport in school sport clubs, and finally performance sport for school youths.

SZS has branches in all provinces and in the majority of communes. According to data from the Chief Central Statistical Office (Sawinski, 1992), 13,980 school sport clubs in a total of 28,381 elementary, technical, and middle schools were

Table 16.1   Sections in Sport Clubs and Number of Members

Sport discipline	Sections in sport clubs	Number of members	
		Total	Juniors[a]
Sport acrobatics	35	2,170	1,101
Boxing	82	3,197	2,544
Artistic gymnastics	18	952	909
Sport gymnastics	23	916	811
Judo	116	12,339	8,292
Road cycling	116	3,071	2,470
Track and field	314	19,595	15,150
Skiing	65	2,670	943
Modern pentathlon	3	101	87
Basketball	224	14,789	10,791
Soccer	1,217	105,261	71,659
Volleyball	393	15,012	11,005
Swimming	89	9,347	7,173
Weightlifting	102	2,795	2,393
Fencing	42	2,271	2,027
Table tennis	428	11,543	8,223
Rowing	35	1,556	1,236
Wrestling, classical style	70	3,894	3,252
Sailing	95	5,038	2,826

Note. From *Report by the Office of Physical Culture and Tourism* (pp. 455-456), by R. Sawinski (Ed.), 1992, Warsaw, Poland: Statistical Publishers Institution.

[a]Juniors are athletes who since 1985 have not been not counted in the seniors category in a given discipline.

active in Poland in 1990. Thus, such clubs functioned in over 49% of schools. While there is a lack of credible information in this area for the following year, because more and more optional classes in schools are being abolished, it is probable that the number of school sport clubs has decreased significantly, or that many have suspended their activities.

There is also a lack of credible information on the number of members in these clubs. However, the latest estimate (Sawinski, 1992), announced that out of 7.5 million students more than 1.2 million girls and boys, or 16.5%, trained in SZS sections in 1990.

Even while approaching this data with the greatest reserve, it is difficult to acknowledge this situation to be satisfactory. While SZS receives financial and organizational assistance from the Ministry of National Education, the Ministry of Health and Social Welfare, and the Office of Physical Culture and Tourism, this assistance is far from sufficient. The cooperation of schools and SZS with the Society for the Promulgation of Physical Culture is even less perceptible.

Another basic problem hindering proper delivery of sport for everyone is the strongly rooted attitude among many teachers and sport authorities that this work should be directed toward the selection of students for performance sport.

As has been stated, the fundamental goal that SZS attempts to realize is universal physical activity of children and youths in coordination with their school responsibilities. The year-round School Sport Athletic Contest (SIS) system, whose activities facilitate the participation of all youths in different forms of sport, is one way SZS realizes its goals. Such school competitions, in addition to their recreational aims, also incorporate training and organizational tasks on the part of the Youth Organizers of Sport and Youth Sport Referees. This system of turning over much organizational-methodological work—drawn from the methodology of Scouting lessons—is treated as an effective form of education through active participation. However, it should be noted that this educational practice is not widespread and has even been diminishing since the early 1990s.

Widespread participation of youths in motor activity is served by the National "Sport for Everyone" Competition, also organized annually by SZS, with the strong support of educational and sport authorities. Its goal is to evaluate the success of school sport programs. The competition concludes with macroregional and central gold medals to the best elementary and secondary schools.

SZS also popularizes different forms of individual sport practice through the publication of handbooks for youths, such as "The Racing Performance Card," "The Index of Physical Performance," and "Check Yourself." The federation has also become involved in assisting schools with their compulsory physical education classes by publishing "Lider" and numerous methodological reports (some in the well-known publication "Sport and Tourism"), as well as organizing training workshops for physical education teachers.

Having functioned for many years, SZS commands the most experience and resources in the organization of sport for children and youths. However, the effects of this systematic work are not very visible. Notwithstanding the federation's cooperation with institutions responsible for the development of performance sport, the range of activities and their effects might be developed a great deal further. The challenge to such a development is primarily the problem of incorporating the school sport clubs into the system of sport training and competitions for youths in the high school tournaments.

Such a comprehensive system of sport for children and youths, whose realization would be undertaken by the School Sports Federation with the full acceptance and close cooperation of the Polish Sport Federations, could be fulfilled by the following elements:

- Training in SKS sport sections within the framework of the stage of versatile preparation.
- The system of interschool competitions for elementary schools.
- The organized sport competitions for secondary schools.
- The partial participation of the federation in the performance sport program.

It is necessary to point out that no organization or institution alone, including sport schools, will solve the problem of basic training. This stage of work with children and youths is especially threatened as a result of the virtual liquidation of optional classes. The negative effects of this will soon appear in small towns and rural areas, where there is a lack of sport clubs outside the schools, and in regions having a weak training base.

In regard to the first element listed earlier, Sulisz (1988, 1991, 1992) has argued for a conception of preparing students to practice sport, along with detailed organizational programs and methodical solutions, in a system of SKS lessons and classes offering versatile and directed preparation of future track and field athletes. It can be treated as a model for detailed solutions regarding individual sport disciplines.

In regard to the second element, a system of elementary school competitions is currently being run with the participation representatives from each school. The basic link in this system is the National School Youth Games. Because of a lack of funds, however, tournaments on a macroregional level are not conducted for these schools. Weaker provinces are thus deprived of a starting line.

Since the abolition of youth athletic meets, there are currently no universally functioning series of competitions for students of secondary schools. In order to compensate for this lack, SZS came out with the idea of organizing competitions for youths up to age 17. The proposal for such a system of competitions, under the name High School Tournaments, was presented to the Ministry of National Education and the Office of Physical Culture and Tourism. If the High School Tournaments are realized, their reach will be determined mainly by the extent of funds and the cooperation of promoters and interested sport federations. Sport authorities are expressing the view that in the current national economic situation, such a series of competitions has a chance for realization on the macroregional level.

Partial participation of SZS in the performance sport program took place in 1990 in 171 interschool sport clubs. In 1991, this number increased to 197 (Sawinski, 1992), grouping around 22,000 talented athletes in many sport disciplines. These clubs, though experiencing great difficulties, have achieved significant successes within the last few years. For example, the MKS Lublin (girls' handball) and MKS Wegrow (girls' volleyball) teams entered League I.

Sport Schools for the Athletically Gifted

Sport schools originated with the idea of developing students' sport careers while also developing his or her complete, unrestricted personality. The Polish sport school as an organizational solution, however, is criticized to this day. Hence, attempts were made at improving the operation of these schools, through which systematic and regular training work, stabilization of the training staff, and individual teaching of student-athletes could be introduced.

The number of sport schools has radically decreased. During the 1992-93 school year, 127 sport schools with 979 departments functioned in Poland, in which 22,923 student-athletes studied. There were 14 sport championship schools, where 1,338 training athletes studied in 106 departments.

These data indicate that learning, especially in sport schools, was conducted under unfavorable conditions, because there were 23 students for each department. In sport championship schools, where individual teaching is emphasized, the ratio was better—13 students for each department.

During the 1992-1993 school year, sport schools functioned in 34 out of 49 provinces and encompassed 35 sport disciplines. The greatest number of schools of this type are found in the provinces of Warsaw (15.7%). These two provinces and the next seven most active together run 84 sport schools.

Most schools include such sport disciplines in their programs as track and field (50 schools), swimming (36 schools), handball (19 schools), volleyball (19 schools), basketball (16 schools), and soccer (12 schools). There is a decided majority of schools in which classes were conducted in only one (49.6%) or two (33.9%) sport disciplines.

The territorial reach of sport championship schools is decidedly smaller, for they are limited to 10 provinces, whereas it is difficult to speak of a decided advantage for any of them. The program of training classes encompasses 19 sport disciplines. Besides swimming, carried on at five schools, and track and field, carried on at three, the majority of these disciplines are limited to the territory of one school.

Thus, it can be stated that the territorial reach of sport schools and sport championship schools, as well as the disciplines and work conditions carried on in them, do not continue to correspond to the principles that have been specified in earlier documents and research analyses (Ziemilska, 1984, 1987).

A certain hope for change in the activities of sport schools is connected with the new conception of their functioning. Legally, a basis for the functioning of the sport school system is given by the Educational System Act from September 7, 1991. The entry about the existence of sport schools was also introduced in the Physical Culture Act and the amended Territorial and Administrative Self-Government Act. However, there is not much in this conception about attempts at structural changes. A positive element in this area is the perceived need for cooperation of many departments and regional self-governments.

However, many formulations regarding the conception itself (the programs of schools and the financing of institutions) are reminiscent of the formal basis for establishment and functioning of the system of educating athletically talented youths concluded in the Ministry of Education Order from May 11, 1977.

Sport Participation

Sport participation and dropout rates vary, and result from reasons inherent in sport itself as well as conditions not directly connected with it. These factors are well presented in reports by Stanczuk (1989) and Ziemilska (1987). The first group of factors, which may be defined as biological, includes: state of health, susceptibility to frequent injury, and inadequate somatic constitution. The second group of factors, which are psychological, includes: inconstancy of emotional and affective states, revaluation of sport activity, lack of developmental perspectives, and discovery of a different area of activity allowing for greater self-realization. The third group of factors, defined as social, includes: the relation of the family to sport activity, interpersonal contacts in the training group, the athlete-coach relationship, and conflict in the fundamental social role of the young athlete—that is, difficulties reconciling learning with sport. The fourth group of factors includes material conditions connected with the training base, sport equipment, medical care, and services on behalf of the young athlete.

Promotional Campaigns

The state of participation by children and youths in sport indicates a great deal of institutional and organizational chaos. On the one hand, it is caused by the process of change taking place in Poland, and on the other hand by the association shaped over the years in many circles of sport as a spectacle to be viewed, and not as a lifestyle, or as one of the means of health and personal competence.

A great hope for reviving the sport activity of youths is connected with the establishment of nonpublic schools, the creation of authentic, authoritative local governments, and the transfer to them by 1994 of the entirety of matters connected with managing schools and their functioning.

The outcome of these changes will be a departure from the hitherto centralized organizations responsible for the development of physical culture, on both a macro and a micro scale, including in this the problem of youth sports. Serving this change further will be the promotion of local and national meets. An example of the former are the streetball tournaments conducted in many localities for the last few years, organized in conjunction with the Polish Basketball Federation and well-known foreign commercial firms.

In June of 1993 the second National Nonpublic Schools Sport Competitions took place in Spala. Since 1990, the Warsaw Amateur Basketball Movement has been dynamically expanding beyond the SZS structures. It is directed by local physical education teachers. A considerable role in the propagation of this sport discipline should be attributed to Polish television, which, through its transmission of NBA games, presents basketball at its highest level.

New sport disciplines are also being propagated which appeal mostly to children and youths. An example of such a discipline is the team game called intercross, developed in southern Poland by activists of the recently created District Federation of Unfamiliar Sports in Legnica.

Out of the proposals contained in many legislative acts, it appears that the regional administrative entities (i.e., on the district level) will be realizing assignments connected with the sporting activity of children and youths. As always, the quality of these activities ought not to be identified exclusively with the record of the act and program, but rather with the elimination of situations of particularism with breaking down of disintegrating divisions as well as meeting the needs of the local environment. It is also anticipated that the newly arising large provinces will take over the role of macroregions, which are to be called sport centers.

A totally different approach to the participation of children and youths in sport may be perceived in the expanding Catholic sport associations in Poland. The founders' meeting of the Salezjan Sports Organization in Salos took place on May 6, 1992. Salezjan educational sport, through sport and game competitions, attempts to develop such values as health, physical fitness, and beauty, as well as the search for the final objective and meaning in life.

One of the more important centers in this movement is Lubin, where the Salezjan Sport Center, Amico, is active. In the Salos National Championships Amico has already achieved its first successes. Ballplayers born in 1975 and 1978 advanced to the finals, taking fourth and third places respectively. For the 1992-1993 season, Lubin submitted teams of older players and younger players for games conducted through the Legnica District Soccer Federation.

For the last few years, youths may also participate in sport in reactivated organizations such as the YMCA and the Sokol Gymnastic Association.

An interesting organizational proposal in the area of physical education and sport is Parafiada, which has been placed on the calendar of Polish sport for good. The Parafiada movement assumes threefold activity aimed at simultaneous formation of the mind, heart, and body. The name Parafiada indicates the range, direction, and place for this activity. The second part refers to the deeply inherent experiences of Olympic agonies in European culture. It is the name of the personal tournament organized since 1989 by the Piarist monastic order, which is the author of the idea and the main organizer of Parafiadas up until now.

The Catholic Sport Association of the Polish Republic (KSS RP), which was recently organized, resolved to make Parafiada V its main tournament in 1993. The association intends to establish sport clubs in parishes, as is practiced in many Western nations.

Previously, Parafiadas took place successively in Krakow (I and II), Bolszewo (III), and Warsaw (IV). The fourth assembled groups of youths from Belarus besides the representatives of many parishes from the entire nation. The establishment of the Parafiada movement was presented at the Fourth World Congress dedicated to the problem of Sport for All (Joniec, 1992), and Parafiada was included on the calendar of world sport tournaments by the Federation Internationale Catholique d'Education Physique et Sportive.

The task of Parafiada V (which took place in Warsaw in late June and early July of 1993) was, among other things, the appointment of representatives of the Catholic Sport Association of the Polish Republic to the Seventh World Youth Day in Denver, Colorado, in the United States, and to the tournament of the Catholic Association of Physical Education and Sport (FICEP).

The presentation at the conclusion of the report of programs and organizational solutions showed the need for looking at sport in a different way and at the same time ordinarily—as a social movement inclining young people toward a healthy lifestyle and specific habits connected with it. However, such an understanding of sport is one we are only starting to learn.

Conclusion

The tendencies, statements, and data discussed in this chapter may be summarized as follows:

- Sport activity of children and youths, which was until now very strongly connected with the selection of athletes for performance sport, is gradually being transformed into a spontaneous and natural form of fulfilling motor activity.
- The realistic functioning of Sport for All will be assisted through organizational solutions characteristic of a decentralized system of sport administration.
- The tempo of these changes will run its course more quickly in environments with reformist tendencies, in which initiatives arising from the ranks as well as spontaneous innovations are connected with the creation of democratic mechanisms.
- Assistance for such a method of procedure will be, after a period of adversity, the creation of an educational conception, normative acts, programs, plans, and procedures connected with the varied needs, possibilities, and interests of children and youths.

References

Joniec, J. (1992, November). *Parafiada as the practical system to realize the idea of sport for all.* Paper presented at the Fourth World Congress on Sport for All, Varna, Bulgaria.

Sawinski, R. (Ed.) (1992). *Report by the Office of Physical Culture and Tourism.* Warsaw, Poland: Statistical Publishers Institution.

Stanczuk, K. (1989). *Reasons for resignation from sports careers by athletically talented youths.* Warsaw, Poland: AWF Publishers.

Sulisz, S. (1988). *Track and field in the School Sports Club.* Warsaw, Poland: SiT.

Sulisz, S. (1991). *Physical education in elementary schools.* Warsaw, Poland: WSiP.

Sulisz, S. (1992). *School physical education and preparation of youths for participation in sport.* Warsaw, Poland: AWF Publishers.

Ziemilska, A. (Ed.) (1984). *Qualified youth sport: Organization of training and health problems.* Warsaw, Poland: AWF Publishers.

Ziemilska, A. (1987). *Youth sports: Conditions and consequences.* Warsaw, Poland: AWF Publishers.

Chapter 17 Portugal

Carlos Gonçalves

There are about 9.8 million inhabitants in Portugal in an area of 92,000 km², or 106 inhabitants per km². There is a considerable variation in the concentration of population in the 18 districts, with the majority spread along the seacoast. Azores and Madeira are autonomous regions with their own governmental bodies.

The Organizational Network

The umbrella organization of Portuguese sport was, from 1933 to 1993, the *Direcção Geral dos Desportos* (Directorate of Sport), a governmental department of the Ministry of Education acting as the normative institution for national sport (see Figure 17.1).

A new Sport Law passed in 1990, which settles the sport system, is being implemented progressively. As a result, in April 1993, the *Instituto do Desporto* (Sport Institute) was created, integrating the Directorate of Sport and the Fund for Sport Development. The main aim of this new governmental body is to stimulate and support the development of sport at all levels.

The *Conselho Superior do Desporto* (Superior Sport Council) consists of 23 members and is a governmental consulting body which is in charge of studying and suggesting sport policy.

The nongovernmental sport structure is mainly based in the 64 national sport federations, the district associations, and the roughly 6,500 sport clubs. In 1993, a new nongovernmental body was created, the Sport Confederation of Portugal, which comprises 32 national sport federations.

The Portugal Olympic Committee, founded in 1910, is responsible for the development of the *Olympic ideal* and for the organization and direction of the activities related to participation in the Olympic Games.

Opportunities for involvement of children and youths, both competitively and recreationally, may be provided by schools, sport clubs, and other organizations such as governmental sport bodies, municipal sport services, and private sport centers.

Funding for Youth Sport

Financial support for school sport comes from one major source: the government (Ministry of Education), which provides about 90% of their total funding. Private sponsorship contributes about 5%. The schools receive some funds from the municipalities for material and transportation. Parents' associations provide only

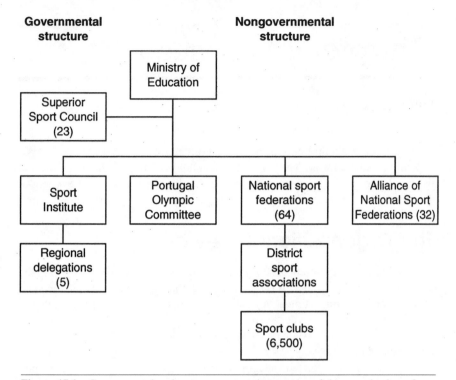

Figure 17.1   Governmental and nongovernmental structures of the organization of sport in Portugal.

a minimal support. There are no registration fees for the pupils participating in competitive school sport. Registration fees, sponsorship, fundraising activities, and special contributions from the municipalities and from the national government for equipment needs are the five main sources of sport clubs.

As for the national sport federations, about 75% of their funding is granted by a governmental body, the Fund for Sport Development (now integrated into the Sport Institute), with revenues from the lottery. Property income taxes and sponsorship are the other significant sources of their funding.

Commercial sponsorship has shown a marked increase over the last 5 years, with various companies wishing to be associated with youth sport. Training programs, minisport events, championship competitions, and fair play campaigns have been the main focus of their attention.

Club Sport Programs

The 6,500 sport clubs existing in Portugal as of 1990 play an important role in the youth sport organization. The emphasis on local, recreational, or competitive sport programs varies with the social traditions and depend on the aims of each sport club. No data are available to estimate the number of youth members and the mean annual fees they pay.

Table 17.1   Estimate of Participation in Competitive Sport Club Activities (%)

Sport % by gender	Boys (n = 103,058) 79	Girls (n = 27,042) 21
Basketball	5	7
Handball	7	8
Gymnastics	1	8
Judo	2	6
Rollerhockey	3	–
Rollerskating	1	2
Rhythmic gymnastics	–	3
Soccer	40	1
Swimming	4	7
Table tennis	2	2
Tennis	2	4
Track and field	12	22
Volleyball	2	9
Other sports	19	21

Note. From *Atlas Desportivo Nacional: Banco de Dados* [National Sport Chart: Data Bank] by Direcção Geral dos Desportos, 1988, Lisboa, Portugal: Author. Copyright 1988 by Direcção Geral dos Desportos. Adapted by permission.

About 130,000 youngsters, or 6% of the population 6 to 18, participated in competitive sport club activities (see Table 17.1).

Soccer is undoubtedly the number one sport among Portuguese boys. Nevertheless, track and field, handball, and basketball are also popular competitive sports among both boys and girls.

Some sports are strongly related to gender, as is evident in the fact that 98% of soccer and 99% of rollerhockey youth players are boys (see Table 17.2).

In all the age groups the young athletes participate at least twice a week (4 hours total) in sport club training sessions. However, the top young athletes participate frequently at least in a daily session (10-12 hours per week). The gymnasts and swimmers participate often in two daily sessions (15-16 hours per week).

According to the latest data available, about 202,000 youngsters were involved at least twice a week, in organized noncompetitive sporting activities practiced in sport clubs, health centers, private fitness studios, or municipal sport grounds (Direcção Geral dos Desportos, 1988). Soccer, swimming, and track and field for the boys and gymnastics, swimming, aerobics, and dance for the girls are the favorite sports. In the noncompetitive sporting activities, with the exception of soccer for the boys, the preferences go to individual or noncontact sports.

Table 17.2   Differences of Practiced Sports According to Gender (%)

Sport	Boys	Girls	Total
Soccer	98	2	33
Track and field	76	24	14
Handball	81	19	7
Basketball	80	20	5
Volleyball	55	45	4
Gymnastics	49	51	3
Swimming	75	25	3
Judo	73	27	3
Tennis	73	27	3
Rollerhockey	99	1	2
Other sports	75	25	23

Note. From *Atlas Desportivo Nacional: Banco de Dados* [National Sport Chart: Data Bank] by Direcção Geral dos Desportos, 1988, Lisboa, Portugal: Author. Copyright 1988 by Direcção Geral dos Desportos. Adapted by permission.

Table 17.3   Participation by Gender in Competitive or in Organized Noncompetitive Sporting Activities (%)

Age groups	Competitive sport (sport clubs)		Organized noncompetitive sport	
	Boys	Girls	Boys	Girls
Less than 10 years	75	25	62	38
10 to 14 years	78	22	68	32
15 to 18 years	84	16	77	23
Total	79	21	69	31

Note. From *Atlas Desportivo Nacional: Banco de Dados* [National Sport Chart: Data Bank] by Direcção Geral dos Desportos, 1988, Lisboa, Portugal: Author. Copyright 1988 by Direcção Geral dos Desportos. Adapted by permission.

Girls represent 21% of the competitive sport participants and 31% of the participants in organized noncompetitive sporting activities (see Table 17.3). The percentage of boys participating in competitive activities is greater, in all age groups, than that of those participating in noncompetitive activities. In contrast, the percentage of girls participating in recreational activities is always greater than that of those participating in competitive sport.

Table 17.4   Age Related Participation in Competitive and in Organized
Noncompetitive Sporting Activities (%)

Age groups	Competitive sport (sport clubs)	Organized noncompetitive sport
Less than 10 years	14	28
10 to 14 years	43	35
15 to 18 years	43	37

Note. From *Desporto Escolar: Relatório do Ano Lectivo 1990-91* [School Sport:
Report on the 1990-91 School Year] (pp. 16-17), by G. Pires, 1991 Lisboa, Portugal:
Ministério da Educação. Copyright 1991 by Ministério da Educação. Adapted by
permission.

The largest percentage of young people participating in either competitive or
recreational sport activities is in the age group of 15 to 18 years (see Table 17.4).
However, there has been, over the last 15 years, a progressive increase in the
percentage of participants in competitive sport among 10-to-14-year-olds, and a
decrease among 15-to-18-year-olds.

At the same time, we observe in this 15-to-18-year-old age group an increase
in the number of youngsters who take part in organized noncompetitive or in
informal sporting activities.

The age at which children begin their participation in competitive sport varies
from 7 (gymnastics) to 10 (e.g., handball, tennis, and volleyball) with the majority
beginning at 8 (e.g., basketball, soccer, swimming, and track and field).

Data available estimate that about 430,000 children and youths participate in
informal sporting activities, namely jogging, soccer, biking, tennis, surfing, and
rollerskating, at least once a week.

Few national sport federations have a youth department with a specific sport
policy. However, some of them have minisport programs with adapted rules (e.g.,
swimming, tennis, judo) or technical skills programs (soccer). The track and field
federation, in cooperation with a national newspaper, has organized the "First
Step" program successfully.

From 1987 to 1992, a plan for coaching education in Portugal was developed,
divided in four levels, with the Monitor One being the first. This was mainly
aimed at those who were going to work with the youngsters.

The degree of Monitor was obtained after a course of 40 hours (containing basic
subjects and sport-specific training) organized by the national sport federations
according to a program designed by the Directorate of Sport. This program was
accompanied by a textbook, the *Handbook of Monitor Coaching Education*.
About 3,200 monitors from 17 sports participated in this program.

The data estimate that about 25% of those working in youth sport have followed
a youth sport coaching education program. The majority of youth sport coaches

learn "how to coach" from their own experiences as players or through the observation of top-level coaches live or via television.

The future education of youth sport coaches depends on the new guidelines for global coaching education. The major trend is to give to national federations the total responsibility in the conception and organization of the program.

School Sport Programs

School sport is considered an extracurricular activity in which pupils can participate as volunteers. At the primary level (ages 6 to 10), in which children are taught by classroom teachers who are not "specialists" in physical education, the Sport Institute, in cooperation with many municipalities, provides a range of sport recreation opportunities for children, including an introduction to games, minisports, and gymnastics. Neighbor schools organize sport meetings from time to time. At the end of each school term or school year, the meetings involve all the schools in each area. There is no organized competitive sport in primary schools. In the school year 1989-90, about 297,000 children, or 40% of the total primary school population, participated in those activities.

As for secondary schools (ages 11 to 18) intramural activities are organized by the school sport clubs (which are multisport clubs), with the support of physical education teachers, who coordinate all the events.

In the 1990-91 school year, about 251,400 pupils between 10 and 18, or 22% of the secondary school population, participated in intramural competitions or in regular recreational sport activities organized by the schools, including 29 different sports, such as soccer, basketball, handball, volleyball, track and field, table tennis, gymnastics, swimming, and tennis (Pires, 1991).

School sport is supervised by a specific sector of the Ministry of Education. Interschool competitions are organized at local, district, provincial, and national levels. Competition levels are organized according to age groups:

- Ages 10 to 12: local and district competitions.
- Ages 13 to 14: local, district, and provincial competitions.
- Ages 15 to 16: local, district, provincial, and national competitions.

Only the 15-16 age group have competitions organized nationally and only in five sports: soccer (five players), basketball, handball, volleyball, and track and field (see Table 17.5).

About 63,200 youngsters, 7% of the total population of this age group (10 to 16), participate in competitive school sport up to the national level. Girls constitute 34% of the participants. The pattern of participation was about 33% among those 10 to 12, 35% for those 13 to 14, and 32% for those 15 to 16. Above the age of 15, youngsters tend to decrease their participation in competitive school sport.

The participation rates by sport and gender are shown in Table 17.6.

Soccer is the most popular school sport (28%), followed by track and field (23%) and basketball (20%). However, for girls, volleyball is the most attractive sport, followed by track and field and basketball. In all age groups, youngsters participate twice a week (4 hours altogether) in school sport club training sessions.

Table 17.5   Estimate of Participation in Competitive School Sport (ages 10 to 16) by Gender and Age Group (%)

| | Age group and gender | | | | | |
| | 10 to 12 years | | 13 to 14 years | | 15 to 16 years | |
Sport	Boys	Girls	Boys	Girls	Boys	Girls
Basketball	62	38	65	35	68	32
Handball	66	34	68	32	68	32
Soccer	91	9	89	11	73	27
Track and field	54	46	58	42	59	41
Volleyball	65	35	54	46	51	49
Total	67	33	66	34	64	36
N=63,200	14,005	6,770	14,580	7,356	13,110	7,379
% by age group	33		35		32	

Note. From *Desporto Escolar: Relatório do Ano Lectivo 1990-91* [School Sport: Report on the 1990-91 School Year] (pp. 16-17), by G. Pires, 1991 Lisboa, Portugal: Ministério da Educação. Copyright 1991 by Ministério da Educação. Adapted by permission.

Table 17.6   Estimate of Participation in Competitive School Sport (ages 10 to 16) by Sport and Gender (%)

Sport	Boys	Girls	Total
Basketball	66	34	20
Handball	67	33	14
Soccer (5)	85	15	28
Track and field	57	43	23
Volleyball	55	45	15
Total	66	34	–
N =	41,695	21,505	–

Note. From *Desporto Escolar: Relatório do Ano Lectivo 1990-91* [School Sport: Report on the 1990-91 School Year] (p. 17), by G. Pires, 1991 Lisboa, Portugal: Ministério da Educação. Copyright 1991 by Ministério da Educação. Adapted by permission.

The relations between school sport and national federations have been difficult, causing frequent conflicts. In the 1992-93 school year the number of pupils affiliated with a sport federation was only two per team, at any level of school sport competition. However, youngsters can take part freely in other sports, different from the one in which they are affiliated with sport federations. In 1990-91, there were 48 school sport teams affiliated with 9 sport federations and competing at this level. Despite the problems of conciliating schooling with the needs of top young athletes, there are no special sport schools.

In school sport it is assumed that if a person has a teaching certificate, he or she is qualified to coach. In the 1990-91 school year, all the teams participating at national level competitions were coached by teachers, 78% of whom were physical education teachers and 22% teachers of other subjects. These teachers receive an extra payment (according to their qualifications as teachers). If necessary, schools may hire non-teacher coaches to meet the needs, based on these teachers' experience in playing or coaching the sport.

One of the major problems in school sport comes from the lack of sport facilities in most schools. In fact, the latest estimates (from the 1987-88 school year) showed that 27% of the schools had no facilities at all, 13% had only outdoor sport facilities, and only about 60% had both indoor and outdoor facilities. However, since 1989 the government, in cooperation with some municipalities, has been leading a specific program to provide community and school sport facilities.

Sport Participation

In 1989 the data available estimated the number of youngsters between 6 and 18 at about 1.9 million (19.2% of the total population).

Despite the decline in the birth rate which occurred in the country during the 1980s, the percentage of children and youths involved in recreational or in competitive sport has increased since 1974 (Direcção Geral dos Desportos, 1988).

Dropout

A study conducted at Oeiras community among sport participants, boys and girls from ages 11 to 15, shows some trends with regard to youth sport participation and dropout. Children and youths were found to be motivated to participate in sport programs for a variety of reasons. The most common reasons given were to improve skills and learn new ones, to succeed or win, to be with friends and make new friends, to be physically fit, to have fun, and to please parents.

The reasons given for dropping out of sport clubs (basketball, swimming, and gymnastics) were: difficulties in reconciling studies with the practice schedules; little participation in competitions (basketball); other more important leisure interests; boredom (monotonous practices, bad ambiance). Decisions about quitting sport were based, however, on a combination of reasons. Socialization processes seem to play an important reinforcing role in participants' leaving sport.

About 78% of those who drop out from basketball mentioned that they would prefer to be on a losing team participating regularly in the competitions than to be seated on the bench of a winning team. Otherwise, 74% mentioned their intentions to be involved again in competitive sport (changing the activity or the sport club).

Dropout increases clearly at the age of 14, after an experience of 3 to 4 years of competitive sport. Girls begin the dropping out earlier and are less ready than boys to be involved again in competitive sport.

Youth Sport Research

There is not a systematic interest in studying the phenomenon of youth sport in Portugal. The most significant studies have been associated with the presence of the graduate programs at the Faculty of Sport Science and Physical Education (Porto University) and at the Faculty of Human Motricity (Technical University of Lisbon). Research has focused particularly on the areas of anthropometric assessment, growth and development, and physical fitness (Costa & Maia, 1990; Janeira, 1989; Sobral, 1988).

Some other descriptive studies have been conducted by sport researchers in topics such as fair play and youth sport (Gonçalves, 1990), children's participation in and motives for dropping out of sport programs (Gonçalves, 1992; Serpa, 1990), and the system of competitions for youngsters (Lima, 1989).

Trends

According to data available in three studies of sport participation carried out in Portugal, it is possible to find some trends (Direcção Geral dos Desportos, 1988, 1990; Gonçalves, 1992):

• The percentage of youngsters who practice competitive sport, in sport clubs, increased about 3% in the last decade. The most significant increase is among girls and in the age group of 10 to 14 years.

• There is a progressive increase in the number of youngsters who give up competitive sport after the age of 14. Several reasons contribute to this tendency. Otherwise the agonistic element is no longer the only motivation for the sport practice.

• There is an increasing number of girls participating more intensively in sporting activities, not only in traditional female activities, but also in those that had been considered specifically for boys.

• There has been much development of sport recreational activities in community clubs, gymnastic studios, and fitness centers. Most sport clubs, on the other hand, became "specialized" in competitive sport and failed to adopt strategies and models in order to allow new sport practices.

• In competition, youngsters tend to favor team sports, but in recreation the preference is for individual sports (viz., swimming), noncontact sports, and others where a taste for experiencing adventure, exploring the unknown, and facing risks are significant motivations for participation.

• Professional practice, as a result of an earlier specialization, namely in soccer, has become more important.

• There has been a marked increase in commercial sponsorship of some youth sport events.

Promotional Campaigns

Specific sport activities are organized for young people by a number of organizations. Since 1986, the ex-Directorate of Sport (now the Sport Institute) has been developing a program titled Sport Holidays for the leisure time of students during school holidays. Traditional games, orienteering, canoeing, basketball, and handball are the most popular sport activities in the program, with about 250,000 participants during 1990. Simultaneously, about 5,000 youngsters participated in a specific program, Sport and Disabled Youngsters, with adapted activities.

Some municipalities, beyond the support given to school sport, have, based on local facilities in their area, conducted youth sport programs with the aim of introducing children and youngsters to sport, through recreational and competitive activities (e.g. city games, sporting weekends) involving the youngsters who do not participate in school sport, or in sport clubs. At this level, soccer, basketball, track and field, chess, volleyball, and tennis are the most popular sports.

Conclusion

Despite the increasing numbers of children and youths taking part in sporting activities, either in competition or in recreation, after 1974, the involvement of the majority of Portuguese youths in sport programs is far from a reality.

Some areas are identified as needing improvement:

- The introduction of more sporting opportunities and facilities in schools, sport clubs, and communities.

- A consistent development model, respecting the patterns of growth and development and the specific needs of young people at the different stages. Youth sport programs should be appropriately designed regarding the organization, the system of competitions, and the education of the large body of adults involved: leaders, administrators, and parents.

- Youth coach education programs, as a significant contribution not only to the adoption of the most appropriate training programs for young elite athletes, but also for those more appropriate for developmental sport at younger ages.

- An increase in research relating specifically to youth sport.

An understanding of the difference between the goals established by children and youngsters when practicing sport and the competitive targets in adult sport will be a decisive factor in the campaigns in favor of youth sport. Besides the fulfillment of the specific needs mentioned above, the development of youth sport will be enhanced by their position in society and by the development of the society in general.

References

Costa, A., & Maia, J. (1990, May). *Sexual dimorphism of youth track and field athletes*. Paper presented at the International Congress on Youth, Leisure and Physical Activity and Kinanthropometry IV, Brussels, Belgium.

Direcção Geral dos Desportos. (1988). *Atlas desportivo nacional: Banco de dados* [National sport chart: Data bank]. Lisboa, Portugal: Author.

Direcção Geral dos Desportos. (1990). *Programa integrado de desenvolvimento desportivo* [Integrated program of sport development]. Lisboa, Portugal: Author.

Gonçalves, C. (1990). Fair play and youth sport participants. In R. Telama, L. Laakso, M. Piéron, I. Ruoppila, & V. Vihko (Eds.), *Physical education and life-long physical activity* (pp. 137-143). Jyväskylä, Finland: AIESEP.

Gonçalves, C. (1992, July). *La practica deportiva de los niños y jovenes* [Children's and youths' sport participation]. Paper presented at the Olympic Scientific Congress. Malaga, Spain.

Janeira, M. (1989, June). *The relationship of somatotype and selected anthropometric measures to basketball performance in young male players*. Paper presented at AIESEP Convention on Movement and Sport, a Challenge for Life-Long Learning, Jyväskylä, Finland.

Lima, T. (1989). *Competicões para jovens* [Competitive sport and the youngsters]. Oeiras, Portugal: Câmara Municipal de Oeiras.

Pires, G. (1991). *Desporto escolar: Relatorio do ano lectivo 1990-91* [School sport: Report on the 1990-91 school year]. Lisboa, Portugal: Ministério da Educação.

Serpa, S. (1990). Motivação para a pratica desportiva [Youth sport participation motives]. In Ministério da Educação, *Desporto Escolar* (pp. 101-106). Lisboa, Portugal: Ministério da Educação.

Sobral, F. (1988, July). *Biosocial dimensions of motor performance: Facts and hypotheses from the Azores growth study*. Paper presented at AIESEP World Congress on Humanism and New Technology in Physical Education and Sport, Madrid, Spain.

Chapter 18 Scotland

Leo B. Hendry
John G. Love

The population of Scotland is slightly more than 5 million, with a fairly equal balance between the genders, and a youth population of over 1 million. According to population estimates, there are 1,168,582 Scots under the age of 18 years (Registrar General Scotland, 1990). Scotland, like Wales and Northern Ireland, is governed by Parliament in London. Nevertheless, Scotland has its own Minister of State and Ministers for Health, for Education, and for Sport, within the Scottish Office in Edinburgh. There are also distinctions between Scotland and England in their separate educational and legal systems. Equally important, the Scots perceive themselves as a separate nation with their own history and traditions. In modern guise one manifestation of this national pride and patriotism coalesces around the national rugby stadium in Edinburgh at the home international matches, with spectators wearing kilts and tartan scarves, waving St. Andrews banners, and singing "The Flower of Scotland"—an unofficial national anthem!

The Organizational Network

Each of the four countries within the United Kingdom has its own sport council with the (English) Sports Council in London taking the lead on certain Great Britain and international issues. Thus, within the United Kingdom various national and local government initiatives have provided a firm baseline for the creation of a network of sport provision which runs from schools to adult society. In 1983, the Sports Council published a discussion paper, "Leisure Policy for the Future," which set out the pattern of leisure-time use in a changing British society and pointed toward the need for coordination among voluntary bodies, commercial and private organizations, local authorities, statutory agencies, the central government, and the leisure industries. The paper also indicated that ordinary people themselves were involved as leisure providers since much leisure is home- and community-based, in which people themselves are the prime movers. The paper emphasized the important role of schools in introducing young people to sporting and other leisure pursuits and motivating them toward active leisure across the lifespan. It did, however, offer a timely warning that for some pupils the association of leisure pursuits with school discipline and control could alienate them from future sport participation. The emphasis on the coordination of various agencies in provision and the important initiating role of schools has been carried forward in such reports as "Sport and Young People" (Sports Council, 1988), which, in its recommendations, indicated varying but coordinated roles for the central government, local authorities, schools, teacher training institutions, the physical education profession, the sport councils and regional councils for sport and recreation, the Central Council of Physical Recreation, governing bodies of sport, local sport clubs and organizations, youth services, coaching associations, the national children's play and recreation unit, parents, and the media.

These English policy documents were matched by a report on school-aged sport in Scotland (Scottish Sports Council, 1988), which again emphasized the coordinating roles of various agencies in the promotion of sport ranging from the primary school through voluntary organizations to the private sector. In looking toward the next century, the Scottish Sports Council (1989a) also produced, after extensive consultation, "Sport 2000: A Strategic Approach to the Development of Sport in Scotland," which again stressed the need for related roles among social agencies, the need for greater cooperation and more flexible arrangements among the public, voluntary, and private sectors, and the need for new ways of funding sporting facilities and delivering services. Given these policies and aims it is possible to identify four main types of organized provision for sport beyond the physical education curriculum in schools: extracurricular school sport, sport clubs, youth groups, and local authority leisure programs and provision.

School Sport Programs

In Scottish schools pupils are offered a fairly traditional range of sports and physical activities. Beyond scheduled physical education, schools offer sports and physical activities within their extracurricular programs, although the range of activities is dependent on staff interests, skills, and commitment. Activities can vary from school to school (Hendry, 1978). It is fair to comment that extracurricular activities focus mainly on intra- and interschool team and individual competitions. The Scottish Sports Council study (1988) found that traditional competitive team sports dominated extracurricular sports, with 68% of schools providing soccer, 43% hockey, and 34% rugby. *Individual* activities were also primarily based on competitive involvement. Activities with little competitive content such as fitness and weight training or dance were only offered by a minority of schools (17% and 16%, respectively). Many schools also offer leisure education programs that run on a weekly basis but are more usually blocked into a two- or three-week program, often in the summer term. These leisure opportunities provide a wide range of possibilities for pupils and extend their range to include noncompetitive games, activities, and outdoor pursuits.

Community Youth Organizations

Community youth organizations—both youth clubs and uniformed groups like Scouts and Girl Guides—include sports within their programs and, on a more casual basis, sport centers and community centers offer facilities for young people's sporting and leisure interests in many areas of the country. In the wake of the Wolfenden Report (1960) and the European Sports Charter (1975), the social and recreational needs of young people have been clearly recognized in Scotland. Implicit in such reports has been the desire to maximize the integrative functions of sport in order to encourage young people to become more socially involved in their local communities. Furthermore, such reports aim to promote healthy and active lifestyles among adolescents which they may take with them into adulthood.

Thus, in summary, physical activities and sports figure prominently in most leisure education programs in school and community and can be seen as a potential route for future involvement with initiatives like the "Ever Thought of Sport?" campaign aimed at young people in Scotland (Walker, 1987). Within this structure the Scottish Sports Council has a crucial and major role in linking with the Scottish Office Education Department, Governing Bodies of Sport, the Scottish Community Education Council, the Scottish Standing Conference of Voluntary Youth Organisations, and a range of other statutory and voluntary agencies (see Figure 18.1). These attempts to promote leisure and sport activities can create involvement patterns, attitudes, and perceptions in young people about sports and leisure pursuits that may persist into later adolescence and adulthood.

Sport Participation

Given this network of sport provision for young people in Scotland, are Scottish children enthusiastic sport participants?

Preadolescent Sport

If we look at the preadolescent period we find that as young people emerge from their childhood years they engage in play activities involving skipping games, ball games, and playground games that are basically traditional, and that these play patterns are influenced by family background. These games are slowly eroded by a more adult concept of leisure. Hendry and Percy (1981) found that by the upper stages of the primary school, social pressures and the influence of the media were pushing boys and girls into much more gender-specific roles in terms of their leisure and sporting activities. As Hendry, Shucksmith, Love, and Glendinning (1993) have shown, there is a decreased involvement in organized clubs and activities by the later stages of primary school (see Figure 18.2), although they still remain popular leisure pursuits for young people in preadolescence.

Such activities include youth clubs, sport clubs, school clubs, youth groups, and church groups, almost all of which make provision for young people's sporting endeavors in a variety of individual and team sports from soccer and netball to swimming, rounders, and athletics. Nevertheless, in terms of overall sport activity, a 7-year nationwide longitudinal study of 10,000 young people (Hendry, Shucksmith, & Love, 1989) found that boys' participation rates were higher than girls'. Swimming (19%), dancing (17%), and gymnastics (12%) were the most popular activities for 9-to-10-year-old girls. This rank ordering had not changed by the end of primary school days, but the participation rates had dropped

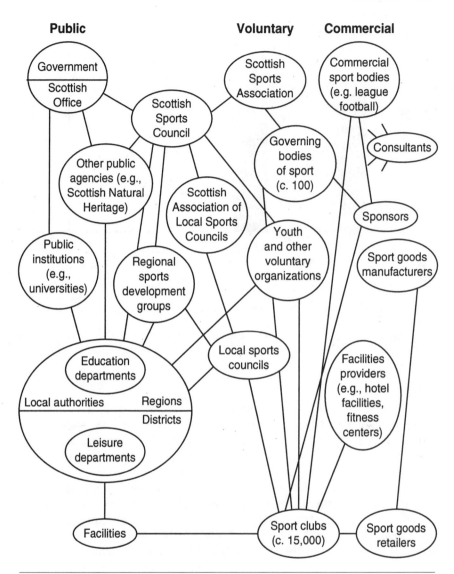

Public   **Voluntary**   **Commercial**

Figure 18.1   The structure of sport in Scotland.
Note. Courtesy of the Scottish Sports Council.

except for swimming (swimming 21%, dancing 11%, and gymnastics 9%). The most popular activities in extracurricular teams/clubs for 9-to-10-year-old boys were soccer (30%), swimming (21%), and martial arts (8%). This ranking did not change for the older boys in the primary survey. Percentages belonging to soccer teams/clubs rose slightly (to 32%) and fell a little for the other sports (swimming 20%, martial arts 6%).

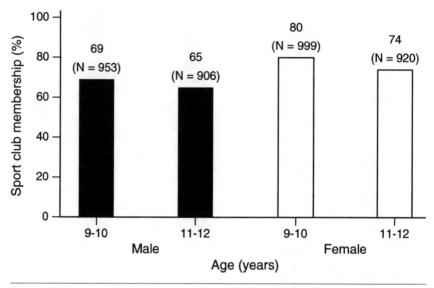

Figure 18.2   Preadolescent leisure activities: Percentage belonging to organized clubs or groups.
Note. From *Young People's Leisure and Lifestyles*, by L.B. Hendry, J. Shucksmith, J.G. Love, and A. Glendinning, 1993, London: Routledge. Copyright 1993 by Routledge. Reprinted by permission.

Hendry, et al. (1993) found that the main reasons given by preadolescent young people for attending sport clubs and other groups are going with friends, learning new skills, doing different activities, and doing things that are "more enjoyable than staying at home." There are significant changes, between the ages of 9 to 10 and 11 to 12 years, in the reasons given for such club membership. Although going with friends and learning and doing activities remain important, the emphasis shifts from the organized element of clubs and groups (sports, uniforms and rules, and the influence of adult figures—sport coaches, leaders, and parents) toward the more informal aspects of group membership (meeting other boys and girls away from the family home). The social element of meeting other children seems to be more important for girls whereas the attendance of boys at clubs and other adult-led activities is more strongly influenced by their parents' wishes. Even at this preadolescent stage there is an undercurrent of adult influence, perhaps especially that of parents, directing young people toward competitive sport in a scaled-down version of adult "models."

Adolescent Sport

In the secondary school setting the evidence available indicates that it is middle-class pupils who "do well academically" who are by and large the young people who take part in extracurricular activities including sports and physical recreation (Hendry, 1978; Hendry et al., 1989, 1993; Reid, 1972). Extracurricular school sport, however, has a differential impact on pupils. For many there is a gradual decline in interest in sport across the secondary school years, as has been noted (e.g., Hendry et al., 1989, 1993; Ward, Hardman, & Almond, 1968), and this decline becomes more marked as pupils reach the minimum school-leaving age (i.e., 16 in Britain) (see e.g., Saunders, 1979). The structure of the programs and the ensuing interactional processes between teacher and taught create a lessening in pupils' involvement. This is especially so for working-class pupils and young women (Hendry et al., 1989; Hendry & Thorpe, 1977; Moir, 1977; Scraton, 1986). It has been argued that this decline in interest in school sports is a reflection of a more general syndrome of school rejection (see Hendry & Thorpe, 1977). What is clear is that school influences provide both important constraints and opportunities for young people's sport and leisure interests.

An early attempt to study psychosocial and other factors related to extracurricular school sport was carried out by Hendry (1978) with over 3,000 adolescents aged 15 and 16 years in 15 comprehensive schools. Pupils were classified on the basis of their involvement in extracurricular voluntary school sport as competitors, recreational participants, or nonparticipants. Just under 60% of young men and around 70% of young women chose *not* to participate in extracurricular sporting activities. Hendry's conclusion was that certain personal characteristics may be used by teachers within the extracurricular program as a basis for differential treatment of pupils, rather in the same way that classroom teachers selectively encourage more academically able pupils. It seems that the interactions between teacher and pupils, either in the classroom or on the playing field, may be crucial in conveying messages of praise or disapproval, attention or neglect, which subsequently influence different pupils' attitudes, interests, and involvement in school activities.

Extracurricular sport for young women in most secondary schools remains dominated by team games, and team games are problematic for female participants. Young women's cultures emphasize the "best friend," or small groupings, and do not necessarily relate easily to the collective team situation. Sport stresses the collective through team games, gym clubs, dance groups, and athletic teams. Young women often reject these situations as incompatible with the expectations of adult femininity (Leaman, 1984). In the studies by Kane (1974) and Hendry (1978), preparation for leisure was stated as a primary aim for sports. This, however, is also problematic for adolescent young women. Recent work in women's leisure has emphasized the problem of defining leisure for women. Women's leisure is constrained by many factors including class, race, age, and, not least, men collectively and as individuals (Deem, 1986). Both Deem (1986) and Griffin (1982) question the very existence of leisure for women as it has been traditionally defined, and this stance is supported by more recent empirical findings by Wimbush (1989). This issue is further complicated by the desire of young women to achieve an "acceptably" attractive physique of adult womanhood. The media reinforce this imagery even when dealing with women involved in sporting activities (Graydon, 1983). Women athletes are presented positively if conforming to the desired image or, alternatively, negatively as having somehow overstepped the boundaries of femininity. Scraton (1985) has suggested that peer group pressure intensifies this culture of femininity, with the consequence that a young woman may be interested in playing netball or swimming in a team, yet experiences pressure from friends that encourages her to drop out or lose interest. In addition, there is a relative lack of women in leadership positions in sport in either professional or voluntary capacities. Hence, young women have few role models.

In general, the evidence suggests that a reputation for success in school sports may provide greater incentives for continued involvement in postschool life. However, a series of postschool studies has shown that despite an association between past and current involvement, there was a pronounced tendency to reduce the extent of participation or to stop participation in sport on leaving school (e.g., Emmett, 1977), although this tendency was less marked among the group who were competitors in school (see Hendry, 1986; Hendry & Douglas, 1975; Hendry et al., 1993). Although some young people do return to sport participation after some years' break, or switch to other physical activities, the more usual pattern shows a declining trend into adulthood (Hendry 1981; Hendry et al., 1993; Moir, 1977; Spry, 1977). Hendry and Marr (1985) sought to establish the principal ways in which a sample of late adolescents spent their leisure time. (These young people had been in their last year of compulsory education some four years before the study.) These 19- and 20-year-olds showed little evidence of return to the types of activity which they had experienced in school. Participation in sports of any kind was limited—less than 30% of males and 16% of females were involved fairly regularly in some form of sport. Schools in the study often explained nonparticipation in extracurricular activities in terms of what they believed to be the shortcomings of adolescents rather than the deficiencies of the schools' own approaches and attitudes to postschool sport and leisure. Hence nonparticipation was seen as stemming from such factors as limited sporting ability, lack of identification with the school, and so on, rather than from school effects and influences. The reasons for the decline in participation in community sports for many adolescents are important to seek and understand.

Hendry, et al. (1993) have offered a number of insights on young people and sport based on the findings from their 7-year longitudinal study of 10,000 young Scots aged 10 to 20, which may have implications for future policy.

Social Networks

The changing focus of the social networks in which young people are involved is important to an understanding of young people's participation in sports and leisure, as the leisure focal theory demonstrates (Hendry, 1983) (see Figure 18.3).

Young adolescents are willingly involved with adult-led clubs and organizations, and this may be an important stage at which adults in Scotland can work with young people. The transition toward more casual peer-oriented activities (given certain gender and social class differences) and then to smaller group leisure pursuits, often, in late adolescence, within commercial venues such as discos, clubs, and pubs (see Figure 18.3), suggests the need for different styles

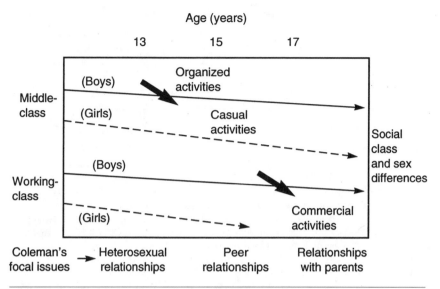

Figure 18.3   Focuses of interest and types of leisure pursuits.
Note. From *Growing Up and Going Out* (p. 166), by L.B. Hendry, 1983, Aberdeen, Scotland: University Press. Copyright 1983 by L.B. Hendry. Reprinted by permission.

of professional associations between adults and youth. It might also suggest the need for different social contexts for these encounters beyond early adolescence. McCusker (1985) has shown the importance of young people's perceptions of the social context of sports to their continuing participation, or their withdrawal to other types of leisure pursuits.

Age, Gender, and Social Influences

From early adolescence, sports and leisure activities are traditionally gender-based (see Table 18.1) and this was found to be so in the study reported by Hendry et al. (1989, 1993). In postschool life, too, gender exerts a more powerful influence on sporting and leisure pursuits than occupational status in that both working and unemployed young people basically wish for similar elements in their leisure time.

The issue here is whether this gender bias, in fact a male bias, in sport should be allowed to continue or whether policies and provision should be adjusted to break down existing gender stereotypes in Scotland.

Organized sport participation as a regular leisure pursuit was popular with just under 60% of all adolescents involved in the study. This statistic is further complicated by the fairly obvious inclusion of age, gender, and social class differences. Put simply, sports were more popular with younger rather than older teenagers, with young men rather than with young women, and with middle-class rather than with working-class adolescents. The Scottish Sports Council survey (1988) established that just 16% of young people were members of sport

Table 18.1   Weekly Participation in All Sports by Gender

	Gender	
Number of Sports	Female $n = 3,052$	Male $n = 3,032$
	%	%
0	55	28
1-3	39	57
more than 3	6	15

Note. Defined as participating in sport at least once a week.
Note. From *Young People's Leisure and Lifestyles: Report of Phase 1* (p. 61), by L.B. Hendry, J. Shucksmith, and J.G. Love, 1989, Edinburgh, Scotland: Scottish Sports Council. Copyright 1989 by Scottish Sports Council. Reprinted by permission.

clubs (21% of boys compared with 11% of girls). Membership was also found to be strongly related to social class, with 29% of young people from families classified as professional or managerial being members of clubs, compared to 9% from families classified as semiskilled or unskilled. With regard to the nature of involvement, the evidence suggests important trends that have a clear gender dimension. Thus among adolescent males, those who engage in competitive sport at the age of 13 remain competitive throughout adolescence and into early adulthood. By contrast, among young women there is a marked shift away from competitive sport involvement toward recreative involvement around the age of 17 (see Table 18.2).

Further, it was found that many young people appeared to experiment with various kinds of sports and physical activities but in an intermittent way, although regular casual activities (e.g., swimming, aerobics at home, or cycling to work) were very popular (see also the Scottish Sports Council, 1988). Perhaps some consideration should be given by providers to the reasons young people have for engaging in sports (mainly social), to the settings they prefer (informal and peer organized), and to their motivations (for enjoyment and/or personal achievement and competence rather than for competition).

Attitudes

The characteristics and attitudes of sport participants were found to differ from those of nonparticipants; in particular, competitors seem to have a range of qualities and positive motivations which set them apart from nonparticipants (and even to some extent from more casual participants). The challenge for Scottish promoters and sport organizations is to design ways of offering a system of sport provision that can incorporate both the desire of many adolescents to engage in physical activities in a less formal way, for enjoyment and social reasons, and the wishes of some adolescents to develop their competitive skills to the highest level.

Table 18.2 Type of Involvement in Sport (in %)

		Age group			
		13-14	15-16	17-18	19-20
Males:					
Nonparticipant		12	10	16	17
Recreational only		35	37	32	38
Competitive		53	53	52	45
	N =	1,028	1,167	511	407
Females					
Nonparticipant		18	22	31	27
Recreational only		36	46	51	61
Competitive		46	32	18	12
	N =	1,038	1,185	475	402

Note. From *Young People's Leisure and Lifestyles* (p. 67), by L.B. Hendry, J. Shucksmith, J.G. Love, and A. Glendinning, 1993, London: Routledge. Copyright 1993 by Routledge. Reprinted by permission.

School Influences

Schools appeared to create both positive and negative effects in young people's sport participation and leisure involvement. They are more effective in generating interest and participation in pupils who are academically able, come from middle-class backgrounds, and have positive attitudes toward school. Sport did not appear to offer an alternative avenue to success for many less academically able pupils. The challenge for extracurricular school sport is to provide a program of activities and a system of teaching and learning that is more positively motivating for young people and enables them to have greater insights and understanding of their own physical activity and sport involvement.

Postschool Sport Participation

There appears to be little continuity between school and community sport and leisure provision. Those who experience sporting success within the educational system are the adolescents most likely to continue sport participation in postschool life. Better links between school and community clubs and sport organizations in terms of information, encouragement, and opportunities might ensure more continued participation into postschool life, especially for young women. Nevertheless, the most significant transitions seem to be happening before the end of compulsory schooling (i.e., 16 years of age) (see Figure 18.4).

This might also demand a changing emphasis in the social and coaching settings of sport clubs so that there are more effective links between school and community.

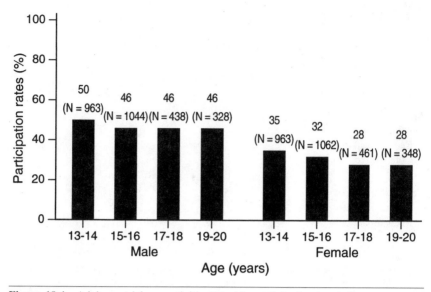

Figure 18.4   Adolescent leisure activities (weekly participation rates): Percentage attending sport clubs.

Note. From *Young People's Leisure and Lifestyles*, by L.B. Hendry, J. Shucksmith, J.G. Love, and A. Glendinning, 1993, London: Routledge. Copyright 1993 by Routledge. Reprinted by permission.

Adults and Youth Sports

Adults can play an important part in adolescents' sport and leisure participation. A study by Hendry and colleagues (1993) shows how parents can be particularly influential in providing norms, role models, pressure, and concrete assistance that affect the sporting involvement of young people (see Table 18.3).

For example, the study highlights the role of parents as role models for their children in sport. Thus the fathers of children on school sport teams are more likely either to play sport themselves or to be involved in the organization of sport. The influence of the family in sport is further confirmed by the finding that parents are second only to friends as fellow participants in sport played by young people outside school. Such influences, however, decrease as young people grow older, so that by the age of 15 to 16 years it is friends who are promoting sport involvement or influencing nonparticipation (see Table 18.4).

Having friends as fellow participants is a major factor in encouraging involvement in both recreational and competitive sport. This fact is related to a particular developmental stage during which the peer group is significant, especially for adolescent young men as focal theory suggests (see Figure 18.3).

As stated earlier, school and teachers were also shown to be important influences affecting the sport involvement of young people. On the one hand, they are capable of promoting sport participation for those pupils able and willing to

Table 18.3 Percentage of Sport Participants Claiming Influence of Family on Involvement (13-16 years)

	Males	Females
	%	%
Competitive sport		
13-14 years	52	27
15-16 years	27	18
	(N = 173)	(N = 152)
Recreational sport		
13-14 years	25	21
15-16 years	10	10
	(N = 243)	(N = 266)

Note. From *Young People's Leisure and Lifestyles* (p. 60), by L.B. Hendry, J. Shucksmith, J.G. Love, and A. Glendinning, 1993, London: Routledge. Copyright 1993 by Routledge. Reprinted by permission.

Table 18.4 Percentage of Sport Participants Claiming Influence of Friends on Involvement (13-16 years)

	Males	Females
	%	%
Competitive sport		
13-14 years	66	50
15-16 years	76	55
	(N = 173)	(N = 152)
Recreational sport		
13-14 years	76	78
15-16 years	80	77
	(N = 243)	(N = 266)

Note. From *Young People's Leisure and Lifestyles* (p. 64), by L.B. Hendry, J. Shucksmith, J.G. Love, and A. Glendinning, 1993, London: Routledge. Copyright 1993 by Routledge. Reprinted by permission.

conform to the more general social and academic aims of the school, while on the other hand they are capable of alienating those pupils unable or unwilling to go along with its mainstream goals.

Adults may also influence, positively or negatively, the involvement of young people in sport in informal settings such as youth groups. Thus athletic clubs, youth clubs, and uniformed organizations, which provide sport as a major part of their activities, all tend to be arranged for adolescents by adults and are often closely supervised by adults. This may be significant because the degree to which adults are directly involved is likely to influence the relationships among adolescents and to have consequences for their sport involvement. Adolescents' involvement in such contexts, though nominally voluntary, may not be genuinely self-chosen and consequently many adolescents may choose *not* to become involved in such organizations and clubs (Hendry, 1983). This may be because in such contexts young people are being overtly socialized and "made ready" for adult society—learning and accepting approved patterns of social behavior and values (Eggleston, 1976). A study by Hendry and Simpson (1977) and a replication study by Hendry, Brown, and Hutcheon (1981) of regular users of an urban sport and community center revealed different reasons for using such clubs. It was clear from the studies that two distinct and separate teenage groups attended the same center, with little or no contact between them: one group following sport activities, the other using the facilities as a social amenity—sitting around the center, chatting, drinking coffee, and listening to pop music. Many of the community area members complained that there were too many rules surrounding the sport area and that the sport area leaders were unable to mix well with young people and were unsympathetic. Rather than subject themselves to the strict discipline and rules, they preferred not to attend, thus opting out of the organized atmosphere of sports for the relaxed informal atmosphere of the community.

Nisbet, Hendry, Stewart, and Watt (1984), in a study of both rural and urban localities within one Scottish region, found that more than 70% of young people in their last year of compulsory schooling had been members of sport clubs or teams at some time in the past, but that only 47% were members at the time of the investigation. (With regard to nonsporting clubs 80% had been members in the past, but just 50% were currently involved. This trend was most evident for uniformed organizations.) Thus while some youths may continue to be attracted to organizations and adult influence, such structured clubs do not touch many adolescents who seek to pursue alternative, subcultural lifestyles. More recently, Hendry, Craik, Love, and Mack (1991) have shown in a nationwide study of a variety of youth work settings that whereas professional youth workers perceived an array of values including decision making, responsibility, leadership, collaboration, and the developments of self-confidence and social skills as the key elements of youth work, young people themselves basically attended sport and other clubs for sheer enjoyment and the desire to be involved in activities such as games and sports. Given the goodwill and enthusiasm of young people for sport and physical activity participation, albeit on a casual, informal basis and in a range of social contexts, what evidence is there of new initiatives emerging on the Scottish scene?

Promotional Campaigns

Problems relating to school-aged sport in Scotland were identified in a Scottish Sports Council report, "Laying the Foundations" (1988), and sport participation across adolescence was shown to decline in the nationwide longitudinal study of Hendry et al. (1993). These issues have also been debated within the School-Aged Team Sport Enquiry Group, which arose from the work on the "Laying the Foundations" report at the request of the Minister for Sport. Team Sport Scotland emerged as a major recommendation of the group's report (Scottish Sports Council, 1989b). Thus Team Sport Scotland is the newest initiative of the Scottish Sports Council for young people. The aims of the Team Sport Scotland initiative can be summarized as follows:

• Developing structures—to help create effective links among the agencies involved in the provision and development of school-aged team sport.

• Developing people—to ensure that teachers, club leaders, coaches, and parents have opportunities and are encouraged to attend training courses.

• Developing activity—to increase opportunities for school-aged children to participate in team games and competitions particularly outside of schooltime.

Team Sport Scotland had funding for a 3-year period from 1991. Its staff consisted of a director and nine sport-specific coordinators—for basketball, volleyball, cricket, netball, boys' soccer, girls' soccer, rugby, shinty, and hockey. Nationally the coordinators' responsibilities included promoting preservice and inservice training courses; producing coaching resource materials; working with the governing body to develop its youth strategy and its communication with schools, clubs, and local sport associations; organizing festivals; and organizing *impact seminars*. The Scottish Sports Council has commissioned an evaluation to determine the effectiveness of Team Sport Scotland in meeting its stated objectives. The evaluation will monitor the work programs and outputs of the nine sport coordinators; survey participants in coaching and inservice courses; interview governing bodies, local authority officers, physical education advisers, and sport clubs; and carry out a number of case studies of specific initiatives. The results of the study will be used as a guide for the operation of any future development of Team Sport Scotland or comparable projects and as an input to a broader program to determine the effectiveness of major policy initiatives by the Scottish Sports Council. Whether such initiatives ensure greater participation by young people in sport awaits further investigation.

Conclusion

The most commonly identified motives for young people in sport have been shown by a variety of researchers to be having fun, improving and learning new skills, being with friends for excitement, being successful, and maintaining physical fitness. Conversely, reasons given for *dropping out* of sport include a lack of playing time, no improvement of skills, no fun, an overemphasis on winning, parental pressure, and dislike of the coach (Fox & Biddle, 1988; Hendry et al., 1989). Research on school leavers (White & Coakley, 1986) reported that negative memories of physical activities and sports included boredom, lack of choice, feelings of incompetence, and negative evaluations from their peers. Girls often associated physical activities with feelings of discomfort and embarrassment and it was frequently the environment itself that was mentioned, such as rules pertaining to dress and showers. Against this background the belief that participation in youth sports will lead to an active life as an adult has yet to be demonstrated (Powell & Dysinger, 1987), and it is likely that the quality of the experience is the crucial factor in the carryover of activity from youth to adulthood (Blair, Clark, Cureton, & Powell, 1989; Simons-Morton, Parcel, O'Hara, Blair, & Pate, 1988). Young people are likely to be influenced in their activity patterns by school, home, and community. These will not be particularly successful if the experience young people have is negative and limited to competitive sport, although, of course, competitive sport does contribute to physical and psychological well-being in some adolescents (Hendry et al., 1989). Policies regarding facilities and provision are important in the Scottish scene but so too is development of nondirective leisure education in which young people "develop skills related to enriching self-determination, pro-activity and meaningful control over their own leisure lives" (Mundy & Odum, 1979, p. 8).

If we are to gain a fuller understanding of the values placed on sport by adult society, and, given these values, of why young people participate—or choose not to participate—in sport, we need to take a multidisciplinary approach to analyzing young people's developing lifestyles and the role of sport within the process of their socialization. This provides a tremendous challenge to us all, both conceptually and methodologically, in attempting to unravel those elements (related to the individual adolescent, his or her ecology, and more general social and cultural factors) which go to make up the various adolescent lifestyles evident in Scotland today.

References

Blair, S.N., Clark, D.G., Cureton, K.J., & Powell, K.E. (1989). Exercise and fitness in childhood: implications for a lifetime of health. In C.V. Gisolfi & D.R. Lamb (Eds.), *Perspective in exercise and sports medicine: II. Youth, exercise and sport*. Indianapolis: Benchmark Press.

Deem, R. (1986). *All work and no play: The sociology of women and leisure*. Milton Keynes, England: Open University Press.

Eggleston, J. (1976). *Adolescence and community*. London: Arnold.

Emmett, I. (1977). *Decline in sports participation after leaving school*. Unpublished draft report. London: Sports Council.

European Sports Charter. (1975). *European "Sport for All" charter*, European Sports Ministers' Conference, Brussels, Belgium.

Fox, K.R., & Biddle, S.J.H. (1988). The child's perspective in physical education: II. Children's participation motive. *British Journal of Physical Education*, **19**(2), 79-82.

Graydon, J. (1983). But it's more than a game—it's an institution: Feminist perspectives on sport. *Feminist Review*, **13**, 5-16.

Griffin, C. (1982). Women and leisure. In J. Hargreaves (Ed.), *Sport, culture and ideology* (pp. 88-116). London: Routledge & Kegan Paul.

Hendry, L.B. (1978). *School, sport and leisure: Three dimensions of adolescence.* London: A. & C. Black.

Hendry, L.B. (1981). *Adolescents and leisure.* London: Sports Council/SSRC.

Hendry, L.B. (1983). *Growing up and going out.* Aberdeen, Scotland: University Press.

Hendry, L.B. (1986). Changing schools in a changing society. In J. Evans (Ed.), *Physical education, sport and schooling* (pp. 41-69). London: Falmer Press.

Hendry, L.B., Brown, L., & Hutcheon, G. (1981). Adolescents in community centres: Some urban and rural comparisons. *Scottish Journal of Physical Education*, **9**, 28-40.

Hendry, L.B., Craik, I., Love, J.G., & Mack, J. (1991). *Measuring the benefits of youth work.* Report to the Scottish Office Education Department. Edinburgh, Scotland: John St. Andrew's House.

Hendry, L.B., & Douglas, L. (1975). University students: Attainment and sport. *British Journal of Educational Psychology*, **45**, 299-306.

Hendry, L.B., & Marr, D. (1985). Leisure education and young people's leisure. *Scottish Educational Review*, **17**(2), 116-127.

Hendry, L.B., & Percy, A. (1981). *Pre-adolescents, television styles and leisure.* Unpublished manuscript, University of Aberdeen, Scotland.

Hendry, L.B., Shucksmith, J., & Love, J.G. (1989). *Young people's leisure and lifestyles: Report of Phase 1.* Edinburgh, Scotland: Scottish Sports Council.

Hendry, L.B., Shucksmith, J., Love, J.G., & Glendinning, A. (1993). *Young people's leisure and lifestyles.* London: Routledge.

Hendry, L.B., & Simpson, D.O. (1977). One centre: Two subcultures. *Scottish Educational Studies*, **9**(2), 112-121.

Hendry, L.B., & Thorpe, E. (1977). Pupils' choice, extra-curricular activities: A critique of hierarchial authority? *International Review of Sport Sociology*, **12**(4), 39-50.

Kane, J.E. (1974). *Physical education in secondary schools.* London: Macmillan.

Leaman, O. (1984). *Sit on the side lines and watch the boys play.* London: Longman.

McCusker, J. (1985). *Involvement of 15-19-year-olds in sport and physical activity.* Proceedings of the Leisure Studies Association Conference (pp. 2.2.3-2.2.13), Ilkley, Yorkshire, England.

Moir, E. (1977). *Female participation in physical activities: A Scottish study.* Edinburgh, Scotland: Dunfermline College of Physical Education.

Mundy, G., & Odum, L. (1979). *Leisure.* New York: Wiley.

Nisbet, J., Hendry, L.B., Stewart, C., & Watt, J. (1984). Participation in community groups. *Collected Resources in Education.* Oxford, England: Carfax.

Powell, K.E., & Dysinger, W. (1987). Childhood participation in organized school sports and physical education as precursors of adult physical activity. *American Journal of Preventative Medicine, 3,* 276-281.

Registrar General Scotland. (1990). *Population estimates Scotland.* Edinburgh, Scotland: Her Majesty's Stationery Office.

Reid, M. (1972). Comprehensive integration outside the classroom. *Educational Research, 14*(2), 128-134.

Saunders, C. (1979). Pupils' involvement in physical activities in comprehensive schools. *Bulletin of Physical Education, 14*(3), 28-37.

Scottish Sports Council. (1988). *Laying the foundations* (Report on school-aged sport in Scotland). Edinburgh, Scotland: Author.

Scottish Sports Council. (1989a). *Sport 2000: A strategic approach to the development of sport in Scotland.* Edinburgh, Scotland: Author.

Scottish Sports Council. (1989b). *School-aged team sport enquiry group report.* Edinburgh, Scotland: Author.

Scraton, S. (1985). *Boys muscle in where angels fear to tread: The relationships between physical education and young women's subcultures.* Proceedings of the Leisure Studies Association Conference, Ilkley, Yorkshire, England.

Scraton, S. (1986) Images of femininity and the teaching of girls' physical education. In J. Evans (Ed.), *Physical education, sport and schooling* (pp. 71-94). London: Falmer Press.

Simons-Morton, B.G., Parcel, G.S., O'Hara, N.M., Blair, S.N., & Pate, R.R. (1988). Health-related physical fitness in childhood: Status and recommendations. *Annual Review of Public Health, 9,* 403-25.

Sports Council. (1983). *Leisure policy for the future.* London: Sports Council.

Sports Council. (1988). *Sport and young people: Partnerships and action* (School Sports Forum). London: Author.

Spry, R. (1977). Leisure and the school leaver in Stoke-on-Trent. In W.M. Fox (Ed.), *Leisure and the quality of life: Vol. 2* (pp. 497-531). London: Her Majesty's Stationery Office.

Walker, S.E. (1987). *Ever thought of sport: Participation in sport by young people in Scotland.* Edinburgh, Scotland: Scottish Sports Council.

Ward, E., Hardman, K., & Almond, L. (1968). Investigation into patterns of participation in physical activity of 11-to-18-year-old boys. *Research in Physical Education, 3,* 18-25.

White, A., & Coakley, J.J. (1986). *Making decisions: The response of young people in the Medway towns to the "Ever Thought of Sport" Campaign.* London: London and SE Region Sports Council.

Wimbush, E. (1989). Benefits and strains of leisure participation for mothers with young children. In R. Maughan (Ed.), *Fit for life* (pp. 155-174). Cambridge, England: Health Promotion Research Trust.

Wolfenden Report. (1960). *Sport and the community*. The Report of the Wolfenden Committee on Sport. London: Central Council for Physical Recreation.

Chapter 19 Spain

Núria Puig
Translated by Richard Rees

Spain is a country which, according to the 1991 census, has 38,425,679 inhabitants. In 1978, when the new Constitution was passed, the country became a parliamentary monarchy—with clearly differentiated legislative, executive, and judicial powers—organized in 17 autonomous communities (Comunidades Autónomas, CCAA) which have their own regional governments. Those have almost exclusive jurisdiction over issues concerning education, health, sport, youths, culture, and social services.

The distribution of the population in the country is very unbalanced, with 50.83% living in the 107 cities with more than 50,000 inhabitants and 56% living in the autonomous communities of Andalusia, Catalonia, Madrid, and Valencia. The pyramid of population is very similar to that of other industrialized societies: the population tends to become older and new couples have only one or two children, if any. The population between 6 and 18 years old is 8,551,196 and between 15 and 29 is 9,828,607. This second group constitutes the focus of this chapter.

Research carried out in Spain into the subject of young people and sport covers an approximate age range from 15 to 29. Beneath this range we find the infant population, whose general characteristics—and consequently those relating to sport—are very different from those of youths. It is therefore impossible to mix these two population groups. Thus, this chapter focuses on the population aged between 15 and 29, the age group which in the Spain of the nineties is experiencing the transition between childhood and adult life.

The Organizational Network

No organizational model exists in Spain for youth sport, because of the way sport is organized in this country. As noted earlier, Spain is a state consisting of 17 autonomous communities (CCAA), each of which enjoys almost exclusive jurisdiction over sport. Consequently, there is great autonomy in the organization of sport in general and, by extension, of sport for youth. All the 17 communities have structures destined to foster youth sport either through the educational framework, outside school hours, or through other organizations (sport federations, governmental youth services, etc.). It is therefore highly difficult to offer a résumé of an organizational system whose extreme complexity is due to the political structure in which it operates. Consequently, it has been decided to abbreviate this section in order to make a deeper analysis of the behavior of Spain's youths in the realm of sport, followed by a commentary on the ambitious nationwide plan, entitled Deporte y Juventud (Sport and Young People), developed by the central government in collaboration with the CCAAs and town and city councils, to foster sport for young people all over the country.

Sport Participation

Sport is one of Spanish youths' favorite activities when it comes to occupying spare time, and it figures sixth on the list after "being with friends," "watching television," "listening to music," "being with the family," and "reading books/ magazines" (García Ferrando, 1993). In 1991, a total of 53% of young men and women in Spain practiced one or several sports three or more times a week. Over the same period, and according to the same measuring criteria, the index of sport practice among the population aged between 15 and 60 was 35% (García Ferrando, 1991). Spanish youths therefore engage in sport far more than their elders do.

This statement is further corroborated by the fact that, when compared to adults, the percentage of young people with previous experience of sport (who no longer engage in it) is greater (28% compared to 26%), while on the other hand the percentage of those who have never engaged in it is far smaller (19% compared to 36%). In other words, the degree of penetration of sport among Spanish youths is higher than it was among previous generations. Moreover, their familiarity with sport and with the values it transmits is greater.

Spanish youths, in fact, have benefited from sport thanks to the profound changes which have taken place in Spain's education system since 1975, the year of Franco's death and of the country's return to democracy. Ninety-six percent of young people today attend physical education classes when at school, while only 4% are never given this opportunity. Although it is true that the survey undertaken by García Ferrando (1993) reveals that today's youths express a relatively poor opinion of these classes ("They were boring," 67%; "They were rather a waste of time," 50%; "They weren't given the importance they deserved," 47%), the fact that they were able from an early age to familiarize themselves with physical activities is the principal factor that explains the differences in attitude toward sport between young people and previous generations, who in their childhood and youth never enjoyed the same opportunities to engage in and become familiar with sport.

By contrast, the differences practically disappear when one examines interest in sport and models of practice. For example, 66% of young people confess to being very or reasonably interested in sport, while the percentage for the population as a whole is 65%.

It is also very interesting to observe how the models of practice are very heterogeneous and reveal the trend, already detected in numerous studies, toward the evolution of sport from a closed to an open system (Heinemann, 1986; Puig & Heinemann, 1992). The pyramid in Figure 19.1 partially illustrates this phenomenon. While 50% of youths claim to practice sport as a leisure activity, without competing, only 4% participate in national leagues. Furthermore, there are intermediate steps which reveal still different models.

This heterogeneity of models is revealed also by other indicators, such as the possession or nonpossession of a federation license (25% against 72%) or membership in some kind of sport organization. Sixty-nine percent of young people consider it unnecessary to belong to any such entity in order to engage in sport; 77.5% of those who practice one or several sports do not belong to a sport association; 62% of these have never belonged to one; and only 20% belong to a club or a traditional association.

This low degree of membership in sport associations reveals the deep changes which have taken place in models of practice, the diversification of which affects the world of sport associations. Engaging in certain models of practice does not require membership in a sport association, and consequently young people do not join them. Therefore, if sport associations do not change with the times and adopt new functions which connect with the sporting interests of young people, they will lose their former role as socializing agents.

This general panorama of the attitudes of Spanish youths to sport would be incomplete without an analysis of the differences existing between ages and sexes. The youth sector as a whole does not behave in a homogeneous way: great differences exist, marked by the way in which socialization affects the phases of transition and the degree to which young men and women accept the stereotypes socially assigned to them.

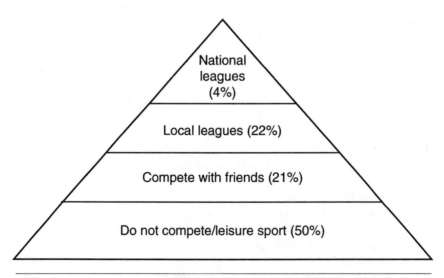

Figure 19.1   Type of sport participation among the youth population.
Note. From *Tiempo libre y hábitos deportivos de los jóvenes españoles* [Leisure Time and Sport Behavior Among Spanish Youths], by M. García Ferrando, 1993, Madrid, Spain: Instituto de la Juventud. Copyright 1993 by Instituto de la Juventud. Adapted by permission.

Dropout

Synchronic studies (mainly surveys) tend to provide cross-sections of reality which impede the view of any diachronic dimension of a phenomenon. This leads either to "optical illusions" with their consequent errors of interpretation, or to loss of information that can be obtained only through longitudinal, or at least biographical, approaches (Puig, 1992).

A clear example of this problem can be derived from an analysis of young people's participation in sport according to age. Table 19.1 shows that there is a marked difference in indices of sport practice between different age groups, in the case of both young men and young women.

The general tendency is to consider these data as indicating a progressive disenchantment with sport as age increases, that is, to assume that young people drop out of sport as they become more integrated into the adult world. While admitting that in some cases this may be true, considerations should be made here that enrich theoretical knowledge in relation to this topic.

In the first place, the need should be noted for an operative definition of the concept of dropping out of sport (Cruz, 1989). Indicators must be developed that would allow a differentiation among *definitive dropout*, *temporary dropout*, and *change of activity*. The survey carried out in 1993 by García Ferrando introduces questions that make it possible to perceive such nuances. Thus, for example, when those who no longer engage in sport were asked if they would return to it (certainly or probably), 46% stated that they would, while 24% were uncertain but did not discount the possibility. Just 22% stated that they would probably or certainly never engage in sport again. Thus, analyzed in this way, the dimension of dropout is relativized because, in many cases, it can be appreciated that the attitude of youths to sport, rather than being stable (sportsman or -woman versus nonsportsman or -woman), is variable. Sport in the youth phase is an *itinerary*,

Table 19.1   Young People's Sports Practice According to Age and Sex (in %)

	Male				Female			
Age	15-16	17-19	20-24	25-29	15-16	17-19	20-24	25-29
Engaged	88	74	66	44	60	45	36	23
Presently not engaged	5	11	20	27	12	27	25	22
Not engaged	7	14	14	28	28	28	39	55

Note. From *Tiempo Libre y Hábitos Deportivos de los Jóvenes Españoles* (Leisure-Time and Sport Behavior Among Spanish Youths] (p. 26), by M. García Ferrando, 1993, Madrid, Spain: Instituto de la Juventud. Copyright 1993 by Instituto de la Juventud. Adapted by permission.

and, according to the circumstances of the transition, the sport itinerary may be continuous or discontinuous.

This observation leads us to a second reflection. There is a tendency to consider that young people drop out of sport because of problems concerning sport provision (technicians, facilities, and so on). While this may be true to a certain extent, dropping out, like any relationship of youths with sport, must be interpreted in terms of young people's "subjective sense of the facts" (Cicourel, 1982), and not in terms of adults' views. Sport is but one activity more in the life of young people, chosen from a number of options throughout their lives. Over a number of years it becomes a priority, later to be replaced, for various reasons, by other activities. The period of transition in life that we are considering here is a phase of discovery, of adventure, during which answers must be found to many questions. Young people choose professions, fall in love, become integrated into the world of work. This may lead them to drop out of sport, although this does not necessarily imply disenchantment with the activity. Although at a given moment they may cease to engage in sport, they may take it up again later. Indeed, the data supplied by García Ferrando throw some light on this question: a high percentage state that they intend to return to sport. Furthermore, the reconstruction of sport itineraries through semidirective interviews produces similar results (Puig, 1992).

In this sense, an examination of the main motives for dropping out reveals that in most cases the sport itinerary was interrupted by other aspects characteristic of the process of socialization: "I came home from work late or tired" (19%); "My studies took up too much time" (19%); and "I was lazy or disinclined" (15%). In relation to the latter comment, a deep analysis should be made of the causes behind laziness or disinclination. Could they not imply also an excess of preoccupations leading to interruption of the sport itinerary? This might be the case of a young man interviewed during the course of our research (Puig, 1992). He was around 25 years of age, a rugby enthusiast, and had played the game regularly except for a 2-year period roughly between the ages of 20 and 22, because it had become incompatible with another of his preoccupations at the time: "discovering nightlife." He realized that he could not cope with going out at night, going to bed late, and getting up early the following day to play. He gave up rugby for a while, but once having "discovered nightlife" to his satisfaction he found a way to incorporate the game once again into his lifestyle.

Thus, we propose that henceforward the subject of dropping out of sport among youths should be operationalized with greater exactitude, that at the same time it be analyzed from the viewpoint of the sport itinerary, and that consideration be given to the fact that during the itinerary, young people must *define the situation* (Allport, 1963; Puig, 1992; Thomas & Znaniecki, 1919; White & Coakley, 1986), which implies that sport practice will be affected in one way or another depending on the circumstances of the socialization process. It is a question, in the final instance, of moving away from adults' views of the world and of sport and penetrating that of the interested parties in this case: young people.

Differences Between Boys and Girls

An analysis of youth sport practice from the viewpoint of itineraries brings to light other suggestive data (Puig, 1992). For example, it has been observed that the type of activity chosen and the level on which it is developed vary according to the different stages of the socialization process. Thus, roughly between the ages of 15 and 17 there is a greater disposition to choose collective sports and to participate in sport competitions. This then varies greatly for many young people at age 18 and onwards, when they enter a new phase in the maturation process characterized by greater self-affirmation vis-á-vis other individuals and institutions. From this point on, many instances occur of young people's breaking away from federative structures and of a search for activities that guarantee greater personal independence from organized structures. Alternative activities and those related to the environment frequently come up in this context.

The relationship with associations also varies as the itinerary develops, being closest when such associations are necessary for the type of sport chosen, offering training sessions, competition organization, touring, and so forth.

Similarly, although the figure of the technician (trainer, coach, monitor, instructor, etc.) is considered by the youth population as a whole to be a crucial motivating factor, this consideration also becomes contextualized, according to age group, by other dimensions. Thus, for example, the older the person is, the more he or she believes that while good technical support is important, personal interest—responsibility toward oneself—is fundamental. By contrast, this is not the case at the beginning of the youth phase, when groups of friends carry greater weight as a motivating factor.

Finally, this overview of young people and sport in Spain would be incomplete if no mention were made of the great differences existing between the sexes, which can be appreciated in Table 19.1. While 68% of young men practice one or more sports, only 41% of young women do so. Because there is a vast body of literature that examines these differences, we shall limit ourselves here to pointing out that they stem basically from values inculcated during the socialization process. In Spain as elsewhere, girls are educated according to one set of values and boys according to another, the latter values being in greater concord with those transmitted by traditional sport.

Nevertheless, at the same time as we witness increasing heterogeneity in models of practice, data obtained from recent surveys reveal changes in women's sport behavior. More women are engaging in sport because of the emergence of models of practice that are in greater accord with the values they have assimilated during their socialization process (García Ferrando, 1991; Vázquez, 1992). Moreover, signs are emerging of the transgression of traditional stereotypes: women who accept the logic of high-level sport without this giving rise to any inner conflict (Puig, 1992), and men and women who enter new practices representing a breaking away from established genres (Buñuel, 1991). These phenomena, however, are so recent that we can speak in terms only of signs, and they should therefore be taken as hypotheses for future research projects.

Promotional Campaigns

Between 1989 and 1992, the Consejo Superior de Deportes (equivalent to the Ministry of Sport) and the Youth Institute of the Spanish government developed the Sport and Young People Plan to foster sport among youths. This measure was considered a priority by virtue of four basic presuppositions (Paris, 1988): (a) sport is a good thing from the educational point of view, (b) sport is a good way to occupy spare time, (c) sport is good for health, and (d) sport as a sector is beginning to generate youth employment.

The plan contemplated seven essential objectives:

- The introduction of physical education into the educational system and support for the development of sport in schools and universities
- An increase in sport practice among young people
- The fostering of sport associations among young people
- The stimulation of awareness among young people of sport in general and of the Barcelona Olympic Games
- The fostering of youth employment through sport
- The fostering of young people's health through engagement in sport
- Support for rehabilitation through sport of young people in situations of risk and social marginalization.

These seven objectives generated 45 specific operations, grouped according to three types:

1. Structural and training operations, directed toward the creation of fundamental structures in all sport systems
2. Awareness and information operations designed to motivate and foster favorable attitudes on the part of young people toward engagement in sport
3. Operations designed to foster participation and provide incentives and mechanisms for young people to engage in sport

Each of these operations was allocated appropriate funds, and the main axes around which they revolved were as follows:

- Physical education in schools, considered as the departure point. Over 30,000 million pesetas (US $215 million) were assigned to provide the country's schools with a sufficient number of properly equipped sport facilities, and to ensure that trained staff would run these centers, training programs being implemented where necessary.

- Sport practice in schools and universities. Support was given to extracurricular sport organizations and university centers in order to consolidate organizational structures that would facilitate sport for young people: facilities, programs of interuniversity sport competition, programs to foster sport in universities, and so forth.

- The 1990 Spanish Sport Law which, while regulating sport in the country as a whole, contemplated specific aspects which would favor sport for young people. Outstanding among these were the design of a new sport association model more attuned to their interests and lifestyles (e.g., via simplification of legalization formalities, inclusion of sport associations of a more recreational nature, etc.), and the introduction of regulations more in keeping with the times as regards sport associations, in order to favor quality instruction and to stimulate youth employment through sport.

While it is still too early to evaluate the effects of the plan fully, its implementation has represented a joining of forces which in itself is a major step forward compared to a past situation in which nothing of the kind was ever contemplated.

Conclusion

To our way of thinking, given that youth sport is intimately linked to the life of young people in general, it is essential that no action destined to foster it should lose sight of this perspective. As was stated earlier, being young means living through a period of transition toward adulthood, and this requires great effort on the part of those undergoing the process. It is impossible to understand young people's sport behavior without taking this background into account. A partial analysis that does not contemplate the way in which socialization processes influence youth sport itineraries might lead to errors of interpretation and, in consequence, to proposals which have nothing to do with the real dimensions of the problem they set out to solve. Youth sport should therefore be fostered in, and not isolated from, the contexts in which young people lead their lives and in connection with their aspirations. In the final instance, this means entering fully into their lifestyles and forgetting, if only for a moment, the adult perspective.

References

Allport, G.W. (1963). *Pattern and growth in personality*. New York: Holt, Rinehart and Winston.

Buñuel, A. (1991). The recreational physical activities of Spanish women: A sociological study of exercising for fitness. *International Review for the Sociology of Sport*, **91**, 203-216.

Cicourel, A.K. (1982). *El método y la medida en Sociología* [Method and measurement in sociology]. Madrid, Spain: Editora Nacional.

Cruz, J. (1989). *Influencia del entrenador en la motivación de deportistas jóvenes: Su evaluación y cambio. Proyecto de investigación* [The influence of the coach on the motivation of young sports people: Its evaluation and change. Research project]. Unpublished manuscript, Universitat Autònoma. Barcelona, Spain.

García Ferrando, M. (1991). *Los españoles y el deporte (1980-1990): Un análisis sociológico* [Spanish people and sport (1980-1990): A sociological analysis].

Madrid, Spain: Ministerio de Educación y Ciencia, Consejo Superior de Deportes.

García Ferrando, M. (1993). *Tiempo libre y hábitos deportivos de los jóvenes españoles* [Leisure time and sport behavior among Spanish youths]. Madrid, Spain: Instituto de la Juventud.

Heinemann, K. (1986). The future of sports: Challenge for the science of sport. *International Review for the Sociology of Sport, 21*, 278-285.

Paris, F. (1988). Perspectivas del deporte para la juventud [Sport prospects for young people]. *Revista de Estudios de Juventud, (32)*, 9-13.

Puig, N. (1992). *Joves i esport: Influencia dels processos de socialitzación en els itineraris esportius juvenils* [Young people and sport: The influence of socializing processes on young people's sport itineraries]. Unpublished doctoral dissertation, University of Barcelona, Spain.

Puig, N., & Heinemann, K. (1992). El deporte en la perspectiva del año 2000 [Sport looking toward the year 2000]. *Papers Revista de Sociología, (38)*, 123-142.

Thomas, W.I., & Znaniecki, F. (1919). Life-record of an immigrant. In W.I. Thomas & F. Znaniecki (Eds.), *The Polish peasant in Europe and America: Monography of an immigrant group Vol. III*. Chicago: University of Chicago Press.

Vázquez, B. (1992). La presencia de la mujer en el deporte español [The presence of women in Spanish sport]. In B. Vázquez (Ed.), *El ejercicio físico y la práctica deportiva de las mujeres* (pp. 9-15). Madrid, Spain: Ministerio de Asuntos Sociales, Instituto de la Mujer.

White, A., & Coakley, J. (1986). *Young people in transition: An exploration of how young men and women make decisions about their sport involvement*. Paper presented at Sport, Sex and Gender, Norwegian Society for Sport Research, Lillehammer, Norway.

Acknowledgment

All the quantitative data in this chapter are taken from the research project carried out by Prof. Manuel García Ferrando on young people and sport in Spain (García Ferrando, 1993). The author of this article would like to express her most sincere thanks to Prof. García Ferrando for allowing her access to this highly valuable information.

Chapter 20 Sweden

Lars-Magnus Engström

There are 8.6 million inhabitants in Sweden in an area of 450,000 km², or 21 inhabitants per km². The opportunities for outdoor leisure activities, both summer and winter, are therefore excellent. Sport, in its broad meaning, plays an important role in Sweden. The Swedish Sports Confederation, founded in 1903, is an umbrella organization of Swedish sport with 1,000 special district federations and 62 special sport federations. The basic unit is the club, and 27,000 sport clubs and 20,000 company sport clubs belong to this organization. The main tasks for the Swedish Sports Confederation are strategic coordination of national sports, promotion of positive opinions of sport, international networking in sport administration, research and development for the Swedish sport movement, and support for national sport federations. The activities are divided into three main programs: competitive sport, recreational sport, and junior sport.

The Organizational Network

More than half of Swedish youths are members of sport clubs. One reason for youth activities being so well-developed is the large body of leaders and coaches, most of whom are unpaid.

There are also many alternatives outside the organized sport system, such as jogging, skiing, hiking, and other activities for recreation and physical well-being.

Students have two to three physical education lessons per week in compulsory school and between one and three lessons per week in upper secondary school. There are voluntary school sport activities as well. About 700,000 boys and girls are members of school sport clubs.

Since the beginning of the 1980s there has been a growing interest in questions concerning the sport activities of children and youths (Blomdahl, 1990; Engström, 1979, 1980, 1986, 1990, 1992, 1993; Patriksson, 1990). The concerns were first discussed at a Sport Research Council symposium held at Bosön, Stockholm, in February 1982. Some of the reasons behind the need to obtain more knowledge about youth sports were:

- The decreasing age at which children enter organized sports.
- The increasing demands put on children regarding performance and commitment to training.
- The excessive emphasis put on tournaments and competition.
- The tendency of sport federations to make children concentrate on only one sport.

- The treatment of many children as outcasts after they did not make the team and their subsequent tendency to quit.

This symposium received much attention from researchers and leaders in the Swedish Sports Confederation and the resulting report was widely read. In the following years, several large conferences were held regarding the same theme: Child and Youth Sport. In relation to the present opinions regarding the training of children in sports, it was quite sensational that behavioral scientists, physicians, and physiologists all agreed on many issues:

- Children should not be looked upon as miniature adults.
- The large variations in maturity among children must be considered, especially during puberty.
- Strength and endurance training should not begin before puberty.
- Learning basic skills and plays should be concentrated on during the years prior to puberty.
- Children's training should be well-rounded—avoiding specialization and selection based on skill too early.

The conclusions were mainly built on sciences like biology and medicine. To look upon sports for children as an important part of their socialization process, where they learn adult lifestyles and norms, had hardly been considered before. Strangely enough, it was not common to look at sports as an important part of a child's upbringing, and even less as a part of our culture. Questions that are often asked today, in contrast, are, "How is youth sport culture changing?", "What are the reasons for the changes?", "Which sports are popular and why do children choose a particular sport?", and "Which children participate in sports and which do not?"

One important purpose is to find out how traditions are established and reproduced in school and during leisure time. How can we explain the variations which exist among individuals concerning attitudes toward physical training as well as the practice of physical activity? In this respect, it is important to identify the opportunities and obstacles that exist in people's living conditions and environments. The development of sports is, like other manifestations of culture, related to people's conditions of life and to the development of society in general. The great and rapid changes that have taken place in society during the last decades are also reflected in the leisure-time activities and sport habits of children and youths. In what way has youth sport changed during the last decades? There are a few distinct trends in this development.

Sport Participation

How many young people are presently active in sport clubs? What branches are the most popular ones? What changes take place with time and increasing age?

To answer the first two questions, we will start from an investigation among approximately 4,000 pupils aged 7 to 20 years from different parts of Sweden. This investigation took place in 1987 (Engström, 1989).

In Table 20.1 the percentage of active members in sport clubs is shown. It is important to notice that these results are from a cross-sectional study, and not from a follow-up study. The changes in a group followed from the time they were 7 to the time they were 20 might be quite different.

We thus find that in the most active age groups approximately two thirds of the boys and about half of the girls are members of sport clubs, that is, clubs not connected to school activities.

The 10 sports which have the most members in the most active age group, 10 to 12 years, are shown in Table 20.2.

Soccer is the most dominating sport. More than every second boy and every fourth girl takes part in this team sport. Next, for the boys, comes another team sport, ice hockey, while the girls in this age group devote their time to individual sports such as horseback riding and gymnastics. Comparatively few youngsters practice classical Swedish sports like track and field, skiing, and cross-country running (running in the forest).

To illustrate the trends, a categorization of all sports can be done into team sports, individual sports, and contact sports, which are all competitive sports, and club sports, which are not competitive (see Table 20.3).

We find that about the same percentage of girls in the clubs take part in team sports, individual sports, and noncompetitive sports. Almost no girls take part in contact sports. Among the boys, the team sports clearly dominate over the individual sports. Very few boys take part in contact sports. Almost every boy belonging to a club is taking part in a competition sport, while "only" two out of three girls do so.

A study of 500 15-year-old boys and girls has been conducted at three occasions (1968, 1984, and 1992) in the same schools located in the area of Stockholm

Table 20.1 Percentage of Active Members According to Gender in Sport Clubs, Ages 7 to 20

Age	Girls	Boys
7-9	37	66
10-12	65	74
13-15	61	71
16-20	49	58

Note. From "Importance and Influence of Behavioural Aspects on the Participation and Attrition of Youth and Sport" by L.-M. Engström. In *Youth Sport: A Social Approach* (p. 78) by W. Duquet, P. De Knop, and L. Bollaert (Eds.), 1993, Brussels, Belgium: VUBpress. Copyright 1993 by VUBpress. Adapted by permission.

Table 20.2   Percentage of Members in Different Sport Clubs, Ages 10 to 12

Girls (N = 224) Sport	%	Boys (N = 226) Sport	%
Soccer	26	Soccer	45
Horseback riding	13	Ice hockey	17
Gymnastics	13	Swimming	8
Dance, ballet	8	Tennis	7
Swimming	4	Golf	5
Track and field	4	Downhill skiing	4
Handball	2	Table tennis	4
Basketball	2	Bandy	4
Cross-country running	2	Track and field	4
Downhill skiing	2	Jogging	3

Note. From "Importance and Influence of Behavioural Aspects on the Participation and Attrition of Youth and Sport" by L.-M. Engström. In *Youth Sport: A Social Approach* (p. 78) by W. Duquet, P. De Knop, and L. Bollaert (Eds.), 1993, Brussels, Belgium: VUBpress. Copyright 1993 by VUBpress. Adapted by permission.

Table 20.3   Activities in Sport Clubs Among Children 10-12 Years Old, With Percentage of Active Members

Sports	Girls (N = 224) %	Boys (N = 226) %
Team sports	27	47
Contact sports	0	2
Individual sports	24	32
Noncompetitive sports	29	3

Note. From "Importance and Influence of Behavioural Aspects on the Participation and Attrition of Youth and Sport" by L.-M. Engström. In *Youth Sport: A Social Approach* (p. 78) by W. Duquet, P. De Knop, and L. Bollaert (Eds.), 1993, Brussels, Belgium: VUBpress. Copyright 1993 by VUBpress. Adapted by permission.

(Engström, 1992). The results from this study give us some information about changes in sport habits among children and youths (see Figure 20.1). The proportion of club members has changed strikingly. In 1968, 17% of the girls and 50% of the boys, aged 15, were active members of sport clubs. Sixteen years later, the number of members had increased considerably, among girls up to 46% and among boys up to 67%. When the last study was done, in 1992, there were still many members, but the percentage had diminished, especially among the boys.

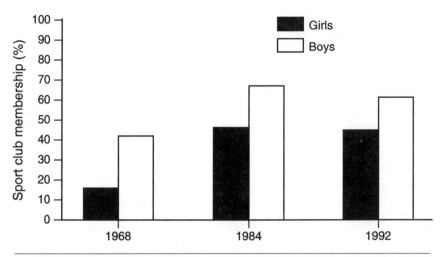

Figure 20.1   The proportion of members in sport clubs among 15-year-olds in the area of Stockholm (1968, 1984, and 1992).

Note. From "Importance and Influence of Behavioral Aspects on the Participation and Attrition of Youth and Sport" by L.-M. Engström in *Youth Sport: A Social Approach* by W. Duquet, P. De Knop, and L. Bollaert (Eds.), 1993, Brussels, Belgium: VUBpress. Copyright 1993 by VUBpress. Reprinted by permission.

There is obviously a leveling on its way between boys and girls concerning membership in clubs. However, the forms of activities that boys and girls participate in are in many ways different (see Tables 20.4 and 20.5).

Soccer was the most popular activity both among boys and girls. Many girls also devoted themselves to horseback riding and handball, while boys were more interested in tennis and ice hockey. The interest in tennis and golf seems to increase while the interest in gymnastics and ice hockey seems to decrease. Besides this, there is no doubt that indoor bandy (i.e., kind of field hockey played indoors) is getting more and more popular.

Consequently, the proportion of club members has increased considerably during the last decades, but what has happened to spontaneous sports, that is, the sport activities taking place outside organized sport? (Spontaneous sports are defined as activities outside clubs, with a strain level at least corresponding to walking and with a regularity of at least once a week.) The changes that occurred between 1968, 1984, and 1992 are shown in Figure 20.2.

Thus, the proportion of those who were active in spontaneous sports decreased considerably between 1968 and 1984. However, the trend changed from 1984 to 1992. The percentage of club members is getting smaller and the proportion of active boys and girls in organizations outside sport clubs (e.g., various gyms, workouts, etc.), as well as the proportion of those who take their own initiative in physical activity, is increasing again. In spite of this, the number of physically inactive young people is still high. This is especially true if the definition of

Table 20.4 Active Female Members in Sport Clubs 1984 and 1992 Among 15-Year-Olds in the Area of Stockholm

1984 Sport	%	1992 Sport	%
Horseback riding	8	Soccer	13
Soccer	8	Horseback riding	10
Dance	8	Handball	6
Basketball	7	Basketball	6
Gymnastics	6	Dance	4
Volleyball	4	Track and field	2
Swimming	2	Swimming	2
Handball	2	Tennis	1
Orienteering	2	Martial arts	1
Tennis	1	Golf	1

Table 20.5 Active Male Members in Sport Clubs 1984 and 1992 Among 15-Year-Olds in the Area of Stockholm

1984 Sport	%	1992 Sport	%
Soccer	22	Soccer	13
Ice hockey	8	Tennis	9
Martial arts	8	Ice hockey	6
Basketball	4	Martial arts	5
Track and field	4	Basketball	4
Badminton	3	Table tennis	4
Handball	3	Indoor bandy	3
Bowling	2	Golf	3
Motorbiking	2	Bandy	3
Swimming	2	Volleyball	3

physical activity is increased to jogging, or corresponding effort, at least once a week. According to this criterion of physical activity half of the young population is active and half is passive (see Figure 20.3).

As a whole, this means that youth sport has in various ways become institutionalized and that those young people who are not members of sport clubs are often physically inactive during their leisure time if we demand a greater effort than walking to count as activity.

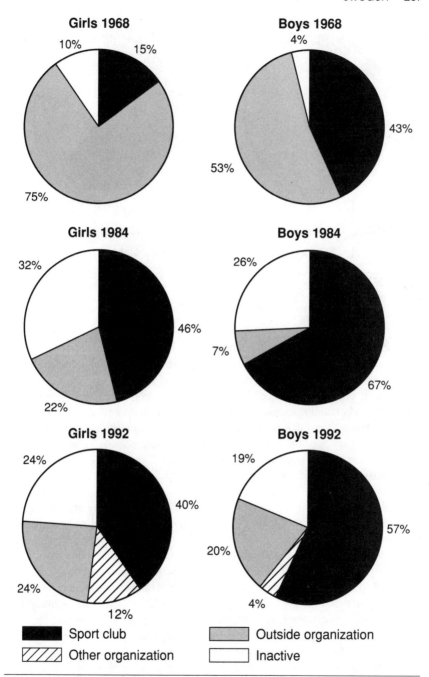

Figure 20.2   Percentage of 15-year-old boys and girls (1968, 1984, and 1992) who during leisure time are active in sports within and outside of clubs or other organizations on an exercise level at least corresponding to walking and with a regularity of at least once a week.

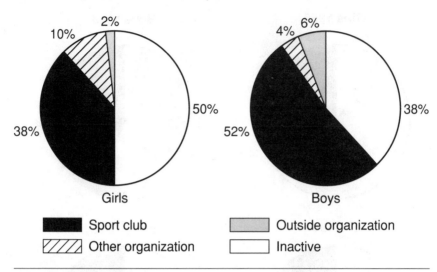

Figure 20.3   Sport activities among 15-year-olds in 1992. Level of strain: Jogging or corresponding activities once a week.

What is the reason for this development?

The situation of children and young people in Swedish society has gradually gone through great changes. The upbringing of children and their everyday situation in general have become more and more connected to institutions of different kinds mainly because in most families both parents are working full-time. Therefore, we have professional caretakers/educators of children in the form of day-care personnel, preschool teachers, comprehensive school teachers, and secondary school teachers. During leisure time, our children are taken care of by leisure-time educators and leaders, youth leaders, and sport leaders in growing numbers. To assist parents, there are pediatricians, welfare officers, psychologists, and other experts on children's problems. Many children attend day-care centers from the age of 1 year, then go on to preschool and compulsory comprehensive school and, in many cases, continue in secondary school until the age of 18 or 19. Childhood and the greater part of youth are thus spent away from the productive side of life. Sports are, consequently, another expression for this child education culture where children's socialization to an increasing degree is taking place outside the family and is tied to different kinds of institutions.

If demands from school, in combination with the pressure of belonging to an organization in leisure time, take a larger and larger place in children's lives, it is easier to understand why spontaneous activities are decreasing.

We are sure that many middle-aged persons remember how they spent many afternoons and many evenings during their childhood at sport grounds, meadows, skating rinks, and even in streets playing all kinds of games and sports. Many adults have learned many sport activities in this way, for example biking, swimming, skating, and so forth. Some have even reached world elite status in spite of, or thanks to, their spontaneous sport activities during childhood and up to their teens. These kinds of sports are now decreasing. Instead, young people are now looking for organized and ready-planned activities.

One further reason for this development has most probably been that the organization of youth sport serves a rational purpose. It could be said that a dominating factor has been that, in order to find the foremost sport stars, one must make an early selection from among those children who are most talented and also encourage them to invest in specialized training in one single sport. Is this rational planning? One of our colleagues, Rolf Carlson (1991), has presented his dissertation on the development of talent for success in top-level competitive sport. Three hundred and fifty-eight athletes in seven sports were involved in this investigation. In all, this study revealed that it is not fully possible to predict who develops to be a top athlete based on individual talent alone. Environmental factors have proved to be of the utmost importance. The analysis furthermore indicates that interactive processes play a major part in the athlete's future development. The social structure, especially the club environment and the coach, turned out to be essential. Becoming a top athlete is favored by the establishment of a good and enduring personal relationship with one coach. Thus, the question is not only, and not even primarily, to find talents, but rather to find the best way of developing talent.

In spite of this knowledge, we find that youth sport also distinctly shows the signs of a more and more professional way of thinking. Among other things, it is noticeable that leaders/trainers have a higher education and more often demand to get paid. Furthermore, many people see youth sport as a recruitment pool from which talents can be developed. Half of the young population start to take part in sports at the age of 7 or earlier and by the age of 10 the majority are active members (Engström, 1990). It is also not unusual that very young team ballplayers are persuaded to change clubs with the prospect of obtaining greater chances for a sport career. In other words, the big city clubs, with strong economic status, are enlisting members from the small clubs, which are often found in the suburbs of the cities or outside the city areas.

Participation in Organized Sport

An important question in this connection is: Who are the children becoming members and staying members in sport clubs? As half of the youths are engaged in the sport movement as early as at the age of 7, interested parents with time and economic resources, for example the opportunity of using a car, are often a necessity. Several studies (Blomdahl, 1990; Engström, 1989) have also convinc- ingly shown that participation in sport among children is very clearly related to the social and economic status of the parents. The relation between the parents' social position and the degree of engagement in sport among children should not only be understood as a result of different financial possibilities. Cultural capital is also of great importance. In a pilot study Larsson (1993) compared a group of 15-year-old children from families with cultural capital (from the father's occupation as, e.g., a teacher or journalist) with children from families with economic capital (from business, etc.) belonging to the same socioeconomic group.

Even if the number of investigated persons is limited in this pilot study, it is quite obvious that young people, especially girls, from homes with economic capital are more often members of sport clubs than those from homes with cultural capital, in spite of the fact that they belong to the same social group as traditionally defined. From these results one could say that the recruitment to child sport does not in the first instance occur among those children who are interested and talented, but among those who have interested and comparatively well-situated parents.

In this context something should be said about the changes in sport habits that occur with increasing age. Patriksson (1987) has shown that the dropout rate from sport clubs is highest among young children aged 8-9, and among youths aged 14-19. The children were studied during 18 months and in that period an average of 13% of the children quit sports completely. Girls were more likely to quit than boys.

In a follow-up study of 2,000 youths between the ages of 15 to 30 years, the number of participants in various sports and keep-fit activities decreased with rising age, especially during adolescence (Engström, 1986). At the age of 15, almost 85% of the boys and 70% of the girls were regularly active at least once a week during leisure time. Five years later, the proportions had decreased to 50% and 30% respectively. The proportion of active men is, however, stabilized thereafter, and at the age of 30 it amounts to about 50%. The proportion of active women increases from 25 to 30 years of age, amounting to about 40% of the total.

There are various reasons for the decline during adolescence. One is the onset of puberty and the growing interest in the opposite sex and another is the great social changes that take place during adolescence. A further reason is the organization of the sport clubs. It is much easier to be a member at the age of 10 or 12 compared to the age of 20.

Value of Sport

Sports can provide different experiences and also satisfy many different needs. Two main groups can be discerned in sport activities: one having an intrinsic value, and one having an investment value. Intrinsic value is to be understood as all those values relating to the here-and-now experiences of sports. It can, for example, be the joy of experiencing the complete performance, of making the perfect turn in a downhill run, of making the perfect stroke in tennis and so forth. It can also be the intensive joy of playing or the excitement and relaxation that practicing a sport so often gives. Those who practice a sport for sport's own sake do it in order to experience something special or to satisfy some basic needs. It is at the very moment the activities are taking place that the needs are being satisfied.

The investment value of sport, on the other hand, involves several purposes of sport activities which are reached through the practicing of sport. A common factor for these activities is that they are used as means of reaching something that in fact is beyond the activity. There are two main lines: the value of sports as an investment in health and physical fitness, and the value of sports as an investment in progress and success. Both these investment values give the participant prestige.

Participation in sports often provides both an intrinsic and an investment value. The larger the input of the investment value, the more the interest is shifted from the activity to the purpose of the activity: success, admiration from the surrounding people, a nicer body, improved health and capacity, and so forth. If the investment is not profitable enough, the activity will probably cease. Today the investment value of sports appears to be the dominating value. This is particularly true among boys and men. Almost all boys become directly involved in the system of competition, where the sign of success is shown in the position achieved by the competing individual or team. Boys to a larger extent than girls learn to practice sports to achieve something outside sports. Sport has become the means and not the end.

With the direction that youth sport has taken, that is, early institutionalized competition for younger and younger children, there is no doubt that the investment value has obtained a greater share at the expense of the intrinsic value of sports. To play games just for the fun of it has become less and less important.

Promotional Campaigns

Several things have been done by the Swedish sport movement to stop some of these negative trends. As was mentioned earlier, the 1982 conference on youth sport started a discussion and a debate about, for example, the problems of early specialization and the overly serious and organized treatment of youth sport, as if children were "small grownups." As a result of these discussions, many sport schools started. The Swedish Sports Confederation and also the Swedish School Sport Federation promoted this idea of sport schools for children to try different sports in a playful way.

In order to prevent youth sport from becoming too serious the Swedish Sports Confederation has also made a recommendation to all the sport federations that deal with youth sport not to organize nationwide competitions for children under the age of 13 years.

Conclusion

The modern forms of physical exercise will not become comprehensible and cannot be understood if they are primarily looked upon as expressions of biological needs for play and movement that human beings have. On the contrary, they are social and cultural constructions, which have to be looked upon in their historical connections and in the light of the power positions of different groups.

Consequently, our main thesis is that sports, youth sports as well as keep-fit sports, have to be seen as an arena where social needs are fulfilled, and where conscious and unconscious investments are made in order to achieve prestige (Bourdieu, 1978, 1986).

To be a member of a sport club entails more than learning a branch of athletics. It also involves learning a number of other skills and attitudes. This kind of learning takes place in a conscious as well as an unconscious way. To be a member of a sport club implies, among other things

- learning the skills of the sport,
- physical and motor training,
- recreation and play,
- social training—cooperation with adults and peer groups,
- learning rules, norms, values, and a lifestyle,
- learning an attitude toward sport and body exercise, and
- learning an attitude toward one's own body and capability.

However, we should not forget that about half of the young generation is outside the sport movement, and physically inactive, and that most adults do not devote themselves to any regular keep-fit activity during leisure time (Engström, 1992). To be physically inactive is also a way to tell other people who you are at the same time as it tells us something about our own sport culture.

Sport is an important normsetter, second only to family and school. On the strength of its range and importance, sport must mediate and re-create essential values for the continued existence of our culture. In other words, it fills the function of reproducing culture. In youth sport, the leader's personality, lifestyle, and behavior are of utmost importance. Youth sport is one of our most important environments for upbringing. It must therefore be valued as such and given its rightful importance in children's lives and development.

The research results and practical experiences of the last decades have been a starting point for the Sport Confederation's Youth Committee in proposing the following plan of action:

- Develop *sport schools* where children can try different sports and get well-rounded training in their vicinity without having to be a member of a sport club.

- Strengthen democracy in a way that makes children more involved in and responsible for the planning of the activities.

- Ensure that the interests and needs of children and youths guide and direct the choice of sporting activities. The main purpose should be to strengthen children's self-confidence and make them develop a positive attitude to physical training.

These normative statements can surely work as important objectives. Whether they can be realized is not only a question of knowledge and intention. Neither are negative trends in youth sport just a consequence of inadequate insight nor of bad teaching and coaching. The structure and development of competitive sports and of society determines the conditions from which the individual can act. To understand what is going on in youth sport, what development can be expected, and what is possible to change is not only a need of better knowledge of the individual or the club, but also of the sport culture and the development of society. Besides research concerning the motor, physical, and personal development of the individual, there is also a demand for building up knowledge whereby sport is studied as a social phenomenon.

References

Blomdahl, U. (1990). *Folkrörelserna och folket* [Popular national movements and the people]. Stockholm: Carlssons Bokförlag.

Bourdieu, P. (1978). Sport and social class. *Social Science Information, 18*, 821.

Bourdieu, P. (1986). *Distinction: A social critique of the judgement of taste.* London: Routledge & Kegan Paul.

Carlson, R. (1991). *Vägen till landslaget* [The path to the national level in sport]. Stockholm: HLS Förlag.

Engström, L.-M. (1979). Physical activity during leisure time: A strategy for research. *Scandinavian Journal of Sports Sciences, 1*, 32-39.

Engström, L.-M. (1980). Physical activity of children and youth. *Acta Paediatr. Scand.* Suppl. 283-101.

Engström, L.-M. (1986). The process of socialization into keep-fit activities. *Scandinavian Journal of Sports Sciences, 8*(3), 89-97.

Engström, L.-M. (1989). *Idrottsvanor i förändring* [Changes of sport habits]. Stockholm: HLS Förlag.

Engström, L.-M. (1990, June). *Exercise adherence in sport for all from youth to adulthood.* Paper presented at the World Congress on Sport for All, Tammerfors, Finland.

Engström, L.-M. (1992, July). *Sport habits as a part of a lifestyle among young people and adults.* Paper presented at the ICPER-symposium, Louvain, Belgium.

Engström, L.-M. (1993). Importance and influence of behavioural aspects on the participation and attrition of youth in sport. In W. Duquet, P. De Knop, & L. Bollaert (Eds.), *Youth sport: A social approach* (pp. 76-89). Brussels, Belgium: VUBpress.

Larsson, B. (1993). *Idrottsvanor och social bakgrund: En studie av 15-åringar i Stockholms län* [Sport habits and social background: A study of 15-year-olds in Stockholm]. Stockholm: HLS Förlag.

Patriksson, G. (1987). *Idrottens barn: Idrottsvanor—stress—"utslagning"* [Children in sport: Sport habits—stress—dropouts]. Stockholm: Friskvårdscentrum.

Patriksson, G. (1990). Sport activity patterns among children and youth in sports clubs. In W. Duquet, P. De Knop, & L. Bollaert (Eds.), *Youth sport: A social approach* (pp. 118-125). Brussels, Belgium: VUBpress.

Part V

Youth Sport in Oceania

Chapter 21 Australia

Henny Oldenhove

Australia is a vast island continent covering some 7.5 million km². It has a population of 17.2 million people, 85% of whom live in urban centers generally situated in coastal areas. The climate ranges from subtropical to temperate, a fact that has encouraged an active outdoor lifestyle evidenced by the involvement of some 6 million people in sporting activities. Australia also has significant multicultural diversity, with more than 20% of the population having been born outside the country.

Australia is a federation of eight states and territories and has federal, state, and local governments. Australian education is the responsibility of state and territorial authorities and comprises state, Roman Catholic, and independent systems. There are 1.76 million 6-to-12-year-olds who attend 8,550 primary schools and 1.28 million 13-to-17-year-olds in 2,200 high schools.

Australians are passionate about their sport. Whether participating or watching, sport is a highly valued cultural tradition, and is considered an essential experience for young people. In Australia, most young people play sport at some stage in their developing years.

Involvement in sport is highly valued by parents and young people themselves. The sporting system is diverse in its offerings to young people and their active participation is vigorously sought. Yet at the same time, there are concerns about how young people are introduced to sport, the quality of the experiences they have, and the pathways that are available to them. These concerns hold whether young people are talented sportspersons or social participants. This challenge in Australian sport is one which is being actively pursued by sporting organizations and governments at all levels. The following description will highlight the issues and detail some of the strategies developed to address these issues. While there is still a long way to go, the direction has been set and it is one which is showing signs of making a difference.

The Organizational Network

Youth sport in Australia is primarily the domain of the school and community club system. This relationship, however, is ill-defined and operates as a loose association where young people themselves determine their involvement in either the school or the club system, or both. This choice is further varied by different practices in delivery at state, regional, and local levels between schools and clubs.

Most young people have ready access to sporting opportunities. While the

245

scope available in small and remote communities is limited compared to their larger counterparts, all communities provide sporting opportunities for young people.

In addition to choosing where to play sport, there is also the choice of which sport. Australia must surely offer the most diverse sporting options available. There are some 140 recognized national sports, most of which encourage youth participation. While this choice enriches and diversifies Australian sport, there is also the dilemma of too few people across too many sports. However, the egalitarian attitude of Australians would make consolidation of sports an extremely difficult task.

Governments at the national, state, and local levels all make a significant contribution to sport. At the national level, the Australian Sports Commission provides support for the achievement of excellence in sport and for broad-based participation initiatives, including a program for youth sport called AUSSIE SPORT. State governments provide similar support to sport at the state level, while local governments provide much of the local infrastructure for sport through the provision of facilities.

Club Sport

There are some 35,000 sport clubs in Australia, ranging across the 140 different sports mentioned earlier, and varying markedly in membership, facilities, and programs offered. Most of these clubs are sport-specific and generally cater to all age groups from the 5-year-old to the mature participant. Most youth participants progress through the clubs' various age groups and through stages of development from modified to adult sport. Since most clubs are established as community-based clubs and cater both to the youth and the senior player, they provide and encourage long-term participation opportunities and actively cater to the entire family. Sporting clubs will be found in all communities, large or small. In some remote outback areas it is not unusual for a team from one club to travel up to 400 km to play against another club!

Clubs cater mainly to competition rather than recreation, particularly for young people, although the competition ranges through modified, graded, and social levels. Young people perceive the sport club to offer a more serious approach to competition than does the school.

Community clubs are the basis for sport delivery. They are supported and linked to regional, state, and national governing bodies. The regional associations are responsible for organizing and conducting the local competitions, setting and overseeing local policies and directions, and encouraging player development. The state associations conduct statewide competitions, coordinate elite talent squads, prepare state teams, provide coach education, and oversee development programs. National sporting associations generally set policy, determine the overall sport development directions, prepare national teams and talent squads, and conduct national competitions. The relationships among national, state, and regional associations are often tenuous and strained, although there is an evolving tendency for all levels of sport to develop more cooperative relationships.

Young people choose to join clubs in order to participate in regular competitions which are played mainly on Saturdays and Sundays, or, increasingly, in midweek in the evenings. Many young people will belong to a number of clubs in order to play a summer and a winter sport or to play a number of different sports.

There are very few multisport clubs in Australia. There is, however, a trend to develop multipurpose facilities. These are often commercially based and tend to cater to the occasional or fitness participant or to lease out their facilities to individual sporting associations for their regular competitions.

The provision of sport for young people in clubs is often provided by parents and volunteers who either choose or are cajoled to coach, officiate, transport participants, or administer the programs. There are some 1.1 million volunteers in Australian sport, many of whom are involved in youth sport. This heavy dependency on volunteers creates a high turnover, and parents often stay only as long as their children are involved. The greatest consequence of this dependency on parents/volunteers is the uncertainty of the quality of the coaching provided to young people.

School Sport Programs

Traditionally, all primary (ages 5 to 12) and secondary (ages 12 to 18) schools have provided sport programs as extensions of their physical education programs. These programs have been conducted either on school time on a sport afternoon, or as an extracurricular activity after school, or on Saturday mornings.

Participation in these extracurricular programs is generally optional and many young people will choose to play for a school team in either the same or a different sport than they may be involved with in the community club. Many choose to play only for the school or only for the club. Teachers involved with these school programs usually do so in a voluntary capacity and receive no compensation in money or time from their employers.

The organization of formal competitive school sport programs is the responsibility of the Australian Schools Sports Council and its state affiliates of primary and secondary school sport associations. The council and the state associations are supported by the education authorities in terms of personnel and program money. These associations are primarily responsible for the organization and conduct of competitive sport at the regional, state, and interstate levels for both primary and secondary schools. Their major international event is the biannual Pacific School Games involving Pacific Rim countries in track and field, swimming, and gymnastics. With limited budgets, participation in all of these competitions is primarily on a user-pays principle.

A 1992 Australian Government Senate Inquiry into Sport and Physical Education in Australian Schools found that physical education and sport are being dramatically reduced throughout schools in Australia (Senate Standing Committee on Environment, Recreation and the Arts, 1992). The inquiry found that these programs are rapidly diminishing as a result of:

- crowded school curricula,
- lack of coherent sport and physical education policies by state education authorities,
- increased devolution of decision making to schools,
- reduction in the number of specialist physical education teachers,
- limited preservice and inservice preparation and support for generalist and specialist PE and sport teachers, and
- reduction of support budgets for competitive school sport.

As a result, the future of a structured and systematic school sport (and physical education) system is in jeopardy. It is, however, quite ironic that the Australian private school system, representing 26% of all schools, has maintained a strong commitment and obligation to providing all their students with a comprehensive and sometimes compulsory sport program.

There is currently no guarantee or measure ensuring that students attending their compulsory years of schooling will be adequately physically educated or have access to an introductory sport program. A National Health and Physical Education Curriculum is currently being developed which will need to address this situation and take into account the recommendations of the Senate inquiry. This curriculum will guide Australian schools in their development of programs and will need to be adequately supported and provided with resources by the education authorities, although there appears considerable doubt that this support will be given.

School-Club Relationships

One of the greatest challenges facing youth sport in Australia is developing a cooperative approach between schools and clubs for its provision.

In 1991 the Australian Sports Commission conducted a comprehensive market research project in relation to young people aged 13 to 18 and their involvement in and perceptions of sport (Australian Sports Commission, 1991). Their report, "Sport for Young Australians," highlighted the importance and interdependence of sport in schools and clubs. It is evident that the two delivery systems are mutually dependent and that neither system is capable of doing it alone.

The research found that young people fell into one of four participation categories. These were nonparticipants (36%), school-only participants (26%), school and club participants (29%), and club-only participants (9%). There was also evidence of significant movement from school sport to club sport, emphasizing the vital role schools can play in nurturing sport participation for young people.

Schools were found to be particularly important in providing an access route for young people from non–English-speaking backgrounds. Many of these young people only play sport at school mainly because of their parents' respect for school-based activities. Schools should also be encouraged to provide a transition path from school to club sport for these students.

There is an increasing tendency and demand for community sport clubs to provide the sporting opportunities that the school system is reducing. Because sport clubs can only offer a sport-specific experience and are heavily dependent on volunteers, there is a need for schools to work in conjunction with community clubs and still provide diverse Sport for All programs through the school.

Sport Participation

The full extent of sport participation (including that of youths) in Australia is not clearly known.

The most commonly used measures are

- sport estimates of registered players,
- a national survey commissioned by the Department of the Arts, Sport, the Environment, Tourism and Territories in the period October 1985 to October 1987 (Department of the Arts, Sport, the Environment, Tourism and Territories, 1988),
- the "Sport for Young Australians" Research Report (Australian Sports Commission, 1991), and
- two state youth-participation surveys in South Australia (Sale, 1991) and the Australian Capital Territory (Clough & Traill, 1992).

The Australian Sports Commission also requests gross registration figures annually. These figures have many limitations, including a tendency for sports to overestimate numbers and the lack of a comprehensive registration system in many sport organizations. There is also no breakdown available for age, gender, school, and/or community, or other important details.

Some trends, however, are notable. There is a decline of registered participation of youth and this dropout is of great concern to sporting bodies. The extent of this dropout is not clear, as many studies are limited to a specific sport and do not take into account

- the participant who shifts from one sport to another,
- the participant who reduces the number of sports he or she is involved with in order to concentrate on one or two,
- the increasing number of sports offered, spreading participants across a greater range of activities,
- the participant who moves away from being a registered sport participant to being an active participant in nonregistered competition,
- the physically active person who is an occasional participant and therefore not included in registration figures, and
- the participant who drops out for a short period of time and then returns in either the same or a different sport.

Participation studies from two states, South Australia (Sale, 1991) and the Australian Capital Territory (Clough & Traill, 1992) indicated that the percentage participation rates for 7-to-12-year-olds is in the vicinity of 55 to 60%. The

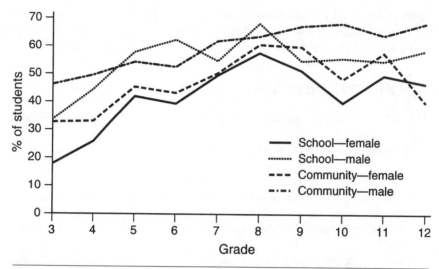

Figure 21.1 Participation rate and age among Australian youngsters.
Note. From *Junior Sport in South Australia*, by B. Sale, 1991, Adelaide, Australia: South Australian Sports Institute. Copyright 1991 by South Australian Sports Institute. Reprinted by permission.

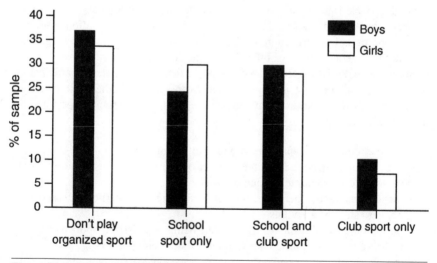

Figure 21.2 Where boys and girls play sport.

way participation fluctuates across age, gender, and participation in school and community sport from grades 3 through 12 is presented in Figure 21.1.

The 1991 "Sport for Young Australians" research analyzed the level of participation for 13-to-18-year-old boys and girls and across ages. The findings are presented in Figures 21.2 and 21.3.

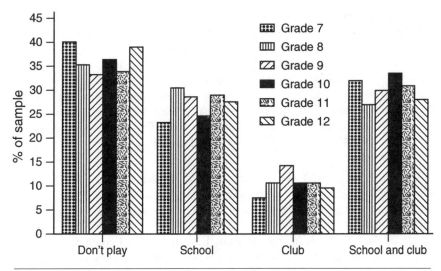

Figure 21.3   Age and participation.

Trends

A number of recent trends are having a significant effect on sport participation.

Policy development. In October 1991 a national conference titled "Junior Sport: Time to Deliver" was conducted by the Australian Sports Commission and the Confederation of Australian Sport to examine the delivery of youth sport in Australia. As a response to growing concerns about the delivery of sport for youth within schools and in the community, the conference addressed the structural and philosophical changes required for a more systematic and coordinated approach.

The 350 representatives from sport, education, and government who attended strongly recommended and supported the need for a National Junior Sport Policy. In addition, the Senate inquiry, which was a consequence of the Junior Sport Conference, recommended that

> the Commonwealth, through the Australian Education Council, and the Sport and Recreation Minister's Council, consult with state and territory educational authorities, and sport and recreation authorities to ensure that written school sport policies are prepared and distributed as a matter of priority (p. 25).

The Australian Sports Commission has recognized this strong demand for policy development and has accepted a role in coordinating these policy outcomes.

The National Junior Sport Policy will seek to provide the necessary framework to achieve this goal. The policy, launched in late 1993, draws together the issues, initiatives, and agencies involved with youth sport and provides a framework of principles to guide the delivery and conduct of youth sport in Australia.

The policy working party brings together the national sporting organizations through the Confederation of Australian Sport, the Council of Directors General of Education representing the state education authorities, the state departments of sport and recreation, the Australian Schools Sports Council, and the Australian Sports Commission to prepare the framework and coordinate the necessary consultation process. States are also working on their own junior sport policies, which will be consistent with the national policy but will enable states to exercise flexibility in detail and implementation. The national sporting organizations will also develop sport-specific policies consistent with the National Junior Sport Policy. The National Junior Sport Policy is a significant step forward for the provision of youth sport and will help to identify and secure the resources required to implement the policy.

Coach education and accreditation. The National Coach Accreditation Scheme (NCAS), run by the Australian Coaching Council, is a highly successful and widely recognized scheme that provides a structure for coach education in Australia.

Under the NCAS, each sport develops Level 1, 2, and 3 coach accreditation courses. In addition to the accredited courses, sports are also encouraged to develop and conduct orientation-to-coaching courses for beginning community coaches and, especially, for generalist primary teachers. In the 10 years since the inception of the NCAS, some 100,000 people have undertaken at least Level 1 accreditation.

These coaching programs have strongly influenced the need for and appreciation of quality coaching. Many sports now regard coaching accreditation as a requirement for their coaches at all levels. Given the special requirements of coaching youths, sports are increasingly recognizing that their Level 1 and 2 courses also need to be provided as Level 1 and 2 youth courses.

Recently, the Coaching Council, in conjunction with state departments of sport and recreation, has established coaching centers in each state to provide greater support and impetus to the delivery of the NCAS scheme at state and regional levels. In conjunction with AUSSIE SPORT there is a major focus on coach education for those working with youths.

The Coaching Council and national sporting organizations have also developed numerous coaching support resources. Their latest publication, ''Coaching Children,'' provides a comprehensive guide to those who coach young people.

Equity and access.   The participation of girls in sport is a major issue in youth sport. There is a clear recognition that *special measures* initiatives are required to encourage greater participation by girls in sport. However, there may also need to be more central changes to systems, practices, behaviors, and attitudes to ensure that equality for girls becomes a reality at all levels and in all activities. The Australian Sports Commission has also initiated a focus to promote the participation of girls through the Active Girls Campaign promoted by the Women and Sport Unit. Still, the issue of girls' participation in sport requires a greater commitment by schools and community sport for genuine equity to be achieved.

Similarly, the participation issues for youths with disabilities, and those from different ethnic, isolated rural, and low socioeconomic backgrounds also require serious attention. At present they are not receiving equitable access to sport.

Talent identification.   The issue of talent identification is one which sport in Australia is slowly coming to grips with. Talent has traditionally been identified through the selection process of watching youths play in organized competition at regional, state, and interstate levels.

Talent identification, rather than selection, programs are currently being examined and developed by several sports. One current scheme operates in rowing. By testing the physiological attributes of youths, the program can identify potential rowers and give them the opportunity for intensive training. The Australian Junior Women's Four, who won the 1990 World Championships, were a product of this identification scheme.

Most talent, however, is nurtured through the hierarchical competition structure and increasingly supported by the implementation of talent squads at regional, state, and national levels. These talent squads are conducted by individual sports and are often supported by government grants and schemes such as the Intensive Training Centre program, state institutes or academies, national training programs, and the National Institute of Sport.

There is a trend emerging with education authorities in the provision of sport high schools that cater to talented youths to aid them in pursuing both their sporting and academic aspirations. The issues of when talent identification is appropriate, at what age to specialize, potential burnout, the ethics of testing large school-based populations, the competition for individuals by sport, and the needs of the individual are yet to be clearly articulated, however. A systematic and integrated process of talent identification and development is an essential aspect of youth sport that must be addressed.

Commercialization of sport.   The growing numbers of commercial centers for sport are attracting many youth participants. These centers enable young people to engage in sport with almost a "fast sport" (like fast food) approach. While it is often more costly, the facilities and the activities are readily available throughout the week and only require a short time commitment. The center also provides a convenient and well-equipped facility for social interaction. Unlike participants in club sport, participants at these commercial centers are not encumbered with training, officiating duties, long season commitments, or the need for parents to drive them everywhere. Older participants can also find valuable part-time work in officiating because this role, unlike at most clubs, is paid for in the commercial centers.

This type of sport provision is not usually affiliated with the parent bodies and thus the opportunity for talented youths, in particular, to progress through the sport ranks is limited and requires them to join the more traditional sport structure. The challenge for parent bodies is to find a harmonious relationship with these commercial centers so as not to fragment their sport and to allow for more mutual transitions between the two. It is also a challenge for the traditional sport system to look at the success of these commercial centers and to address what components attract youth with the view to incorporating them into their own practices.

In some states there are a number of licensed sporting and social clubs that derive considerable income from alcohol and gambling. These clubs often expand their activities beyond this core and it is not unusual for a licensed soccer or social club to provide, and encourage their members into, other sporting activities, either inside or outside mainstream sport. These clubs are also supportive of programs for youth.

Social changes.   The traditional weekend, when most sport is played, is gradually being eroded. As work practices change, the opportunity to play sport needs to be more flexible. With the increase of retail hours into seven-day shopping and greater employment opportunities in the tourist and service industries, many youths, and the necessary volunteer providers, are being excluded from the traditional sport competitions. This trend in flexible work practices is starting to affect sport participation. Sport will need to look at how it can accommodate these lifestyle changes and start to shift some of its competitions into evening and midweek time slots or find a greater shift to the "fast sport" model. The most accessible time for youth sport is in the hours immediately after school, but unfortunately this is the time when most adult volunteers are still at work.

Barriers to Participation

Studies have indicated that there are a number of barriers to sport participation (Australian Sports Commission, 1992a). The Sport for Young Australians report highlighted the following issues and reinforced the similar findings of numerous other studies (see Figure 21.4).

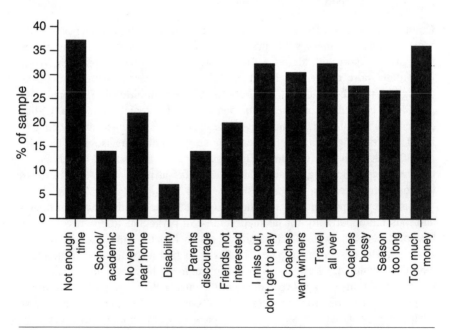

Figure 21.4   "Turnoffs" to sport.

Time.   Not having enough perceived time was the single most often repeated "turnoff," or reason for not playing sport.

Cost.   The second highest turnoff to sport was that it costs too much. Some young people, primarily in underprivileged schools, identified cost as a reason they did not participate in sport.

While parents from lower socioeconomic areas generally give their children more pocket money, they provide less financial support for their involvement in sport than parents from high socioeconomic areas, who support their children's participation in sport by funding sporting activities, club fees, equipment, and clothing.

Travel.   Having to "travel all over the place" to play matches was, along with "missing out" (not getting a chance to play), the third-highest barrier to participation.

Self-esteem.   Many young people who do not participate in sport would like to but do not feel they are good enough. The researchers noted from the group discussions that some young people who did not want to leave felt they had been "forced" to stop participating. These young people had been enjoying their sport until they were classed as "not good enough to continue"—they did not have the opportunity to play at the level of their ability. They felt humiliated in front of their peers, suffered great emotional hurt, lost self-confidence, and continued to feel a sense of unfairness. They were defeated by the "win at all costs" ethos and while it continues most will not participate in organized sport again.

For young people currently not playing sport, access within sport rather than to sport was also important. Young people would be more interested in sport if there were more opportunities to play, that is, more teams or relaxed substitution rules which give all players a fair go. Most young people do not like sitting on the substitution benches waiting and hoping for a chance to go on.

Coaching.   The experiences young people have with coaches have a direct impact on their level of participation. The research indicated that one out of three youth participants will drop out of sport because of a coach. This usually relates to not getting a go, the coach having favorites, a too-heavy emphasis on "winning at all costs," and poor instruction.

Gender differences.   While age and gender do not influence overall participation of 13-to-18-year-old students, they do affect what sports are played, where they are played, and the amount of time spent playing. Girls predominantly still play sports traditionally considered women's sports and boys take part in traditional men's sports.

The results nevertheless indicate that boys have a greater range of opportunities and easier access to sport than girls. Girls are not equally encouraged or recognized in their sport participation and resources are not equitably shared.

Ethnicity.   Ethnic background also has an impact on the level of participation and the types of sports this age group plays. Children from non–English-speaking backgrounds play organized sports mainly at school. In some of the communities surveyed, children from non–English-speaking backgrounds represented over one third of the school's total population.

Schools have an important role to play in encouraging parental support for sport and providing opportunities for children from all ethnic backgrounds to participate in school and community sports.

Study.   It was found that a small proportion of young people drop out of sport in the later years of school to concentrate on their studies. However, most of them indicate a readiness to resume some form of sport once they have finished studying.

Work.   Students working part-time or in family businesses have additional difficulties. While some young people have part-time jobs that can fit comfortably around sport schedules, other jobs, particularly those in family businesses, bring with them expectations and obligations that make it difficult to find time for sport.

Competition.   The current competition structure and "win at all costs" philosophy is considered to be the main reason young people quit sport or do not start playing sport.

Team sports are preferred, but organized team sports are currently associated with being too competitive, too organized, and too serious, especially by the female participants.

Clubs and associations.   Lack of grounds and facilities may not be a major barrier to becoming involved with sport—but lack of coordinated, accurate, and easily available information concerning the location of clubs, or contact people for clubs, may be. Both parents and children, but especially parents, want the sport near home or school—and played as soon after school as possible. Weekend games are preferred over midweek evening games. Young people also have a strong desire for opportunities for social interaction, but many clubs inhibit these opportunities by their lack of organization and indeed by their competition-based structures.

Promotional Campaigns

The most significant impact on youth sport in Australia has been that of AUSSIE SPORT. While national sporting organizations have initiated several sport-specific programs, AUSSIE SPORT has provided a framework and a catalyst for a focus on youth sport development.

AUSSIE SPORT is a national initiative of the Australian Sports Commission, which aims to enhance youth sport by influencing the practices of key agencies in the development and delivery of sport. Since 1986 the Australian Sports Commission, through AUSSIE SPORT, has been developing a range of strategies, programs, and promotions which seek to enrich the lives of young people through quality sporting experiences which will encourage lifelong participation.

AUSSIE SPORT was launched in 1986 and has expanded considerably since the early days, when it commenced by introducing the concept of modified sport for primary-school-aged children. Since 1989, AUSSIE SPORT has adopted a much broader charter and now targets young people from 3 to 20 years old.

AUSSIE SPORT is coordinated nationally by the Australian Sports Commission and is delivered in partnership with state departments of education and of sport and recreation through state AUSSIE SPORT units, with involvement and support from national sporting organizations. These state units supplement and complement the national approach in a number of different ways.

The key focus of AUSSIE SPORT is one of advocacy and facilitation. It is this role, along with the development of supporting programs, promotions, and resources, that is influencing the attitudes and practices of those agencies that develop and deliver youth sport. Since 1986, the impact of AUSSIE SPORT has included

- an adoption of AUSSIE SPORT philosophies and program elements into school sport curricula by 96% of primary schools, across eight state education authorities including state, Roman Catholic, and independent schools,
- the registration as AUSSIE SPORT clubs of over 5,000 sport clubs,
- the undertaking of the introductory Level O coaching courses by 9,000 coaches,
- the attendance of AUSSIE SPORT inservice courses by 8,000 teachers,
- the training of 4,000 youth leaders through the AUSSIE SPORT leadership programs,
- a "benefits of sport" media campaign and a mailing to primary school boards and principals on how to deliver an effective school sport policy and program,
- the annual distribution of 100,000 copies of "Codes of Behaviour,"
- the production of a magazine, AUSSIE SPORT "Action," which is distributed to all Australian schools and AUSSIE SPORT clubs,
- a national youth sport conference, "Time to Deliver," which led directly to the National Junior Sport Policy development and the Senate inquiry,
- the securing of two national sponsors to support, expand, and deliver AUSSIE SPORT programs, and
- the appointments of more than 60 full-time and 250 voluntary field officers who are advocating AUSSIE SPORT in the community.

Research into the impact of AUSSIE SPORT suggests that while no direct causal relationships can be established, involvement in AUSSIE SPORT has had a positive effect on young people's enjoyment of sport and on their desire to continue to participate in sport (Australian Sports Commission, 1992b; Robertson, 1992).

There are five strategic areas in which AUSSIE SPORT seeks to influence and provide assistance. These are public education, school education, sport clubs/associations, school-club linkages, and youth leadership. These strategic areas are supported by a number of national AUSSIE SPORT programs that are sequential in development and act as models for inclusion into existing programs. The programs progress from play to basic movement and sport-related skills as well as focusing on leadership at older age levels. The programs are designed to be supportive to programs of the school and club.

• Sportstart is a resource designed to help and encourage parents and caregivers provide, and be involved with, play opportunities for young children. Sportstart reinforces basic movement skills for children.

• Sport It! is a primary school program sponsored by Pizza Hut (Aust.) which enables teachers to implement a series of fundamental motor skills lessons in six skill areas.

• Modified Sport Program is sponsored by Kellogg (Aust.) and is the initial AUSSIE SPORT program that advocates modified games for children. In cooperation with national sporting organizations, The Modified Sport Program promotes some 43 modified games.

• The Active Girls Campaign is a joint initiative of the Women and Sport Unit and AUSSIE SPORT that aims to encourage a greater participation in sport by adolescent girls.

• Sport Search is a sport counseling package for 11-to-17-year-olds. The aim of the program is to provide students with feedback regarding sports they may enjoy and achieve success in.

• Sportsfun is a school based leadership program that develops young people's leadership skills. It provides an after-school sport experience for children and is conducted by these secondary leaders.

• CAPS (Challenge, Achievement and Pathways in Sport) is a sport-based leadership program that encourages young people aged 14 to 20 to become involved in training programs in the areas of coaching, administration, umpiring/refereeing, officiating, sport health, and participation. All the AUSSIE SPORT programs are supported by extensive resources and materials of high quality.

The national sporting organizations, in conjunction with AUSSIE SPORT, have developed beginner coach manuals and instructional skill videos. They have also produced support and promotional materials for their modified sport versions such as Minkey (hockey), Kanga Cricket (cricket), Roo-ball (soccer), and so forth.

The developments in the area of coach education and accreditation through the Australian Coaching Council have also had a major impact on how youth sport is conducted.

Conclusion

The participation of young people in sport is highly valued in Australia. Ironically, it is sometimes this high status afforded to sport that brings about practices not considered desirable for youths. The "win at all costs" ethos, so often influencing the practices of coaches and parents in a negative way, quite clearly has a detrimental effect on many youths. Although these factors are still prevalent in youth sport, they are becoming less acceptable as a broader awareness of the importance of quality sport experiences and appropriate practices influences those who provide youth sport.

These changes have not occurred by accident. They are a result of a concerted effort by government, sporting, and educational organizations based on sound research and genuine need. Coordination and cooperation by all key agencies has been essential to achieve a common aim and direction for enhancing youth sport in Australia.

The future of quality youth sport in Australia will be largely determined by the successful implementation of the National Junior Sport Policy, which provides the framework for concerted and cooperative action. In implementing it there is a need for education and the sporting community to work together as one. Without this coordinated responsibility, youth sport will once again become fragmented and disparate. There will always be a strong focus on youth sport in Australia— now is our chance to get it right. The direction has been set, and it is the youth of Australia who will judge the outcome through greater enjoyment and involvement in sport.

References

Australian Sports Commission. (1991). *Sport for young Australians: Widening the gateways to participation*. Canberra, Australia: Author.

Australian Sports Commission. (1992a). *Youth sport—The next step: Physical and sport education*. A Report by the Senate Standing Committee on Environment, Recreation and the Arts. Canberra, Australia: Author.

Australian Sports Commission. (1992b). *AUSSIE SPORT evaluation*. Canberra, Australia: Author.

Clough, J., & Traill, R. (1992). *A mapping of participation rates in junior sport in the Australian Capital Territory*. Canberra, Australia: ACT Government.

Department of the Arts, Sport, the Environment, Tourism and Territories. (1988). *Physical activity levels of Australians*. Canberra, Australia: Australian Government Publishing Services.

Robertson, I. (1992). *Children, AUSSIE SPORT and organised junior sport*. Canberra, Australia: Australian Sports Commission.

Sale, B. (1991). *Junior sport in South Australia*. Adelaide, Australia: South Australian Sports Institute.

Senate Standing Committee on Environment, Recreation and the Arts. (1992). *Physical and sport education*. Canberra, Australia: Commonwealth of Australia.

Chapter 22 New Zealand

David G. Russell
Justine B. Allen
Noela C. Wilson

New Zealand is a small country with an impressive international sporting record spanning nearly a century—from Anthony Wildings's Wimbledon titles around the turn of the century to the Eisenhower Trophy of the amateur Golf Team in 1992. Consisting of three main islands in the Southwest Pacific Ocean and 300,000 km^2, New Zealand has a temperate climate with well-defined seasons but without great extremes in temperatures.

The population of 3.4 million is composed primarily of British stock and indigenous Maori. There are 680,000 New Zealanders aged 6 to 18 years. After the Second World War there was an influx of Dutch immigrants, and a sizable number of Pacific Islanders and Asians have immigrated over the past two decades. New Zealand as a nation traces its modern history from the Treaty of Waitangi between the Maori and Queen Victoria in 1840. Immigration from Britain, particularly from England and Scotland, followed. This early British influence on the young country is still evident in its parliamentary system of government, its exotic flora and fauna, and its sport. Rugby and cricket, so important in the boys' schools of the last century in the "Mother Country," are still the preferred winter and summer team sports among young New Zealand males (15 to 18 years), with a third playing the former and 28% the latter. Netball is the only team sport of any major consequence among females of the same age group (played by 26%). Tennis is the preferred individual sport among this age group (preferred by 39% of females and 40% of males).

Among younger New Zealanders (5 to 15 years), 80% are reported to participate in sporting activities (see Table 22.1). Among this group, a higher proportion participate in swimming than in any other activity (boys 42%, girls 51%). As for the 15-to-18-year-olds, rugby and cricket (both 16%) are the most reported team sports. Netball is similarly popular among these younger (5 to 15 years) girls (21%).

The Organizational Network

The term "sport" in New Zealand generally refers to physical activities which are or can be competitive on an organized basis. The Life in New Zealand survey (LINZ), from which most of the data in this chapter are derived, questioned respondents about organized sport and informal, social sport (Russell & Wilson, 1991, Appendix D).

Table 22.1   Sport Participation of 5-to-15-Year-Old New Zealanders (%)

Gender	5-7	8-11	11-13	14-15	All
			Age (years)		
Boys	62	86	86	88	81
Girls	69	87	83	73	79
All	66	87	85	81	80

Organized sport was defined as "activities or sports organized by an association or club for competition" (Question 25). Informal social sport was defined as participation "on an informal, social basis away from home . . ." (Question 26).

Young New Zealanders participate in sport in large numbers. Children typically start playing sport at a young age. For example, the members of the 1992 All Blacks (New Zealand's Rugby Union Team) first played on teams at the mean age of 5.6 years. As Table 22.1 shows, 62% of boys and 69% of girls aged 5 to 7 years play some form of sport, so rugby players are not unique. Schools have not generally provided sporting opportunities at this young age, so how do these children play sport? About the middle of this century, primary (elementary) schools organized competitions in the major sports for children as young as 8 or 9 years. In the late 1950s and early 1960s in New Zealand, as in many countries, there was a change of attitude toward competition. Cooperation became more important. The large school-based sporting competitions lost favor and sport clubs became the focus of competitive sport for children. For example, the local rugby clubs organized competitions and children started playing competitive rugby as young as 4 years. So there developed a dual system of school and club sport (Russell & Abernethy, 1984). Russell and Isaac (1986) investigated the participation of 11-year-old children in school and club sport using data derived from the "Dunedin Multidisciplinary Child Development Study" (McGee & Silva, 1982). These data show that, in the southern city of Dunedin, 80% of 11-year-olds, both boys and girls, play some form of competitive sport at their schools, and 73% of boys and 40% of girls at clubs. Russell and Isaac also reported that the age at which children start playing competitive sport for clubs is significantly younger than for school sport.

In 1984, then-Minister of Recreation and Sport Hon. Mike Moore called for a review of sport and recreation in New Zealand. That report, "Sport on the Move" (Scott, 1985), addressed what it perceived as a lack of commitment on the part of the education system to sport. However, the main outcome of the Scott Report was the establishment of the Hillary Commission for Recreation and Sport.

The Hillary Commission provided the vehicle whereby the issue of school sport could be addressed. One of the early initiatives of the Commission was

KiwiSport, a system of modified sport which takes into account children's developmental and skill levels. KiwiSport is based on Australia's AUSSIE SPORT (Goodman, 1992) and is designed for primary school children. A second initiative, SportFit, is designed for high school students, and was introduced in 1990 on a trial basis. Its purpose is to build on the success of KiwiSport to encourage continued sport participation into the teenage years. Both KiwiSport and SportFit are the result of close cooperation of the various national sporting bodies, the school system, and the Hillary Commission.

These two initiatives lie alongside club sport, and the more traditional competitive school sport at the high school level, as vehicles to encourage sport participation among young New Zealanders (see Figure 22.1). They will be discussed in greater detail later in this chapter.

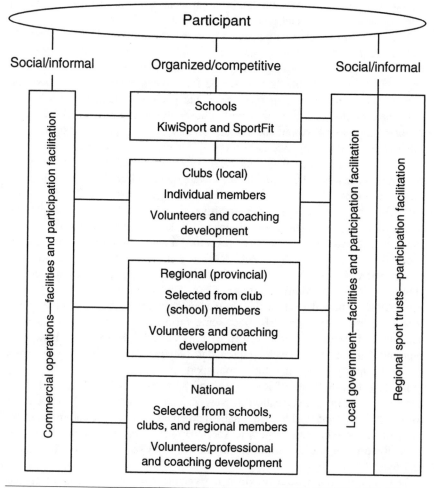

Figure 22.1   Structure of sport in New Zealand.

But what about elite sport? By elite sport we mean international-level sport. National sporting bodies are responsible for the development of their athletes for the international level. They are assisted in a variety of ways. Coaching New Zealand (CNZ), the national association of coaches, provides coaching courses and assists national bodies to prepare and run coaching courses. Besides their national coach, many sporting bodies also employ a technical director and some have established coaching academies. The Hillary Commission's Draft Strategic Plan "Moving a Nation" (Hillary Commission, 1993) specifies as a target to "assist all major sports to enhance their performance via coaching academies" by 1997-98 (p. 11). In addition, a number of sports have established youth development squads. The most recent example of the effectiveness of this approach was New Zealand's winning of the Eisenhower Trophy for the World Amateur Golf Championships in Vancouver in 1992. The members of that team came up through the New Zealand Golf Association's Titleist Youth Development Squad. At a regional level, many sport associations also employ regional coaching directors.

Both sporting bodies and individual athletes may receive financial support. Sporting bodies receive funds from the Hillary Commission based partly on their registered membership, and for Commonwealth and Olympic Games preparation from the New Zealand Olympic and Commonwealth Games Association. Individual athletes who have achieved world ranking or who are judged to have that potential may receive direct funding from the New Zealand Sports Foundation. This foundation receives its funding primarily from corporate sponsorship. Thus, young elite athletes may have available considerable direct financial support from their national organization, the Hillary Commission, and the Sports Foundation.

Sport Participation

To provide an overview of the population, we will consider children from 5 to 15 years. Secondly, we will consider children aged 15 to 18 years, and, thirdly, the 19+ years group. The data are derived from the LINZ survey of the health-related lifestyles of the New Zealand population (Russell & Wilson, 1991; Wilson, Russell, Spears, & Herbison, 1991). These data are from three samples. The data on 5-to-15-year-old children are derived from reports of adult respondents concerning the activities of children of these ages in residence. The second sample, 15 to 18 years, is a snowball sample (see Goodman, 1961) derived from those selected from the electoral rolls. The 19+ years sample was similarly derived from the country's 97 electoral rolls. The compliance rate for LINZ was 80% (Wilson et al., 1991).

5-15 Years

As we have seen (see Table 22.1), sport participation among New Zealand children is 66% at 5 to 7 years and 81% at 14 to 15 years. Table 22.2 gives the participation rates for the more popular sports among 8-to-15-year-old children.

These data refer only to sport outside school hours. Only those activities attracting at least 5% of this age group are included.

The most popular winter team sport for girls is netball (21%). The next most popular team sport is field hockey (5%). Girls' participation in summer team sports is low, with less than 5% in any one sport. Of individual activities, swimming (51%), cycling (17%), and tennis (14%) are the most popular among girls. For boys, soccer (17%) and rugby (16%) are the most popular winter sports, and cricket (16%) the most popular summer team sport. Nine percent of 14- and 15-year-old boys play softball/baseball. Preferred individual activities among boys are the same as among girls: swimming (42%), cycling (21%), and tennis (17%).

Two things stand out in these data: first, participation in any activity is quite consistent among 8-to-13-year-old boys, but drops from 87% among 8-to-11-year-old girls to 73% at ages 14 and 15. Second, with the exception of tennis for boys, and netball and track and field for girls, participation rates drop from 11 to 13 years (primary school) to 14 to 15 years (high school).

These data suggest that boys of these ages tend to drop one sporting activity to participate in another, while girls drop out. It is possible that boys participate

Table 22.2   Sport Participation of New Zealand Children Aged 8-15 Years (%)

Sport	Boys			Girls			All
	8-10	11-13	14-15	8-10	11-13	14-15	
Badminton	4	4	9	2	3	4	3
Basketball	2	8	7	4	6	5	4
Cricket	23	24	14	2	4	4	12
Cycling	26	23	20	19	19	10	20
Dancing	1	0	1	20	7	6	5
Gymnastics	2	1	1	13	6	2	4
Hockey	3	6	5	5	5	7	5
Horseback riding	4	1	3	12	13	13	8
Martial arts	6	4	5	1	2	0	3
Netball	2	1	1	22	28	23	14
Rugby	17	23	17	1	1	0	11
Skateboarding	9	12	9	0	0	1	6
Soccer	21	18	14	1	2	1	9
Softball	4	5	5	6	6	1	6
Swimming	47	42	34	69	54	28	46
Tennis	13	21	27	13	19	17	18
Track and field	6	9	7	7	8	10	8

Note. From *Life in New Zealand Commission Report: Vol. 3. Physical Activity* (p. 54), by W.G. Hopkins, N.C. Wilson, D.G. Russell, and G.P. Herbison, 1991, Dunedin, New Zealand: University of Otago.

in a wider range of physically active pastimes at a younger age and therefore have the confidence to attempt new activities. The attitudes of older New Zealanders may also influence this situation: of the males who started a new leisure activity over the previous 12 months, 40% cite as a reason to "compete with others," compared with 22% of women (Cushman, Laidler, Russell, Wilson, & Herbison, 1991). On the other hand, 83% of women and 73% of men took up a new activity "to feel better mentally/spiritually" and a significantly greater proportion of women than men "to relax and reduce stress." This tendency of women to take up leisure activities for reasons other than competition could be reflected in their dropping out of sport as they mature. Perhaps sport in general is considered too competitive by these young women and they gravitate toward other nonsport and noncompetitive pastimes.

15-18 Years

What about the young adults between 15 and 18 years? LINZ data (Hopkins, Wilson, Russell, & Herbison, 1991) show that one in three males plays rugby union and about one in five plays basketball, rugby league, or soccer as a winter team sport (see Table 22.3). The preferred summer team sports among males of this age are cricket (28%) and softball/baseball (17%). As for females, netball is the most popular, played by about one in four and basketball by less than one in five. Females' most preferred summer sports are cricket (17%) and softball/baseball (13%). It is worth noting that a small proportion of 15-to-18-year-old New Zealanders play the major national sport of the opposite gender (4% males play netball and 5% females play rugby union). This is a relatively recent trend with formal competitions (leagues) having been established only in the last five years.

Preferred individual activities show marked differences and similarities. There is a major difference in participation rates in two activities which are often available in the same facility: aerobics and weight lifting. Four percent of males and 39% of females participate in aerobics, and nearly 30% of males but only 7% of females in weight lifting. Motorized activities show similar gender differences with three to four times as many males participating in motorcycling/trailbiking and motorboating than females. However, by far the most popular individual activities among both genders in this age group are swimming (females 55%; males 40%), cycling (46% and 38% respectively), and tennis (39% and 40%). There are major gender differences found in the individual activities of archery/shooting (13% male, 1% female), snooker/pool (39%, 15%), skin/scuba diving (13%, 3%), and skateboarding (13%, 4%).

Individual activities that can be undertaken in a noncompetitive environment with friends predominate among females' preferences, with more than a third participating in aerobics, cycling, swimming, and tennis. This reflects the LINZ finding that friends constitute the major source of leisure companions among both males (82%) and females (81%) (Cushman et al., 1991).

Table 22.3   Sport Participation Among New Zealand Youths 15-18 Years (%)

Sport	Males	Females
Aerobics	5	39
Archery/shooting	13	1
Softball/baseball	17	13
Basketball	21	18
Canoeing	7	5
Cricket	28	17
Cycling	38	46
Golf	12	4
Hockey	5	9
Horseback riding	4	12
Martial arts	6	6
Motorboating	21	5
Motorcycling/trailbiking	24	9
Netball	4	26
Rink sports	2	5
Rowing	3	5
Rugby league	20	2
Rugby union	33	4
Sailing	8	6
Skateboarding	13	4
Skin/scuba diving	13	3
Snooker/pool	39	15
Snow sports	5	5
Soccer	18	5
Squash	16	11
Surfing/skiboarding	23	8
Swimming	40	55
Table tennis/badminton	20	18
Tennis	40	39
Ten-pin bowling	8	7
Track and field	14	10
Volleyball	16	16
Water skiing	6	7
Weight lifting	29	7

19+ Years

For all 19+ year-old New Zealanders the most popular individual activities are those enjoyed by at least 10% of the population. For team sports, the most popular are defined as those played by at least 5%.

Tables 22.4 and 22.5 show the participation rates in sport among males and females 15 years and older. Those sporting activities with rates of less than 5% are not included.

Table 22.4   Sport Participation Among Male New Zealanders (%)

Sport	Age (years)					
	15-18	19-24	25-44	45-64	65+	All
Aerobics	5	12	6	3	0	6
Archery/shooting	13	7	5	4	0	6
Basketball	21	11	2	1	0	5
Cricket	28	17	11	3	0	11
Cycling	38	22	14	8	3	16
Golf	12	9	10	17	13	12
Lawn bowls/croquet	1	0	1	12	24	5
Motorboating	21	26	7	6	5	11
Motorcycling/trailbiking	24	12	6	3	1	8
Rugby union	33	15	6	4	1	10
Sailing	8	8	4	7	4	6
Skindiving	13	11	5	2	0	6
Snooker/pool	39	31	18	19	16	23
Soccer	18	4	5	2	1	5
Softball/baseball	17	6	5	1	0	6
Squash	16	12	9	1	0	7
Surfing/sailboating	23	17	4	2	2	8
Swimming	40	42	23	13	10	25
Tennis	40	24	13	5	2	15
Track and field	14	8	7	2	0	6
Weight lifting	29	17	8	2	0	10

Note. From *Life in New Zealand Commission Report* (Vol. 3: Executive Overview) by D.G. Russell and N.C Wilson, 1991, Dunedin, New Zealand: University of Otago. Copyright 1991 by Hillary Commission. Adapted by permission.

Most notable about these percentages are the differences in variety of sporting activities among a significant proportion of New Zealanders, since males participate in about 21 compared with about 8 for females. While a smaller proportion of females than males in this age group participate in sporting activities (males 74%, females 59%), it is clear that women in general do not appear to be attracted to certain sports. It is perhaps significant that New Zealand women do not participate in team sports in large numbers and, generally, not in competitive individual sports perhaps with the exception of golf (12%), which, of course, may be played noncompetitively. The LINZ data support this: two thirds of women agree that there is too much competitiveness in leisure activities today (compared with just over half of men), and nearly three quarters believe that sporting bodies are too concerned with having the best players and winning (Cushman et al., 1991).

Table 22.5   Sport Participation Among Female New Zealanders (%)

Sport	Age (years)					
	15-18	19-24	25-44	45-64	65+	All
Aerobics	39	35	17	6	1	17
Cycling	46	28	14	5	1	17
Golf	4	2	3	9	5	5
Netball	26	13	5	1	1	7
Snooker/pool	15	16	4	2	2	6
Swimming	40	42	23	13	10	25
Tennis	39	14	10	7	0	12
Volleyball	16	9	3	1	0	5

Of the team sports, the traditional sports of cricket (11%), rugby union (10%), and netball (7%) are the most popular among this age group. Of the individual activities, swimming is the most popular (25% of men and women) and reflects the accessibility of the country's beaches, rivers, and lakes, and nearly 40 years of effective swimming teaching in New Zealand elementary schools, a large proportion of which have their own learner pools. The former point is supported by the fact that 50% of New Zealanders use beaches, rivers, and lakes as leisure facilities, second only to shopping centers (56%) and slightly ahead of restaurants (47%) (Cushman et al., 1991).

Overall, it appears that New Zealanders generally prefer noncompetitive, individual activities in an environment that encourages socializing. Among men (25%) and younger women (about 15% for 15-to-24-year-olds), the popularity of snooker/pool, a popular game in pubs and clubs, illustrates this point.

Dropout

There are two ways to assess dropout from sport. One is to consider changes in individual physical activity levels; the other is to consider the proportion of participants who stop an activity. The problem with the latter is that an individual may change sport activities rather than stop playing sport altogether. As we suggested earlier, 5-to-15-year-old boys appear to change from one sport to another whereas girls may drop out as they reach adolescence.

Hodge and Zaharopoulos (1991) estimated that nearly 450,000 children aged 5 to 19 years participate in organized sport in New Zealand but that there is a significant drop in adolescent (15 to 19 years) participation. They questioned nearly 400 high school netball players and over 800 high school rugby players to determine the dropout rate from these sports, whether their dropping out was sport-specific (a change in sporting activity) or sport-general (stopped playing sport), and the reasons for dropping out.

Twenty-three percent of their netball sample were classified as dropouts. Of these, 72% were sport-general dropouts, ceasing to play competitive sport. The three most often specified reasons for dropping out were other things to do, the need to get a job, and too much emphasis on winning.

In contrast to netball players, only 7% of the rugby sample were classified as dropouts. Of these, 46% were sport-general dropouts. The three main reasons specified were other things to do, loss of interest in rugby, and a loss of enjoyment.

In terms of changes in activity levels, the LINZ data (Hopkins et al., 1991) show that virtually none of the 15-to-18-year-olds are less active than they were a year ago. However, perhaps surprisingly, 75% of females claim to be more active, compared with 61% of males. This may be the result of two factors. First, it is possible that the activity levels of young males is already high and that it is unlikely that they would be more active now than previously. Second, if this is not the case with young females, and if the health message of the benefits of physical activity are having an effect, then perhaps the trend is reasonable. Nearly 70% of females (and 68% of males) 15 to 18 years old specify "to keep healthy" as a reason to participate in physical activity. Further, 38% of females in this age group specify "weight control" as a reason for participating in physical activity, compared with 21% of males.

In summary, 81% of New Zealand boys and 79% of girls aged 5 to 15, and 74% of men and 59% of women 15 years and older participate in sporting activities.

Promotional Campaigns

In our introduction we referred to two initiatives of the Hillary Commission, KiwiSport and SportFit. These are two very successful programs that are having a major influence on New Zealand sport.

KiwiSport

Ninety-four percent of New Zealand primary schools participate in KiwiSport (Hillary Commission, 1992). This modified form of activity is available in 26 sports. (Table 22.6)

KiwiSport is a skill-based sport education program designed to be part of the primary and intermediate school curriculum for children 7 to 12 years old. It offers a wide variety of sports modified to suit the physical, social, and emotional level of development of this age group. These sports offer children a broad range of skills and cater to their abilities and interests.

The aims of KiwiSport are to

- encourage participation in a variety of sports,
- improve the amount, equity, and variety of sport activities available to children,
- encourage skill development in a variety of sports,
- promote fair play and good sporting behavior while discouraging a win-at-all-costs attitude among children,

Table 22.6   Sport Modified for Primary (Elementary) and Intermediate (Junior High) School Children

Sport	KiwiSport	Sport	KiwiSport
Badminton	Kiwi Badminton	Skiing	Kiwi Ski
Basketball	Mini-Ball	Soccer	Mini-Soccer
Bowls	Kiwi Indoor Bowls	Softball	Kiwi Softball
Cricket	Kiwi Cricket	Squash	Kiwi Squash
Golf	Kiwi Golf	Surf lifesaving	Kiwi Surf
Gymnastics	Kiwi Gym Fun	Table tennis	Kiwi Table Tennis
Hockey	Mini-Hockey	Tennis	Kiwi Tennis
Judo	Kiwi Judo	Track and field	Run-Jump-Throw
Lifesaving	Kiwi Aquapass	Trampolining	Kiwi Trampoline
Marching	Kiwi Marching	Triathlon	Kiwi Tri
Netball	Kiwi Netball	Volleyball	Kiwi Volley
Orienteering	Kiwi Orienteering	Wrestling	Kiwi Wrestling
Rugby league	Mini-Footy	Yachting	Kiwi Yachting
Rugby union	Kiwi Rugby		

Note. Adapted from information provided by the Hillary Commission for Sport, Fitness and Leisure, 1994.

- promote enjoyable and satisfying competition, and
- establish a sound foundation for activity throughout life and for higher level sport.

KiwiSport has developed from the idea that learning in sport, like that in reading, mathematics, and art, should be progressive. Consequently, sports presented as KiwiSports maintain the same basic skills as traditional sports but are modified to suit the ability levels of the participants. For example, in KiwiVolley the ball is softer and can bounce once before being played. The most noticeable modification is the scaling of equipment and playing area to suit the size and abilities of young New Zealanders. For example, in basketball and netball the goal is lowered. In Mini Hockey, the field is half the normal size, the hockey sticks used are shorter and lighter, and the ball used is softer. Further, the rules have been simplified with emphasis placed on individual skill and development. KiwiSport games are played on equal terms with no distinction made between female and male participants.

Fair play and good sporting behavior is an integral part of KiwiSport. The responsibility of leaders and others connected with the program in promoting fair play is strongly emphasized.

Early research on the perceptions of those involved with KiwiSport clearly show that school children enjoy their playing (Colmar Brunton Research, 1992). A 1992 report on KiwiSport activities in schools showed that nearly all primary and intermediate schools (94%) play KiwiSport. Further, KiwiSport is mostly played in sport periods and lunchtimes rather than after school or on the weekends. While this report indicates that teachers are the main providers of KiwiSport, in the last 12 months there has been greater input from parents, outside coaches, principals, KiwiSport coordinators, and sport club representatives. Each region within New Zealand has a KiwiSport Coordinator whose role is to establish a support network for KiwiSport, to assist in maintaining and improving the quality of the KiwiSport program, to develop training programs and distribute support materials and resources, and, finally, to promote the KiwiSport program and its concepts in the local community. An important finding of this report is that the KiwiSport program is viewed favorably by schools, sporting organizations, parents, and children. Among the strengths of KiwiSport are that it

- offers a wide variety of activities,
- teaches skills that children can practice and master,
- is aimed at the child's level of ability,
- has good training manuals and videos,
- has simple rules,
- is easy to teach, and
- shifts the focus from winning.

There is potentially a problem with the expansion of KiwiSport into sport clubs. KiwiSport's objectives are skill acquisition and enjoyment. Schools understand this. Clubs, on the other hand, are perceived to emphasize competition and winning (Cushman et al., 1991). The danger is that clubs may be influenced by these adult attitudes and expectations, which are contrary to KiwiSport philosophy.

The KiwiSport slogan sums up the program and thinking behind it admirably: "In KiwiSport the people are more important than the game."

SportFit

SportFit is a sport education program for high schools. The emphasis of physical education in secondary schools within New Zealand is moving away from traditional skill-based physical education toward sport education, encompassing the total sport experience. The recently introduced SportFit program for secondary schools and organizations that assist in promoting high school sport (regional sport trusts, colleges of education, polytechnics) is leading this renewed emphasis on sport participation for teenagers. Regional sport trusts exist in all main centers and are funded by their local communities and by the Hillary Commission. Their function is to service the needs of sport in their area. The aims of the SportFit program are to increase participation in school sport and to improve the quality of sport programs in schools. The program defines sport in the broadest terms, including outdoor pursuits and physical recreation (which can include cultural activities), as well as the traditional school sports.

SportFit is a Hillary Commission program designed specifically for the benefit of all secondary school students. The Commission believes that providing high-quality school sport programs to all students can establish positive attitudes and skills that will benefit young people after they leave school. Schools and organizations taking part in the SportFit program are provided with partial funding (usually a 50/50 partnership) for up to 2 years. This funding is used for full- or part-time sport coordinators, time allowances for recreation and sport teachers, and school-based programs to reduce participation barriers for groups such as females, Maori, Pacific Islanders, people with disabilities, or those from remote schools. This funding provides for preservice and inservice courses and other training opportunities for sport leaders such as teachers and coaches.

This Hillary Commission support offers schools the chance to improve their existing sport programs as well as implement new initiatives. Early feedback suggests that the majority of schools involved feel that the SportFit program is worthwhile and intend to continue with it.

A recent Hillary Commission survey of New Zealand secondary school students clearly showed that SportFit provides 90% of the students with the opportunity to participate in sport. The survey also showed that New Zealand parents are very eager for their children to play sport. Further support is found in the LINZ data, which show that 77% of females and 61% of males 15 to 18 years old want to become more physically active. To date the SportFit program has proven to be very successful. Some of the achievements reported by participating secondary schools include

- increased student numbers participating in sport (greater number of school sport teams),
- new opportunities for students (greater variety of sports offered in schools),
- lunchtime activities,
- interclass competitions,
- increased and improved opportunities for student leadership within sport (school sport committees, organization of competitions, coaching courses),
- better access to sport equipment,
- increased staff and community participation in school sports, and
- improved support (financial and educational) for coaches, administrators, and managers of school sport teams.

Conclusion

Given the current structure of sport in New Zealand and the achievements of the school system, the national sporting bodies, and the Sport Foundation, all supported by the Hillary Commission for Sport, Fitness and Leisure, the Commission's objective of a 10% increase in the numbers of people reporting frequent physical activity through sport and leisure by 1998 is reasonable (Hillary Commission, 1993). If met, this would lead to improvements in the overall health of the country and result in substantial savings to the national economy (Russell, Berkeley, Fraser, Wilson, & Allen, 1992).

References

Colmar Brunton Research. (1992). *KiwiSport quantitative baseline study: Vol I. A report on KiwiSport activities in New Zealand schools.* Wellington, New Zealand: Hillary Commission for Sport, Fitness & Leisure.

Cushman, J.G., Laidler, A., Russell, D.G., Wilson, N.C., & Herbison, G.P. (1991). *Life in New Zealand Commission report: Vol. 4. Leisure.* Dunedin, New Zealand: University of Otago.

Goodman, G. (1992). *AUSSIE SPORT leaders trainers manual for junior and senior leaders.* Canberra ACT, Australia: Department of Education & the Arts and Australia Sports Commission.

Goodman, L.A. (1961). Snowball sampling. *Annals of Mathematical Statistics,* **34**, 148-170.

Hillary Commission. (1992). *KiwiSport: An introduction for teachers and coaches.* Wellington, New Zealand: Author.

Hillary Commission. (1993). *Moving a nation: Draft strategic plan for 1993-1997.* Wellington, New Zealand: Author.

Hodge, K., & Zaharopoulos, E. (1991). *Participation motivation and dropouts in high school sports: Executive summary report.* Dunedin, New Zealand: University of Otago.

Hopkins, W.G., Wilson, N.C., Russell, D.G., & Herbison, G.P. (1991). *Life in New Zealand Commission report: Vol. 3. Physical activity.* Dunedin, New Zealand: University of Otago.

McGee, R.O., & Silva, P.A. (1982). *A thousand New Zealand children: Their health and development from birth to 7.* No. 8, Special Report Series. Auckland, New Zealand: Medical Research Council of New Zealand.

Russell, D.G., & Abernethy, B. (1984, July). *Children's participation in school and club sport: Some implications for talent identification.* Children to Champions. Keynote Address at the Pre-Olympic Symposium, Los Angeles, California.

Russell, D.G., Berkeley, M., Fraser, G., Wilson, N.C., & Allen, J. (1992). *The cost of inactivity.* Report No. 92-20, LINZ Activity and Health Research Unit. Dunedin, New Zealand: University of Otago.

Russell, D.G., & Isaac, A. (1986). Patterns of sports participation of Dunedin 11-year-olds: A descriptive study. *New Zealand Journal of Health, Physical Education and Recreation,* **19**, 8-10.

Russell, D.G., & Wilson, N.C. (1991). *Life in New Zealand Commission report: Vol 1. Executive overview.* Dunedin, New Zealand: University of Otago.

Scott, R. (1985). *Sport on the move: Report of the Sports Development Inquiry Committee*. Wellington, New Zealand: Ministry of Recreation and Sport.

Wilson, N.C., Russell, D.G., Spears, G.F.S., & Herbison, G.P. (1991). *Life in New Zealand Commission report: Vol. 2. Survey protocol*. Dunedin, New Zealand: University of Otago.

Acknowledgment

The authors are grateful to Paul Tredinnik of the Hillary Commission for Sport Fitness & Leisure for his valuable input to this chapter.

Part VI

Conclusion and Discussion

Chapter 23 Worldwide Trends in Youth Sport

Paul De Knop
Lars-Magnus Engström
Berit Skirstad

Sport is the most popular leisure-time activity among youths. In most of the countries in our study, half or more than half of all children in their early teens are active in various sports. Most of these activities take place in sport clubs or in extracurricular training in schools. From all the reports included in this book, it is quite obvious that sport is an important activity among youths all over the world.

Characteristics of Youth Sport

More boys than girls are active. This is especially true in traditional sports and team sports, of which competition is a fundamental part. This finding is not surprising. These kinds of sports are built on traditionally male values, of which competition and performance are important parts. A boy who is successful in competitive sport strengthens his masculine identity, while it is most unsure to what extent sport success influences the identity of women. Sometimes success in sport may even mean a risk for the female identity. Moreover, sports segregate the sexes as do few other phenomena. It is very seldom that boys and girls take part in sports together.

Some of the most common sports are soccer among boys and swimming among both boys and girls. Among activities outside sport clubs, jogging, cycling, and walking are the most popular. The most common sports are almost always universal. There are hardly any great sports in any country that are played solely in that country. Sport has thereby become international, not least with the help of television, with practices and rules that are understood by almost all individuals regardless of nationality and language.

The most common motives for taking part in sports are intrinsic values like enjoyment and social reasons. These motives are more common than investment values like success in competition and better performance.

In those countries where studies about social recruitment to sport have been conducted, middle-class children are overrepresented. Membership in a sport club is related to gender, social class, and family situation.

A few countries have indicated that they have special organizations for finding and training talents. That does not mean that other countries have no interest in this matter. On the contrary, the ambition to find talents is often very high, but the methods used to develop future top athletes might be different. Most often, talented children remain in their mother clubs up to their teens and at the same time take part in various national and international tournaments.

The most striking observation from these reports, however, is the similarity among countries concerning the organization and content of youth sport.

Trends in the Development of Youth Sport

Going through all the reports, a number of trends are noticeable. For example, the number of opportunities for participating in sport for youngsters has increased substantially in the last 10 years. However, few individuals are able to be successful in several sports, as was possible in earlier generations. Sport has become more specialized and differentiated at the same time as the demands of performance have increased.

Sport has also become institutionalized. The traditional sports, like team sports, are not played spontaneously to the same extent as before. In some countries spontaneous sports have almost disappeared. Children's knowledge about and performance in sport have become more and more differentiated and the extent and intensity of physical activity have become more varied. Today it is possible to identify two extreme groups of children. In one group, children are training intensively several times a week, some even every day. In the other group, children are not physically active at all during their leisure time. Thus, physical capacity and skill in sport can vary considerably among children and the variations tend to increase—making these two groups clearly distinct.

During the last decades more and more children have applied for organized sport. The increase has been remarkable, especially among girls. Even if boys devote themselves to sport more than girls, the difference between boys and girls in both the type and extent of involvement has decreased, mainly because the girls' sport habits have come to resemble the boys'. This trend is especially noticeable in Sweden, Norway, Finland, and Germany.

Currently the flow to organized sport, however, seems to have stopped and even diminished in many countries, for example in Sweden and Germany. On the other hand, activities, often in commercial venues, whereby people train their bodies, increase their physical capacity, and try to improve their appearance have increased. What is significant about these commercial training institutes and gyms is that they offer possibilities for social contacts, yet demand no far-reaching obligations or other undertakings. It is in the clients' own interest to train, they can come and go as they like, and they are not dependent on the engagement of parents.

Another noticeable trend is the decrease in the age of beginners in sport. In many countries 50% of the children start to play sports at the age of 7 or 8 or even younger. The number of dropouts is, on the other hand, increasing with increasing age, especially among girls. Sport participation, on one hand, is a dynamic process whereby young people's involvement is characterized by moving in and out of a wide range of activities with a considerable amount of experimentation. On the other hand, there is a trend of specialization in sport, where all the concentration and physical effort must be given to one, or at most two, sports. Interest in many of the traditional sports like gymnastics and athletics seems to be decreasing, while the interest in new sports like judo and girls' soccer seems to be increasing.

The single most often repeated reason for not playing sport is "not having enough [perceived] time." Other reasons, often mentioned, are "no interest anymore" and "other leisure activities."

Current Problems

From these findings, and from explicit points in the reports from the countries taking part in the study, we can identify the most crucial problems in youth sport.

The dropout problem among teenagers, especially among girls, is reported from all countries where researchers have studied this phenomenon. During adolescence there is an increasing decline in the number of participants. The interest in organized sport seems to have peaked in many countries and to be decreasing, which many sport organizations regard as a problem.

Another problem is that adult sport has influenced youth sport to a large extent. The norms and values of adults are dominating. One example is that the rules for team sports, from the beginning designed for adults, are the same even if the children are only 8 years of age. Another example is that youth sports involve activities that are far too specialized, with too much one-sided training. In many sports children are looked upon as though they were small adults.

Youth sport has become more serious and less playful. Children are not allowed to play to the same extent as before. This problem is increasing as the age of children's entry into sport decreases. Youth sports have become too organized. The different sports are competing for the children's interest, leading to a decrease in the age when children typically join sport clubs and also to a lack of cooperation among the clubs.

Sport is also often not equitable, because involvement is related to the age and gender of children and youths and to the social positions of their parents. This segregation is not intentional but due to the predominant types of sport (most organized sports often suit boys) and to the organization of sport clubs (with their increasing seriousness in competition with increasing age). It is also due to the fact that many children are dependent on their parents, for financial and logistical support (e.g., transportation), meaning that in many cases a certain economic standard is a prerequisite.

Finances are another increasingly controlling factor. Rents and equipment are more and more expensive, as are fees for coaches and athletes. Recruiting of successful athletes also raises financial issues, when even youths are lured to new clubs with large sums of money. Another important problem is a trend toward increased commercial sponsorship of youth sports.

Ethical questions have been another focus in many countries. This is not only a problem among top athletes but also among children. Questions have been brought to the fore regarding whether sports really educate children: (a) to follow the rules and regulations of athletics, (b) to show respect to fellow-competitors and officials, (c) to demand the same from oneself as from others, and (d) to show a sense of justice and to be loyal and generous.

Western competitive sports have developed a greater degree of seriousness, focusing on results, and have concurrently developed a more widespread and polished system of competition. These developments are also in large part true in youth sport. The increasing financial and social meaning of victory (compared with getting other prizes) in top sports leads to harder behavior within (and without) the limits of the rules, and an increasing temptation to use illegitimate drugs (e.g., doping) to achieve a desirable victory. This development among top athletes is in the view of many people even a threat against youth sport.

It is reported from several countries that there are problems in getting qualified leaders for youth sport. In this connection, education as well as financial problems are mentioned. There is a heavy dependency on volunteers, which creates a high turnover and an uncertain quality of leadership and coaching.

Finally, youngsters who are not active in organized sports are seldom active on their own, either. The number of young people who are physically inactive has therefore increased, along with disparities among children concerning physical activity and, consequently, physical capacity.

Policy Measures

The problems of sports are linked to the problems of society and therefore cannot be solved solely within the sport system. One paradox is that at the same time as attempts are being made to find ways for children to develop their talents to international standards, there are also attempts made to create good and playful learning situations that suit children, enable them to develop at their own speed according to their own interests, and may lead to a lifelong interest in sports as a mean to good health and fitness. It seems as if, despite these efforts, competition and good performance have become the dominating factors in organized sports.

Nonetheless, as a reaction to this development many alternative sporting activities have been initiated within and outside the sport movement, including

- sport schools where the main goal is to provide possibilities for children to try various sports in a playful way that differs from the more traditional ways of training for sports,
- special programs that look to children's need for body movement and play rather than to suit the demands of different sports;
- sport equipment that suits children;
- open-door activities;
- fair play campaigns;

- campaigns for special target groups, including girls, talented youths, youths with disabilities, and immigrants;
- sport during holidays (sport camps); and
- cooperation among youth associations, local groups, neighboring clubs, and, last but not least, educational leaders.

Although it is reported that a cooperative and coordinated approach to the provision of youth sport between schools and clubs is one of the greatest challenges facing youth sport, it is hardly found as the theme of a campaign.

The Future of Youth Sport

Youth sports can serve many purposes. They can be a meaningful occupation for many children and give them a lifelong interest in physical activity as an important part of a healthy way of life and as a source of joy and relaxation. They can also provide a platform for future elite sportsmen and -women and become a means of self-realization and success for young people with a talent for sports. For many children, sports are also an important environment for upbringing and fill an important function in society's cultural reproduction, whereby significant values in our culture are re-created and carried over to the next generation.

It is, however, very doubtful whether youth sports, with the development that has been described in these pages, can to a full degree fulfill any of these purposes. Our definite opinion is that the course must be changed and, with this in mind, we would like to conclude with the following comments:

Sport for children must be made more accessible. It should be located close to residential areas. The opportunities to try different sports must be increased considerably, thus creating better conditions for varied physical activity and diminishing the importance of parents' interests and life conditions.

Play and learning must come first, that is, the intrinsic value of sports must have priority. To stress the investment value one-sidedly is a misdirected ambition from adults and as a matter of fact an alien element forced upon children's world of sports.

Training must be individualized and rich in variations. A too-firmly controlled and formalized training can counteract its purpose. The activities of sport clubs should aim at trying to develop every child's talent in the best way possible instead of simply trying to find talents. A selection of individuals, as well as any pronounced specialization, should not occur before young people have reached their teens. The great variations in the maturing process among individuals make all prognoses made before the teens very uncertain.

A child's relation to sports, to his or her own body, and to the experience of his or her own physical ability is the result of a learning process. To learn a sport is, however, not only a question of learning motor skills. It is also a question of learning norms and a set of values, learning how to behave oneself, and learning a style of life. Children are socialized into sports and thereby also into the value system of sports. Youth sports are one of our most important environments for upbringing. Sports must therefore also be valued as such and given their rightful importance in children's lives and development. Perhaps sport is the most important normsetter, second only to family and school. On the strength of its range and importance, sport must mediate and re-create essential values for the continued existence of our culture. In other words, it fulfills the function of reproducing culture. Therefore, it is of utmost importance that sport should follow a sound ethical code. In youth sports, the leader's personality, style of life, and behavior are also important.

Perhaps one of the greatest challenges facing youth sport now and in the near future is to set up a cooperative and coordinated approach by schools and clubs with the purpose of offering sports as an educational environment for all children that will enable them to develop at their own speed according to their own interests.

Index

About the Contributors

Editors

Paul De Knop

Paul De Knop earned a PhD in physical education from the Faculty of Physical Education of the Free University of Brussels (VUB), Belgium. He is a professor at the same faculty and is the head of the Youth Advisory Centre for Sport, an interdisciplinary research and advisory center. His teaching includes areas of sport, leisure, and physical education from a sociopedagogical perspective. He is secretary-general of the ICSSPE Sport and Leisure Committee, a member of ISCPES, ICSS, and NASSS, and a member of the board of the BLOSO. His research interests include youth and sport, sport and ethnic minorities, sport and tourism, and sport management.

Lars-Magnus Engström

Lars-Magnus Engström holds a PhD in education (pedagogy). Since 1983 he has been a professor at the Stockholm Institute of Education, Sweden. His research interests include follow-up studies as well as cross-sectional studies of children, youth, and adults and have focused mainly on sport and keep-fit activities. He is treasurer of the ICSSPE's Committee on Sport and Leisure, one of the founding members of the European College of Sport Science (ECSS), and a member of the board of the Swedish National Center for Research in Sports.

Berit Skirstad

Berit Skirstad is an associate professor at the Norwegian University of Sport and Physical Education in Oslo, Norway. She has been academic head of the Department of Social Sciences since 1993 and has held executive board positions nationally in skiing, orienteering, and sport-for-all organizations, and internationally in the Education and Promotion Committee of the International Orienteering Federation. Former secretary-general and since 1985 president of the Sport and Leisure Committee of ICSSPE, she was also president of the Norwegian Association for Sport Research from 1987 to 1991. Her research interests are sport organization and administration, leisure sport, and sport for all.

Maureen R. Weiss

Maureen R. Weiss is a professor of social psychology of sport and exercise in the Department of Exercise and Movement Science at the University of Oregon. Her research has focused on the psychological and social development of children and adolescents through participation in sport and physical activity, with particular interests in the areas of self-perceptions, motivation, observational learning, peer relationships, coaching influences, and moral development. Research and its applications are implemented frequently through Dr. Weiss's role as Director of the Children's Summer Sports Program at the University of Oregon, a sport-skill development program serving youth 5 to 13 years of age.

Weiss has published over 60 articles in refereed journals and 8 book chapters, was guest editor for a special issue of *Pediatric Exercise Science* on social psychological factors influencing children's physical activity, and coedited two books with Daniel Gould, *Competitive Sport for Children and Youths* and *Advances in Pediatric Sport Sciences, Vol. 2: Behavioral Issues*, both published by Human Kientics. She has been a faculty member at the University of Oregon for 14 years. Dr. Weiss has been an invited scholar and lecturer in Israel, Belgium, Canada, England, New Zealand, Thailand, and Australia, as well as for numerous universities and professional organizations across the United States.

Authors

Justine B. Allen was a research assistant with the LINZ Activity and Health Research Unit at the University of Otago, focusing on the investigation of New Zealanders' lifestyles, and is currently a graduate student at the University of Victoria, Canada. She is studying toward a master's degree in the psychology of sport, with particular interest in youth sport issues. She is actively involved in field hockey as both a player and a coach.

Michael Bar-Eli holds a PhD in sport sciences—psychology and sociology from the German Sport University, Cologne, Germany. He is an associate professor in the Department of Management at Ben-Gurion University in Israel. He is also a senior researcher and head of the Sport Mangement Program at the Ribstein Center for Research and Sport Medicine Sciences, Wingate Institute, Israel.

Wolf-Dietrich Brettschneider earned his PhD in 1975 from the University of Paderborn, Germany. He is a professor at the Free University of Berlin. His research interests include sport pedagogy, physical education, and sport and youth culture. He is acting director of the Institut für Sportwissenschaft at the Free University of Berlin and chair of the educational commission of the German Sport Federation.

Albert Buisman graduated with a teaching degree in 1961 and held several functions in elementary and secondary education. From 1963 he was in a graduate program at the University of Utrecht (The Netherlands), where he received a master's degree in education. In 1970, he became a lecturer at the University of Utrecht, Faculty of Social Science, Department of Education/ Sport, Movement and Health, where he performs research in value clarification in the field of youth sport. He is also involved with the training of coaches.

Lamartine P. DaCosta is a doctor of philosophy and professor of physical education at the University of Rio de Janeiro and the University Gama Filho (Brazil), as well as visiting professor at the University of Porto, Portugal. He is also a former consultant in sport, education, and health projects located in Kuwait, Tanzania, Argentina, Paraguay, the United States, and Peru, and author or coauthor of several books in sports, education, and management.

Carlos Gonçalves is a master of science in education, specializing in the methodology of physical education. Since 1979 he has been head teacher in physical education and sport at Linda a Velha Secondary School (Portugal). He is in charge of the Fair Play and Youth Sport Program, Oeiras Municipality. His research topics are the analysis of teaching in physical education, teachers' and coaches' training, teacher effectiveness, child and youth sport, and school sport.

Cart T. Hayashi, PhD, is an assistant professor in the Department of Health, Physical Education, and Recreation at Texas Tech University. Dr. Hayashi's areas of specialization within the social psychology of sport and exercise are cross-cultural and developmental differences, perceived competence, and motivation. His experience with youth sport includes serving as instructor in the Children's Summer Sports Program at the University of Oregon and at a summer youth program in Hawaii.

Leo B. Hendry, MSc, MEd, PhD, FBPS, CPsychol, is professor of education, University of Aberdeen. He has been involved in a number of nationally funded research projects, including an SOED study, "Towards Community Education" (1981); a 7-year longitudinal study of 10,000 Scottish adolescents (1992); "Working with Young People on Drug Misuse and HIV/AIDS" (Grampian Health Board, 1991); and "The Benefits of Youth Work" (SOED, 1991).

Bjarne Ibsen holds a PhD in political science. He is an associate professor at the Danish State Institute of Physical Education, Copenhagen, Denmark. His research interests include sociological studies of the voluntary sector (clubs and associations), volunteering, sport participation, and leisure policy.

Teus J. Kamphorst was executive secretary to the board of the Interdisciplinary Department of Development and Socialization of the Faculty of Social Sciences of the University of Utrecht, The Netherlands. His main field of interest is leisure and socialization. He has written about 15 books and reports and about 100 book chapters and articles on leisure and related subjects. He was one of the founders of the Leisure Recreation and Tourism Abstracts information system, a board member of the World Leisure and Recreation Association, and executive secretary and lately president of the Research Committee on the Sociology of Leisure of the International Sociological Association. He is presently director of the World Leisure and Recreation Association International Centre of Excellence (WICE).

Lauri Laakso earned a PhD in physical education from the University of Jyväskylä, Finland, and has been an associate professor at the same university since 1985. His research topics of interest are physical activity, sport motivation, evaluation, and sport participation.

John G. Love is lecturer in sociology at the Robert Gordon University in Aberdeen, Scotland. He was formerly a research fellow in the Department of Education at the University of Aberdeen. His research interests include young people and he has been involved in two major studies of young people in Scotland: ''The Young People's Leisure and Lifestyles'' study (1985-1992) and the ''Benefits of Youth Work'' study (1990-1992). Dr. Love coauthored the final report of the latter study and the book *Young People's Leisure and Lifestyles* (1993), which reports on the findings of the former study.

Jo M.H. Lucassen studied human movement sciences at Amsterdam Free University (The Netherlands), and was graduated in 1982 in the field of planning, organization, and management in sport and recreation. He has executed research projects for the Ministry of Welfare, Health and Culture, the National Foundation for Games and Sport, and the Netherlands Sport Confederation, and was lecturer for the Netherlands Sport Academy and the Institute for Professional Coach Education. He has worked as policy-advising executive for the Netherlands Association of Sportcoaches and Volunteers (NFWS) and the Ministry of Welfare, Health and Culture, and is presently policy and management advisor for the Netherlands Olympic Committee/Netherlands Sport Confederation.

W. Kerry Mummery earned an MSc in physical education from the University of Saskatchewan and a PhD from the University of Alberta. Since September 1993 he has been a research associate at the Alberta Centre for Well-Being. He has 16 years' experience as a professional competitive swim coach and served twice on the coaching staff of the Canadian National Youth Swimming Team.

Henny Oldenhove has a bachelor's degree of education in physical education. After 9 years as a teacher in physical education, she became the senior project officer of the National Girls and Physical Activity Project. Since 1988 she has been working for the Australian Sports Commission, first on the topic Women and Sport and since 1991 in the Aussie Sport Unit.

Laila Ottesen holds a master's degree. She is an associate professor at the Center for Sport Research in Copenhagen, Denmark. Her research topics of interest are the analysis of sport habits, studies of youth, and leisure policy.

Núria Puig is licentiate in modern history from the University of Barcelona and has two doctoral degrees: one in sociology (University of Paris) and one in sciences of education (University of Barcelona). She is a professor at the INEF of Catalonia, Barcelona, Spain. Her research topics of interest are the sociology of sport and sport facilities. She is also an associate editor of the *International Review for the Sociology of Sport*. Until 1991 she was secretary-general of the International Sport for All Federation (FISpT) and from 1979 to 1983 a member of the Spanish Olympic Committee.

Hai Ren earned an MEd from the Beijing Institute of Physical Education, China, in 1981, and a PhD from the University of Alberta, Canada, in 1988. At present he is associate professor and executive director of the Centre for Olympic Studies of the Beijing University of Physical Education. His main research fields are Olympic studies and the sociocultural aspects of sport.

Kenneth Roberts is professor of sociology and head of the Department of Sociology at the University of Liverpool, United Kingdom. He has written several books and numerous articles on the sociology of leisure. He codirected a large-scale study of indoor sport facilities and users, and the Liverpool branch of the Economic and Social Research Council's 16-19 Initiative. He is currently directing a series of studies among young people in East-Central Europe.

Nicholas Rowe holds a BA (Hons) in urban and regional planning and an MPhil (Edin) in urban design and regional planning. Since 1983 he has been a sport and leisure researcher for the Sports Council. His research topics of interest are large-scale participation surveys, physical activity for health and fitness, evaluation studies, performance in sport, and sport and ethics. He is also chair of the Council of Europe Research Experts Group on Young People, Sport, and Ethics.

David G. Russell is professor of kinesiology at Otago University, New Zealand, director of the Life in New Zealand Activity and Health Research Unit, and deputy chair of the Division of Sciences at the University of Otago. Dr. Russell was director of the National Survey of New Zealand School Pupils conducted for the New Zealand Education Department. His current research interests include New Zealanders' lifestyles and elite athlete commitment, the latter as part of the Project on Elite Athlete Commitment (PEAK), which is a joint research program between Otago University and the University of California at Los Angeles.

Hans-Gerhard Sack earned his PhD in 1973 from the University of Giessen, Germany. In 1983 he earned a master's degree in psychology from the Technical University of Berlin. He is a professor at the Free University of Berlin. His research interests include sport psychology, and work and organizational psychology. He is a member of the Scientific Committee of the German Sport Federation.

Uriel Simri earned a PhD from West Virginia University, and was a lecturer at the Zinman College (Israel) until 1991. For 20 years he was the scientific head of the Wingate Institute, and he has been guest professor and lecturer at several universities abroad.

Mari-Kristin Sisjord is working on a postdoctoral scholarship at the Norwegian University of Sport and Physical Education in Oslo, Norway. In April 1994 she received her doctoral degree in sport sociology at the same university. Her research interests are the sociology of sport and youth and sport.

Seweryn Jerzy Sulisz earned his doctoral degree in physical education in 1974. Since 1974 he has been assistant professor of theory and methodology of physical education at the Academy of Physical Education, Warsaw, Poland. His research interests include the physical development and motor activity of children, youth and sport, and the methodology of physical education.

Risto Telama earned a PhD in sport science from the University of Jyväskylä, Finland. He is professor of sport pedagogy in the Department of Physical Education at the same university. He is a member of the editorial board of the *Scandinavian Journal of Medicine and Science in Sports*, chair of the Finance Committee (Treasurer) of the AIESEP (International Association of Physical Education in Higher Education), an AIESEP delegate to ICSP (International Council of Sport Pedagogy), a member of ISSP and ICHPER, and an honorary member of the Finnish Association of Physical Education Teachers. His research interests include sport pedagogy, physical education, social-ethical issues in sport, youth sport, and nature and physical education.

Gershon Tenenbaum earned his PhD at the University of Chicago, United States. He was director and researcher in the Ribstein Center for Research and Sport Medicines, Wingate Institute, Israel. Currently, he is an associate professor at the University of Southern Australia, Department of Psychology. His main research interests are in the fields of psychometrics, cognition, and motivation in sport psychology.

Marc Theeboom earned a PhD in physical education at the Faculty of Physical Education of the Free University of Brussels (VUB), Belgium. Since 1994, he has been a part-time professor and doctor-assistant at the same faculty. He has conducted research on topics such as leisure education, sport and underprivileged youth, and physical education. His main academic interests are in the youth sport domain, with an emphasis on sport pedagogy.

Bart Vanreusel earned a master's degree in sport studies at the University of Massachusetts, United States, and a PhD in physical education at the Faculty of Physical Education and Physical Therapy of the Catholic University of Leuven, Belgium. He is a professor at the same faculty and head of the research unit on Social and Cultural Kinanthropology. His teaching includes areas of sport, leisure, and physical education from a sociological perspective. He is also responsible for the outdoor education program at his faculty, and is an extended board member of the International Committee for the Sociology of Sport. His recent publications are on sport participation, longitudinal studies of the relation between sport and physical fitness, the social meaning of sport, and sport and the environment.

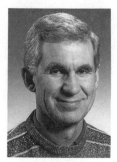

Leonard M. Wankel earned a PhD in physical education at the University of Alberta, Canada. Since 1977 he has been a full-time professor in the Faculty of Physical Education and Recreation, University of Alberta. His teaching and research areas are the social psychology of sport, physical activity, and leisure; sport and the community; youth sport; physical activity, health, and well-being; motivation and satisfaction; and exercise adherence. He has served on a number of provincial and national committees and task forces devoted to improving the delivery of sport and physical activity programs to Canadian youths. He is a founding member of the sport psychology committee for establishing the (Canadian) National Coaching Certification Program and a master instructor for the NCCP program.

Anita White earned an MA in education (University of Sussex, England), and an EdD in the sociology of sport (University of Northern Colorado, United States). She has been a lecturer in physical education, sport, and recreation and a researcher on young people, sport, and gender. Since 1990 she has been head of development of the Sports Council.

Noela C. Wilson is a research fellow in the LINZ Activity and Health Research Unit at Otago University, New Zealand. Dr. Wilson was project coordinator for the Life in New Zealand Survey, the purpose of which was to provide a data base on the major health-related lifestyle factors of New Zealanders. Her current research interests are New Zealanders' lifestyles, netball injury prevention, and exercise during pregnancy.

Helena Wittock graduated in physical education from the State University of Ghent in 1989 with a research thesis entitled "Epilepsy and Sports," and one year later she graduated in sport management from the same university. Since 1991 she has been affiliated with the Faculty of Physical Education of the Free University of Brussels (VUB), Belgium as an assistant, involved in teaching and research concerning sport management, event management, and the organization of sports. Her research interests are in sport sponsorship, strategic planning for sport federations, and other management-related topics.

Yasuo Yamaguchi earned a PhD from the University of Waterloo, Canada. He is an associate professor in the Faculty of Human Development of Kobe University in Japan. His major areas of research are sport socialization, aging and sport, cross-cultural study of sport, and sport and the community. He is a member of the board of directors of the Japan Society of Sport Sociology.

Xiaolin Yang worked as a researcher at the Beijing Research Institute of Sports Science in China. Since 1989, he has been working on a scholarship at the University of Jyväskylä, Finland, where he received his master of science degree in sport in 1991 and his licentiate of science in sport in 1993.

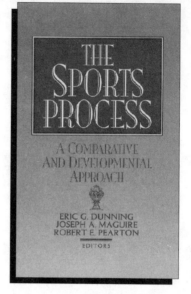